TENNESSEE WILLIAMS
and Friends

by GILBERT MAXWELL

THE WORLD PUBLISHING COMPANY
Cleveland and New York

Published by The World Publishing Company
2231 West 110th Street, Cleveland 2, Ohio

Printed in the United States of America

LIST OF PHOTOGRAPHS

List of Photographs

For permission to use material in this book grateful acknowledgment is made to the following:

The Condé Nast Publications Inc., for an excerpt from "The Meaning of the Rose Tattoo," by Tennessee Williams, in Vogue, March 15, 1951; Esquire, Inc., for an excerpt from "The Agent as Catalyst," by David Newman in the December 1962 issue of Esquire Magazine. Reprinted by permission of Esquire Magazine copyright © 1962 by Esquire, Inc.; Holt, Rinehart and Winston, Inc., for excerpts from Laurette, by Marguerite Courtney; Life Magazine, for an excerpt from an article by Edwin Bronner in the issue of August 31, 1962. Copyright Time Inc.; The Miami Herald, for an excerpt from an article by David Kraslow in the issue of January 11, 1952; New York Post, for part of a letter from the issue of May 4, 1958, from Tennessee Williams to Robert Rice. Copyright © by New American Library, 1958. Reprinted by permission; The New York Times, for the following material: "On a Streetcar Named Success," by Tennessee Williams, The New York Times Drama Section—November 30, 1947; "An Appreciation," by Tennessee Williams—December 15, 1946; "The Past, Present and the Perhaps"—March 17, 1957; and Drama Mail Bag—March 4, 1956. Copyright © 1946, 1947, 1956, 1957 by The New York Times Company. Reprinted by permission; G. P. Putnam's Sons, for excerpts from Remember Me to Tom, by Edwina Dakin Williams as told to Lucy Freeman. Copyright © 1963 by Edwina Dakin Williams, Walter Dakin Williams and Lucy Freeman; Random House, Inc., for two excerpts from The Glass Menagerie, by Tennessee Williams, copyright © 1945.

FOREWORD

In New York in the year 1940 that brassy block between Fifth and Sixth on Fifty-second was known to all columnists and hipsters as Swing Street. There, on Saturday nights and Sunday afternoons, groups of college kids from Princeton, upstate, and Long Island sat in the smoky dives, drinking, talking jive, listening to one name band or another; and like as not, if you looked in any way hep, some furtive figure would ease up beside you whispering, "Hey, man, couldja use a little tea?"

In Swing Street Donald Windham and Fred Melton, two Atlanta friends of mine, lived upstairs over a basement club where their current obsession, a happy, sad little old clown of a woman called Crazy Daisy, performed. They were part and parcel of Swing Street, these two—and on a certain bright spring day I climbed the dark stairs of their crumbling brownstone to meet a Mississippi fellow who wrote poetry, plays, and short stories.

There was a kitchen half to my friends' one-room walk-up, and as I came in I saw a young guy seated at the dining table. I could tell, even before he stood up, that he was not tall. He had on a pork-pie rain hat and his face underneath it was round, with a handsomely chiseled nose and one eye that was bright blue, as the other would have been except for the opaque cataract that disfigured its pupil.

Fred Melton said, "Tennessee, this is Gilbert Maxwell," and it strikes me now he must have subconsciously phrased his introduction that way for though I was a poet with two published volumes and Tenn was as yet unknown—Fred had introduced *me* to *him*. But then, Melton was always perceptive, for I remember his drawling to me one day later that spring, "Gilbert, I've decided Tennessee is a visitor from another planet," and indeed this statement embodies a truth far less far-out than the uninformed might imagine.

Well, there we were, young Williams and I, meeting in a furnished flat above a hot blues joint on Swing Street—and in that milieu, rather more his than mine, he gave me a wide smile and a warm-voiced greeting.

We drank beer, not booze, that afternoon (we always did at Fred and Don's since they needed the Ruppert empties to collect on for next morning's breakfast), and Tenn and I made out just fine, straight from the start.

I told some stories about a few droll characters in my home town, and T.W.'s incredible laughter rose shrill, sliding down from a high, spontaneous *who-o-o* to a shaking guffaw.

He told me then, "You should've been at my house in St. Louis the day Mother had a tea for the late regent of the D.A.R. She'd asked our colored maid to get into the spirit of the occasion—and the maid did, with a vengeance. She triumphed in a physical struggle with the D.A.R. chapter's regal secretary out in the hall, seized the regent's memorial candle, and marched in holding it high while the secretary sat and wept piteously on the stairs."

All of us there in the room laughed long and loud at this anecdote—and since it's the sort of story any Deep South man with a sense of the morbid-absurd adores, I felt an instant rapport with Williams. The Deep South citizen is generally a strange breed of cat. It's a rare thing when he walks alone and when he does it is seldom from choice. He is a garrulous, convivial creature by nature—and nothing suits him better than to talk family-and-folks down home with one of his own kind, just met. Give him a half hour with anyone born below Baltimore and he'll make contact, as T.W. and I did that day, running fast through the family names of six states to come up finally, crying, "Why, do you really know Dick Orme?" "Well, for God's sake, sure . . . I used to see him all the time at Madge Surtee's Better Ole, and also, his Cousin Callie's a real close friend of my friend Ellen Woolf in Atlanta. . . ." On and on, until the two people talking finish up friends, or maybe even find out they are cousins, six times removed. So it goes with Southerners who meet anywhere—in New York, in Paris, in the bazaars of Cairo—and always such abstract contacts are enough to begin a casual association.

With Tennessee and me, however, time and talk were to form a relationship rooted in something far deeper than the circumstance of our having mutual old friends from down home—for we were to find there was an eerie likeness in our family backgrounds, as well as in certain events of our childhood.

Tennessee Williams was born March 26, 1911, in a small hospital near the Episcopal rectory of his maternal grandparents, the Reverend and Mrs. Walter E. Dakin, at Columbus, Mississippi; I, one year and one month earlier, February 13, 1910, into the stoutly religious household of my maternal grandparents, James Madison and Frances Robinson Gilbert, in Washington, Georgia.

At his christening, Tenn was named, after his paternal great-grandfather, Thomas Lanier Williams—and though I have usually suppressed the information, my mother burdened me with the middle name of Tupper, after my father.

Tenn's paternal great-grandfather fought under General Andrew Jackson. My great-uncle Bill fought under General Stonewall Jackson, and my mother's father, Jim Gilbert, under General Robert E. Lee.

Tenn contracted diphtheria at the age of five; I, malaria at three and a half. Diphtheria's after effects caused Tenn to abandon the

company of kids his age, and because of his salesman-father's being
so much on the road, he virtually grew up without a father, so
dependent upon his grandparents, his mother, and his sister that
he emerged from his cloistered world to enter school "delicate and
sissified."

As a result of malaria I had regular bedridden bouts with my
stomach every summer until I was fourteen. My mother left my
father while I was still wearing three-cornered pants and returned
to the home of her parents where I grew up away from my old
man—so, I too, having become dependent upon my grandparents,
my mother, and a girl cousin who lived with us, was a sissy little
boy when I started grammar school.

Thomas Lanier Williams and I, too weak, timid, and introspec-
tive to join in healthy games with kids our own age in school,
suffered abuse at their hands—and both of us gradually retired
into a make-believe world of books and motion pictures. We retreated into public libraries, read heavy books by great authors,
starting at the age of eight, and all through childhood and adolescence sought escape in movie houses from a world of poverty
and misunderstanding that seemed often too harsh to have the
reality of that fanciful world dancing before our eyes on a silver
screen.

Tennessee has said, "When I was little I used to want to climb
into the screen and join the action. My mother had to hold me
down." And while I had no urge to get into the scene with the
actors up there, I did frequently leave the Strand in my home
town feeling as though I looked just like one of my favorite stars.
To this day, Tenn and I are childishly ardent movie fans. We go
to pictures together and always sit in the loge where we can
whisper and laugh without disturbing too many people, or being
summarily ejected for becoming helpless with glee when a film
turns out to be unintentionally funny. Tenn buys movie magazines
in lots of half a dozen, and when I hopefully asked him once,
"You just look at the pictures, don't you?" he answered, "Lord,
no. I read every damn word of the interviews." I no longer read
fan magazines, but I cannot resist leafing eagerly through them at

drugstore stands, and looking, in nostalgia, as Tenn does, too, for pictures of old silent films and their glittering stars.

Working in Hollywood has not dimmed Tenn's ardor as a movie fan, and this pleases me, since our mutual enthusiasm for films is a naive blessing we've always shared.

We are friends also because of other tastes that we have in common—but most subtly I think because of similarities in our unhappy backgrounds. As I go further into this book I shall note similarities in the traps, the beneficent or evil events of our early lives. For I feel that the reader should also become fully acquainted with me as a man who, in the often malicious, ill-starred company surrounding Williams, has somehow emerged at this writing from storms of jealousy, hate, gossip, and malediction, as an old, close, and (I hope) trusted friend.

TENNESSEE WILLIAMS
AND FRIENDS

ON A BOOKSHELF IN THE LIVING ROOM OF TENNESSEE WILLIAMS' New York apartment stands a triple-photograph frame containing three poses of an extremely pretty young woman. She is wearing a large hat with a white motorist's veil tied in a huge bow under her chin. Her fine profile is uptilted, delicate, aesthetic. The eyes are luminous and the slightly retroussé nose is balanced by the aforementioned chin in which the discerning observer will note determination. This is Edwina Dakin Williams, a descendant of aristocratic Quakers who were Tories during the American Revolution, as she looked when, in the town of Columbus, Mississippi, she met Cornelius Coffin Williams, scion of an old east Tennessee family.

Cornelius had left the University of Tennessee law school after his first year there to become a second lieutenant in the Spanish-American War.

Edwina had made two debuts in Vicksburg, Mississippi (meeting society with two friends, the Moore sisters, each of whom in different years asked Edwina to come out with her), when Cornelius, by then associated with the Columbus Telephone Company, fell in love with her at the dress-rehearsal of an amateur production of Gilbert and Sullivan's *The Mikado*. The couple were married by Edwina's father in St. Paul's Episcopal Church, of which Mr. Dakin was rector. In time, Cornelius became manager of three Mississippi Gulfport telephone exchanges and moved with his bride to Gulfport, where, having lost his job through hard times just before the birth of his first child, Rose, he did a right-about-face and became a successful traveling salesman for a men's clothing concern.

Cornelius—hard-working, aggressive, garrulous, hard-drinking, a man's man, convivially known to his drummer friends as C.C.—was to become a trial to his gently bred, soft-voiced wife. Still, the problems which arise in any union cannot altogether be created by one partner alone, and though Edwina plainly had much to put up with in her husband, C.C.'s position with the Dakin family in the early years of this marriage was, in turn, not an easy one.

After Rose was born, the young salesman was on the road a great deal, so Edwina lived with her parents in Columbus, Mississippi, for five and a half years, in which Rose and Tom grew close to her and the Dakins.

The story Edwina tells about Tom's howling loud enough for her to hear him halfway down the block the first day she took him to kindergarten in Columbus is significant, for Tennessee has told me, "When I was little, I loved my mother so much, if she went out somewhere without me, I was wretched until she came home."

When Tom was three years old, Mr. Dakin transferred to Nashville, Tennessee, where he became rector of the Church of the Advent.

After Nashville, the family lived for a few months in Canton, Mississippi; then Mr. Dakin was called to Clarksdale, a delta town where he was to remain for thirteen years. There, at the age of five, Tom contracted diphtheria and almost died.

In telling of this near catastrophe, Edwina has said:

> I slept with him for nine nights, following the doctor's direction to keep his throat packed in ice, changing the ice all night, so he would not choke to death. . . . When his fever returned to normal, I allowed Tom to get up. Then I noticed that, instead of walking, he would sit on a little stool and push himself around the room to reach his toys. There was evidently something wrong with his legs. Again I called the doctor. He said the diphtheria had affected Tom's kidneys and paralyzed his legs; he called it Bright's disease. . . . For the better part of two years Tom could not use his legs.*

Tennessee told me recently, "I believe Mother must be wrong about that. I doubt that my legs were paralyzed. I think they were just so weakened I couldn't use them."

No matter what the reason may have been for the disability, its results were both tragic and beneficent. Since the boy could not play outdoors, his mother began to make up stories and games for his diversion and to read aloud to him, turning, when she had gone through all the children's books, to Thackeray, Dickens, and Scott. Mr. Dakin, who could recite "The Raven" by heart, also read to his grandson from great writers, concentrating because of his fascination with the macabre upon the works of Poe. And so the whole diphtheria experience had a deeply significant effect upon young Williams' growth and development.

Already so attached to Edwina at the age of three that he had to be withdrawn from kindergarten, Tom, when he was unable to walk, grew even more dependent upon her, as well as upon his gentle grandparents, his shy older sister, and Ozzie, his Negro nurse; and quite naturally, both children became closer to each other, to Edwina, and the grandparents than to their father who was so often away.

---

* Edwina Dakin Williams, *Remember Me to Tom* (New York: G. P. Putnam's Sons, 1963), pp. 23–24.

In her book, Edwina says:

> Cornelius was not around a lot those years, when he turned from
> selling men's clothing to selling shoes. He never paid much atten-
> tion to the children, anyhow; my father was more like a father to
> them. One summer, when we vacationed in Tennessee, I did not
> see my husband at all. Occasionally, he would pick me up at the
> rectory and we would drive off in his car for the weekend. I
> remember the ancient Ford, in which he carried his shoe samples,
> spinning around in one circle of mud after another in this
> macadamless world of Mississippi mud roads.*

The picture, as she presents it, is not a pretty one, but Tennessee remembers weekends at the Peabody Hotel in Memphis
when both his parents, enjoying their holiday from the rectory,
bounced him happily on their knees while they sang him a rollicking song about a steamboat comin' round the bend. One scarcely
knows what to think of the Williams-Dakin ménage at this time,
when one compares Edwina's later contradictory statement that in
those years she "saw only the charming, gallant, cheerful side of
Cornelius" with this equally contradictory recollection of Tennessee's:

> My grandfather was a clergyman. It was really he that sup-
> ported us, although my father must have made good money on
> the road. My grandfather was a kind man. He was soft spoken
> and gentle. Somehow he created about the whole house an
> atmosphere of sweetness and light. Everyone in the house seemed
> to be under his spell. . . . Only on those occasional week-ends
> when my father visited the house were things different. Then the
> spell of perfect peace was broken. A loud voice was heard, and
> heavy footsteps. Doors were slammed. Furniture was kicked and
> banged. . . .
>   Often the voice of my father was jovial or boisterous. But
> sometimes it sounded like thunder.†

---

* *Ibid.*, p. 25.
† *Ibid.*, p. 26.

What is to be said for Cornelius, who never made a public statement regarding the situation in which he found himself?

It seems doubtful that Tom and Rose in these years received either from Edwina or her parents an unbiased impression of their father, and since Cornelius *did* slam doors, speak harshly, kick and bang furniture about, what possible conclusion is there, except that he had considerable provocation for reacting with such violence before returning, with a sigh of relief, to his lusty life on the road? Undoubtedly he felt like a stranger in the rectory, and—being human—resented a state of affairs which he had no power to alter, since he had to be on the road earning a living for himself and his family.

Perhaps the personality of the man who found himself in this maddeningly frustrating fix can best be summed up in a statement which Tennessee made to me: "He was a hard man to live with, Gil, but I know now he loved us and that he was deeply in love with mother."

Tennessee also understands now that his diphtheria handicap had much to do with his early estrangement from Cornelius. At five, forced because of weakness to withdraw from the society of active children, he began to make up stories and to convert them and their characters into fanciful games which he played with his sister. He and Rose lived in a cloistered world alien alike to their hearty, blustering father and to other children, so, when Tennessee emerged from that world to enter school in St. Louis, it was natural that he should seem "sissified" to C.C. and to his active, first-grade playmates.

In 1919, when Cornelius quit the road to become sales manager for the Friedman-Shelby branch of the International Shoe Company in St. Louis, he moved his family from the rectory in the leisurely town of Clarksdale, Mississippi, to a rooming house in a city of strangers where the background and prestige of his and Edwina's families had no significance whatever.

Edwina, after a siege of mumps contracted from Tom, went forth, pregnant, in search of a permanent dwelling. She found a ground-floor six-room apartment on Westminster Place, so dark that lights were kept burning the greater part of the day, and this is the place upon which Tennessee, permanently obsessed by the memory of its gloom, later based the setting of *The Glass Menagerie.*

Far more important, however, than the apartment's darkness— the transition for the children from a spacious house with grounds in a friendly country town—was the situation involving them and Cornelius, thrown constantly together under the same roof for the first time. The adjustment was painful and there seems no reason to doubt Tennessee's statement that the hegira to Missouri proved to be a shattering experience for the entire family.

From the start, both the Williams children despised St. Louis, but in the beginning it was Tom who suffered most keenly. At the Eugene Field School he underwent considerable abusive treatment at the hands of bullies bigger and stronger than he. He was unable, because of his shyness, his small size and physical weakness, to join in active games, and his mother recalls a day when the child came home with his ankles bruised and blackened. When she questioned him he told her that while he'd been sitting on a bench at recess watching a group of boys at play, each of the small monsters in passing had given him a kick on the ankle.

Many a child has suffered a similar experience, and, recognizing the innate cruelty of children, one can easily understand why a gang of healthy brats with a parentally ingrained mania for conformity—seeing a timid, withdrawn child as a freakish misfit— should feel impelled to torment him. A bookish, dreamy boy who sits alone at recess watching rowdy kids at their games is bound to bring out the gang's innate sadism. As extroverts, they feel toward him a kind of bewildered contempt, and they are damn well determined, somehow, to make him over into their patterned image.

All this, of course, sums up to a case of deep-layered misunderstanding between the tormented and his tormentors. They have no conception of their victim's psyche, so they cannot know that his reactions toward them are subtly complex. He cannot join in their games or scraps, not just because he is frail, but because he is scared of being hurt—and even more scared of showing it. He does not always refuse to fight simply because of cowardice, but rather because he is terrified of the derision he must undergo if he emerges as loser. Being more sensitive than his foes, he can foresee that he will be licked in a fight, so he takes to his heels instead.

Feeling meekly inferior, he does not realize that in being different he may also be mentally head and shoulders above his companions, and so, ironically, he is persecuted for an unrecognized self-quality which his enemies sometimes do half sense, with resentment and perhaps a baffled unease.

This is a situation which teachers, gang members, and the scared, confused misfit himself cannot comprehend. For the persecuted child, however, there is a compensation. If he happens to be creative by nature, he may well turn out to be a more sensitive, original artist than he would have been had he not been mistreated. It may even be argued that if Tom had been able to become a group member he might not have turned out to be an artist of any kind. At any rate, to have been thrust into the hostile world of a big, cold city, to have undergone humiliations and physical cruelty at school, then to have come home to a father who often remarked as his son came timorously into a room, "Here comes Miss Nancy," was quite enough to make this boy who would one day become Tennessee Williams the devious, bewildering adult that he is today. At the age of fifty-four Tennessee cannot, will not, enter a room full of strangers without having emboldened himself beforehand with three stiff drinks. Subject to claustrophobia, he will not taxi from New York City to LaGuardia Terminal without his pocket flask, and he is literally terrified of a trip through the Holland Tunnel. He is suspicious of his dearest friends and convinced at times that he is not only being used, but abused, by one and all of them.

This deplorable state of affairs—almost certainly the outcome of that unusually wretched early school and home situation—is maddening, infuriating, and amusing to all of us who love him. On the other hand, I am reminded of a salty old gentleman of my acquaintance, who, not having cottoned to a most amiable, well-adjusted friend of mine he'd just met, amused me with a comment that I shall not forget.

I said, "Bill tells me that he never, in all his life, heard his parents speak one unkind word to each other," whereupon my old codger replied, "An admirable state of affairs, no doubt, but unfortunately one which is not always productive of an interesting human being."

So, for good or ill, because of his unhappy childhood, we have in Tennessee Williams a fine playwright who is also a contradictory personality. It is my conviction that if he had not suffered as a youngster, we would have had in our day some kind of writer named Thomas Lanier Williams, but we certainly would not have the artist who took the provocative nom de plume of Tennessee.

In January, 1919, Cornelius and Edwina Williams' third child was born in St. Louis, and christened Walter Dakin, after his grandfather. Soon after his arrival Edwina contracted influenza in the flare-up known as the Great Epidemic. Her lungs were affected, and since Cornelius was going West on business for the shoe company, she accompanied him. Mrs. Walter Dakin came to St. Louis to care for the children and life went on much as it had before. They were snubbed and misunderstood by their playmates, ridiculed for their Southern accents, scorned by children of wealthy parents because the Williams family had only one car and lived in an apartment rather than a spacious house.

Tom was now reading every sort of book he could find—the Waverley novels, all of Dickens, and Shakespeare. He loved the Bard at his most violent, being particularly entranced by *Titus Andronicus*, in which the venomous king cooks his foes into a stew and devours them, and it may well be (as one of his previous biographers has suggested) that T.W.'s preference for this work had a far-reaching effect, since we have evidence of similar types of violence in his adult writings. For instance, there is a short story called "Desire and the Black Masseur" in which a giant colored man, the masseur, eats up a timorous little Caucasian office worker and whisks his bones, wrapped in newspaper, down to a lake—to say nothing of the play, *Suddenly Last Summer*, wherein a sexually oral poet is devoured by a group of dark youngsters some of whom he had been previously devouring. However, Tennessee's creative preoccupation with violence is amazingly at variance with his true nature. He is deeply involved with violence in his work because of a fear and abhorrence of it (he once looked aghast at me when I told him of a fight I'd had with a friend, and whispered, "My God, I don't know what I'd do if someone I loved struck me"); and it is possible, of course, that this attitude toward mayhem may be directly traceable, not to anything he has read, but to the schoolboy bullies in St. Louis.

In their nine years of residence in the Missouri city, no member of the Williams family was happy, and it is of this period that Edwina has said, "Before we arrived in St. Louis I saw only the charming, gallant, cheerful side of Cornelius. For a while he tried to keep the Mr. Hyde from me. But he could hardly hold secret his excessive drinking, not when he would come home emitting fumes of alcohol and in a cross and ugly mood."

In contrast, she has also remarked, "My husband was an earnest worker and loyal to his company. My sons have inherited some of his best qualities—honesty, perseverance, integrity." And though she deplored his drinking habits and his poker games, she admits that he never failed to be at his office on Monday morning, adding in his defense:

I don't think he liked the new job in St. Louis. He was really a salesman at heart, with a love of the open road and the human contact between customer and salesman. Now he was tied down not only to the routine of family life, new to him, but also to a desk. He probably felt a deep dislike for the tremendous pressures he had to exert on the salesmen and the ruthless hiring and firing necessary to keep up sales. He had a fondness for the lonely salesman of the road, and suddenly found himself tyrant to the salesman. I think perhaps he hated himself for what he had to do each day and when he came home at night took out his self-hate on us, for we symbolized confinement of another sort. Also, because of us, he had to take this higher-paying job, one he didn't really want or like.*

Tennessee, feeling his mother has at times been over-zealous in recounting C.C.'s bad qualities, has told me that Cornelius was

* *Ibid.*, pp. 34–5.

sufficiently fond of all his children to take them on occasional outings. He also recalls his father's taking him each Saturday of his life to the barbershop, and one can hardly help suspecting the senior Williams of a gesture of defiance in these weekly jaunts, since he despised the golden curls which Edwina was always loath to have shorn from the head of her elder son.

Tennessee remembers his father as a lonely, isolated man, and Edwina herself has borne him out in this statement, saying, "Cornelius loved two breathing things: Dakin and the dog in the house." In her book, speaking of her husband's attachment to a bulldog named Jiggs, she tells of returning from a visit to her parents to find Jiggs ill and Cornelius suffering from a monstrous hangover. On this occasion, he moaned, "It was a draw who would pass out first before you got here—me or Jiggs," so it appears that he had missed her considerably.

On the day Jiggs died Cornelius wept, and, shortly after the canine's funeral, pasted on his bedroom wall a cartoon of a wire-haired terrier captioned, "A friend's a friend who knows your faults and doesn't give a damn"—a gesture which would also seem to indicate a certain wry, rather pathetic, indirect defiance.

When Tom Williams was eleven his mother bought him a typewriter and he began to write. At fourteen, to Edwina's delight and her friends' amusement, he entered a contest sponsored by Smart Set magazine, and won a prize of twenty-five dollars for a first-person article entitled, "Can a Good Wife Be a Good Sport?"

Edwina first told about this at a dinner party at my house in Miami, and I remember Tenn's squirming gleefully about on the couch, taking an occasional sip of his highball, puffing on his cigarette and spilling ashes all over his person as he eagerly watched her face. Edwina is a born raconteuse; her timing is excellent, she knows when to reach a climax, stop, and top off her tale with a tag line—and I have often wondered how much of her narrative talent may have been passed on to Tennessee through association. He has written her into the character of Amanda in The Glass Menagerie and of Alma Winemiller in Summer and Smoke, capturing the qualities of her personality, her wit, the nuances of her voice and gestures; and watching her on the night she told the story about the prize, I seemed to see something more: as he grew up, Tom Williams was so closely identified with his mother as almost to be part of her. So, if you add to this his almost uncanny ability to listen to and absorb any scene or personality which his sixth sense tells him he may use at some future date, you begin to understand why even his most outlandish characters emerge on paper (not to mention the stage and screen) as astonishingly lifelike beings.

Shortly after his success with *Smart Set*, Tennessee won a ten-dollar prize offered by Loew's State Theatre in St. Louis for the best review by a member of the audience of the silent version of *Stella Dallas*, starring Belle Bennett and Lois Moran. He was writing short stories and poems during his high-school days, and in his junior year he sold a story called "The Vengeance of Nitocris" to *Weird Tales* for thirty-five dollars. In this piece, Nitocris, an Egyptian queen, had a vast underground dining chamber, with hidden sluice gates to the Nile, built beneath her palace, invited her foes to a banquet, got them drunk, retired, opened the gates, and drowned everybody in the flood that filled the hall.

During Tenn's high-school years, his rector grandfather took him to Paris one summer, and, as a part of his education, to the Folies Bergère, where he looked with awe and curiosity upon the spectacle of a number of naked ladies. Apparently, though, he never emerged from his cocoon of shyness at University High in St. Louis, since throughout his years there, according to his English teacher, he was "not socially inclined toward the group." She goes on to say, "He had too many thoughts of his own. His grades were average. There was no evidence of brilliance in his work. I fear he was not well adjusted. In the period I knew him he never was clear about tomorrow's lesson. Tommy belonged to another world."

He did indeed—and one of the central figures in that world was a fair-skinned, auburn-haired girl named Hazel Kramer, one year his junior, a little taller than he. She was a child of divorced parents, living with her grandfather, who held a position subordi-

nate to that of Cornelius Williams in the International Shoe
Company's sales department.

Cornelius always held a dim view of Tom's attachment for
Hazel, but Edwina approved of her, and sometimes, when C.C.
was out of an evening, gambling with his salesmen cronies, she
would go along at Tom's invitation to the movies with him and
Hazel.

Tenn recalls, with a kind of wistful nostalgia, that on these
jaunts Hazel would walk slightly stooped in the shoulders, striving
to match her height with his own. He was in love with her, and
there is to be found in one of his stories, "The Field of Blue
Children," a convincingly real description of a virgin college boy,
who is a poet, making love to a coed.

Edwina has said, "If Tom had Hazel in mind when he wrote
'The Field of Blue Children' . . . I think he was drawing quite a
bit on his imagination," and she goes on to state her belief that
"the two enjoyed only a Platonic relationship." Tennessee, however, has told me of a weekend that he and Hazel spent in Chicago, far from parental chaperonage or disapproval, from which
they returned to St. Louis only when he'd "run out of money in a
night club."

He and Hazel had hoped to enter the University of Missouri
together, but when Cornelius got wind of this he went into furious
action. Vowing that the girl's presence on the university campus
would cause his son to neglect his studies, he informed Hazel's
grandfather that he would not let Tom go to Missouri U. if Hazel
was to be there; whereupon the old gentleman, afraid of losing his
job with the shoe company, hastily dispatched his granddaughter
to the University of Wisconsin.

Tom went on to Missouri, outwardly acquiescent, but inwardly
enraged. He continued writing at the university, and in his fresh-
man year received honorable mention in the Dramatic Arts Contest for a play with a missionary background, called *Beauty Is the
Word.*

When, in his third year at school, he failed R.O.T.C., Cornelius, proud of his military antecedents and his Spanish-American

War record, became infuriated. He yanked his son out of school, brought him home to St. Louis, and placed him in a sixty-five-dollar-a-month job with the International Shoe Company. However, there seems to have been some legitimate justification for this act, since these were depression years and C.C., watching his few stocks drop alarmingly in value, "constantly felt the financial bottom dropping out of his world."

He had never had the slightest patience with Tom's writing, so one can imagine his reactions as he now observed his dreamy, withdrawn son and pondered upon his future. There was no way of knowing how long the worldwide economic crisis might last, and he may well have asked himself, "What's to become of this dreamer son of mine who has no trade (not to mention his mother, his sister, and his younger brother) in case the depression goes on, and some disaster such as chronic illness or death happens to me?"

Tennessee has said of mornings spent in dusting shoe samples at the warehouse and monotonous afternoons spent in typing columns of figures, "It was a job designed for insanity—a living death." He has told me, "It was nothing but three years of penal servitude," but he has also stated that the shoe corporation, to work for, "was no worse than most and considerably better than some"—and this period was, after all, a time of trial for many young men. I myself was having no easy time of it, working sporadically at all sorts of menial jobs in New York, and thousands of other kids in their early twenties were riding the rails across this stricken country or walking the streets of its towns and cities, half-starved, with no kind of employment in sight. Therefore, even though I can feel a certain sympathy for young Tom as the square peg in the round hole, I have, as well, some understanding of C.C.'s attitude.

Tennessee, too, seems to have realized that something more than disgust with him for failing R.O.T.C. prompted his father's actions at this time—for here is part of his letter to Robert Rice which appeared, along with Rice's last article on Tenn's life, in the New York *Post*, May 4, 1958.

You present [my father] in a terrible light. He was not really
that bad. Since his death about a year ago, I have changed my
feeling toward him. After he quit "the road" my father was a
terribly unhappy man who could only escape his unhappiness
through the bottle, poker, and through the great affection and
esteem of the salesmen who worked under him. In his favor I
would like to make these points. My father was a totally honest
man, he was never known to tell a lie or to take unfair advantage
of anybody in business. He had a strong character and a sense of
humor. He lived on his own terms which were hard terms for his
family but he should not be judged so long as he remains the
mystery that he is to us who lived in his shadow. Maybe I hated
him once, but I certainly don't anymore. He gave me some valu-
able things: he gave me fighting blood, which I needed, and now
he has given me, through the revelations of my psychoanalysis,
a sense of the necessity to forgive your father in order to forgive
the world that he brought you into: in my opinion, an important
lesson which I hope I have really learned. Forgiving, of course,
does not mean accepting and condoning, it does not even mean
an end to the battle. As for his being devoted to money, as my
younger brother is quoted as having said of him, all American
businessmen seem to have that devotion, more or less, mostly
more, and I think it is a sort of reverse sublimation. Disappointed
in their longing for other things, such as tenderness, they turn to
the pursuit of wealth because that is more easily obtainable in
the world. My father got little of either.

This is a brave latter-day attempt on Tennessee's part to understand the stranger-relationship existent between Cornelius and
himself. I am sure that it took some doing for him to arrive at the
rationalizations apparent in the letter, and I find no fault with any
part of it except the statement, "Forgiving, of course, does not
mean accepting and condoning."

Cornelius was always monstrously unfair to his elder son, and
while I am aware, knowing Tennessee as I do, that he can accept
the fact that people are partial monsters, he can never accept nor
condone any real or imagined great wrong done to him or to those
he loves.

I suppose if I were asked whether or not I'd forgiven my own monstrous old man (who, incidentally, did less for me in his lifetime than C.C. did for Tenn), I should probably say that I had. Still, I cannot, to this day, accept what was, as compared to what might have been, if my father had behaved differently toward me, nor can I condone his actions which so drastically affected my childhood and adolescence. And of course I cannot accept or condone them, chiefly because I have never been able to understand such behavior on the part of a man who should have been a responsible, affectionate parent to me.

This being the case, I can only conclude that Tennessee (even as I) has never forgiven his father for certain acts which may justifiably be unforgivable.

As to C.C.'s having finally separated his son and Hazel Kramer, however, I offer this observation: it is a matter of record that confinement in a warehouse did not keep Thomas Lanier from working all night at his writing, which represented the only life he knew at the time; and since I have yet to see my friend pursue any literary or romantic objective with less than complete, unswerving tenacity until he obtained it, I submit that if he had really wanted to wed Miss Kramer, neither frugal circumstances nor Cornelius Williams' opposition could have stopped him from doing so.

Undoubtedly, he loved this girl. However, his writing came first in the thirties, even as it does today, and during the three years he spent "in penal servitude," he created many stories and plays. He has said, "It was in those years that I first began to write seriously," and indeed he did—driving himself beyond endurance with coffee and cigarettes and going without sleep.

In February, 1935, he learned that Hazel Kramer had married—and one month later, just before his twenty-fourth birthday, a general condition which he has described as "a big underground rebellion" resulted in catastrophe.

No one—perhaps least of all, Tennessee—knows how great a part the news of Hazel's marriage may have played in his rebellion against C.C. and the shoe factory, but—for whatever reason—one Sunday in March when he was riding home with Rose from Loew's State Theatre, he was stricken, as they passed St. Luke's

Episcopal Hospital, with heart palpitations, numbness, and short-
ness of breath.

Rose stopped the taxi, ran to the hospital for help, and watched
aghast as he was carried into the building, apparently paralyzed.
She then telephoned her mother to relay the news—and of her
later reactions, Edwina has this to say:

> Rose sailed magnificently through the crisis of Tom's attack. But
> that night at home she broke.
>   She lost control of her senses, wandering from one room to
> another in a panic. She woke up her father screaming in terror,
> "You're going to be murdered! We're all going to be murdered!"
> It was as though Tom's slight breakdown had destroyed the
> slender thread by which she had been hanging on to a reality she
> could no longer grasp.*

Tom remained in the hospital for a week, gradually recovering
some semblance of normalcy. When he came out Cornelius was
finally convinced that the atmosphere of St. Louis and the shoe
factory, coupled with Tom's dogged will to succeed as a writer
even if it meant working twenty-four hours a day, must inevitably
mean the death of him, so he was sent to stay with his grandparents in Memphis, Tennessee.

The doctors had assured him his collapse was due to exhaustion,
and not, as he'd thought, to a heart attack. Nevertheless, there was
born in him at this time a haunting fear that he might die at any
time of a cardiac condition, and this bugaboo has continued to
plague him down the years. On the other hand, fear of such a fate
did not cause him, that summer in Memphis, to give up smoking,
swimming, or writing for long hours—even as no warning by
nature or doctors has since impelled him to abandon cigarettes,
drink, exercise, sex, or overwork—and so it was in this summer of
1935 that he wrote his first full-length play. This was a comedy
called *Cairo! Shanghai! Bombay!* and he was led to write it, at the
Memphis rectory, by a girl named Dorothy Shapiro, who was
working with a group of players at the Rose Arbor—a little theater

---

* *Ibid.,* p. 70.

owned by a lady named Roseboro. Feeling that Tom, as a currently melancholy writer, needed a lively creative interest, Dorothy suggested he try his hand at something her gang could present, and he agreed to the project. She and Tom dreamed up a plot involving the merry adventures of two sailors on shore leave who picked up a couple of girls, and Tom wrote the script, with Dorothy supplying the prologue and epilogue.

The play, staged late in the summer, was warmly applauded and, what's more, left such an indelible imprint on the mind of Mrs. Roseboro, who staged it, that she wrote Tennessee a few years ago, saying she still considered it the best of all his efforts.

The production of this play made a lasting impression upon young Tom, too, for he has said, "That was when I first realized this was a medium that was most attractive. I discovered the thrill of people reacting to my work before my eyes"—and any writer will understand the significance of this statement. Writing is lonely work, and, much as he loved it, Tom Williams, having already learned this at twenty-four, now welcomed hearing and seeing at the Rose Arbor the effect of a creative work of his upon a receptive audience. In other words he was publicly sharing a work created in solitude—which has always been the only work-sharing of which he is capable. In all the years I have known him, this writer has not talked directly with me nor with anyone else about any story or play of his, during the process of creation. He has, however, read finished stories and plays aloud to a few close friends, and there is to be found in the published version of *Camino Real* a touching preface wherein he speaks, in wistful, mild defense of the critics' reaction to this play, of his having tried merely to share with an audience a few things he felt impelled to say.

In the fall, when Tom Williams returned to his parents' home, he had not fully recovered from his minor breakdown, but he did have, in his head and at his fingers' ends, a new-found, provocative form of writing to sustain him. He also signed up for some courses at Washington University in order to earn the few credits necessary for his entrance into that school's senior class, and now, for the first time in St. Louis, he met a small group of poets—among them Clark Mills McBurney, whose published work has since appeared under the name of Clark Mills.

Clark lived near the Williamses in Clayton, a St. Louis suburb, and he and Tom soon became warm friends. In a preface to some poems of his own, published by New Directions, Williams has written, "It was Clark who warned me of the existence of people like Hart Crane and Rimbaud and Rilke, and my deep and sustained admiration for Clark's writing gently but firmly removed my attention from the more obvious to the purer voices in poetry. About this time I acquired my copy of Hart Crane's collected poems, which I began to read with gradual comprehension."

His discovery of Hart Crane was a major event in his life, for Crane's poems became gradually a kind of obsession with him. Before reading Crane he had been infatuated, along with most of his generation, by a lady of whom (directly addressing the Reaper) he had written:

> Rudely you seized and broke proud Sappho's lyre,
> Barrett and Wylie went your songless way.
> You do not care what hecatomb of fire
> Is split when shattering the urn of clay;
> Yet, Death, I'll pardon all you took away
> While still you spare me—glorious Millay!

Tenn and I still share a love of Edna St. Vincent Millay as woman and poet—and I shall never forget his excitement, just after I met him, when I told him about meeting her in the late fall of 1933. Out on my job collecting bills for a night club, I had stopped at the St. Regis Hotel desk to leave a dun, when someone with a bouquet came up, telling the clerk, "These flowers are for Mrs. Eugen Boissevain."

I ran home, grabbed a copy of my first book of poems, which had just come out, trotted right back to the St. Regis and left it at the desk for Millay with a flyleaf inscription from her own "The Lamp and the Bell," "For you, because you are to me a burning lamp, a flame the wind cannot blow out." I had no phone, but I had left my address, and she sent me a note of invitation by messenger that afternoon. So it was that I went at five o'clock to spend with that small, red-haired, green-eyed pixie, the most ecstatic two hours I had known in the twenty-three years of my life.

In the winter of 1958, at lunch during the *Sweet Bird of Youth* rehearsals with a rather condescending young man from *Esquire's* staff, Tennessee and I found ourselves defending Edna (who, God knows, needs no defense), and I recall Tenn's ending his eulogistic convictions as to the permanence of her best work with the vehement phrase, "I say this to you, my young friend, and I'm prepared, if necessary, to say it to the editors of the *Partisan Review*." Whereupon the young man murmured, with sardonically lowered lids, "Oh, *they'd* doubtless agree with you"—a remark which deflated us only slightly. We are both loyal to this gifted sorceress—idol of our adolescence—and I only wish I could say that we share a similar idolatry for Hart Crane. But, alas, when Tenn has read aloud to me from "White Buildings," crying, "Now surely you think that's magnificent?" I have always been forced to react with a sorrowful shake of the head—having no more than a cold admiration for this poet's technical skill and laborious striving for perfection.

Tenn, however, wore out the volume of Crane's collected poems which he'd removed from the Washington University library, carting it around in his suitcase through the first half-dozen years of his wanderings over this continent, and he has quoted from the poet at least twice in connection with his own work. He prefaced *Sweet Bird of Youth* with:

> Relentless caper for all those who step
> The legend of their youth into the noon

and *Streetcar* with the following:

> And so it was I entered the broken world
> To trace the visionary company of love, its voice
> An instant in the wind (I know not whither hurled)
> But not for long to hold each desperate choice.

There are reasons for Williams' obsession with Crane's work and his biography, which will escape no one familiar with that tragically fated young man's history. Crane, insidiously involved with his mother, loathing his father who confined him in the family's candy factory, escaped into "the broken world," there to be cult-ized by a small group of his contemporaries; then, after some years that involved a series of alcoholic-sexual orgies, he leaped from the rail of a ship into the Gulf of Mexico. Tennessee will never attempt suicide, but the identification of himself with Crane as he was in his young years at home was plainly inevitable, for this poet spoke to young Thomas Lanier Williams in St. Louis as he has probably seldom spoken to another man, anywhere.

In describing Williams at this time, Clark Mills has said, "Tom had fanatical and inexhaustible energy in his writing. His persistence was almost grotesque. It was Dionysian, demoniac. He wasn't aiming basically at material success. He wrote because it was a fatal need. Here was this lost member of his family trying to learn playwriting entirely in the dark. He may have written one hundred unsuccessful plays." And, as I've already suggested, this description of Williams' dedication to his work was no exaggeration in 1935, even as it would not be today. Tenn still has fanatical, inexhaustible energy, as well as an almost grotesque persistence, Dionysian and demoniac. He no longer needs to—indeed, according to his doctors, should not—work as hard as he does. But by now of course the work is an absolute compulsion—a need which is greater than the need for rest or sleep or even the body's "grave, evening demand for love."

So, the tormented artist continues to slave obsessively, and for me it is sad to realize when he says forlornly, "The work is all I have," that he really believes this to be true.

He has often told me that being famous and rich has brought him little happiness, and though I could go on for hours about the relative amounts of happiness which are, consciously or unconsciously, enjoyed by those who have money and fame as compared to those who have not, I think it is true that Tenn doesn't enjoy his life as he probably did back in those days with Clark Mills—though certainly that time, too, held its share of disappointments.

For instance, in a letter to his grandparents in April, 1936, Tom speaks of his parents' being laid low with bad colds, and of his having received a small poetry prize which he is adding to his savings acount of twenty-odd dollars in the bank. He adds wistfully, "If I get a little more from my writing I may be able to attend summer school," and continues:

> Dad has been talking about taking Mother and Dakin on a touring trip East this summer—to Washington and Virginia and home by way of Knoxville. I hope he decides to do it—it would be a wonderful thing for Mother—and you could come up here with us, though I'm afraid this place would not be much cooler than Memphis.*

The quotation is indicative of both the home situation and Tom Williams. His father was doing nothing to help him at twenty-five to get on, at summer school, with the education he yearned for, nor had it occurred to C.C. that his elder son needed a vacation from the summer heat of St. Louis. Yet there is no sign of bitterness, no complaint about being shunted aside and left out, in Tom's letter: he is just happy that his mother and Dakin, Cornelius' favorite child, are going on a pleasant trip.

On the lighter side, however, I have been amused to learn from Benjamin Nelson's book that in 1936 part of Tom's enjoyment, nay, "his great passion, aside from writing and from the interest of the previously named writers, was plump girls." Nelson tells us that Mills recalls the young man's being "smitten . . . wholly enraptured" at a party by a very fat girl "no one else would look at." Then Nelson goes on to cite a story, later published in 27 *Wagons Full of Cotton*, about a blimp of a Southern farm belle who has a liaison with a whip-wielding overseer, naively asserting that it illustrates Williams' "peculiar but passing infatuation" with porcine *jeunes filles*.

If Nelson had known his subject as I do, he would have been

---

* *Ibid.*, p. 81.

bound to realize that this girl at the party was already taking form (even as he flattered her and fawned upon her) in the mind of our crafty Thomas as a physical prototype of the farm girl he would write into his story that summer.

Mrs. Williams has agreed with Nelson that T.W. did have a "passing infatuation" with obese girls, but since I have known him, he has never shown more interest in fat females than he has in thin ones. He has always admired young, beautiful people and been intrigued by freaks and misfits; however, for the record, as well as for Nelson's consolatory enlightenment, I will here affirm that T.W. does definitely have a gleaming eye for most girls, fat or lean, who have voluptuous bosoms.

In that fall of 1936, Tom Williams' second play, *The Magic Tower*, a romantic piece about a pair of young marrieds living in an attic, was staged at a little theater in a St. Louis suburb called Webster's Grove, and for this effort the playwright, expectant of a cash award, received a sterling silver cake plate which he presented to Edwina. (Two years later he would have taken it straight to the nearest hock shop.)

He now became a senior at Washington U., with his grandmother Dakin largely supplying his tuition. He also fell in with a fine Bohemian little-theater group of whom he has said in his preface to *27 Wagons:*

> Dynamism was what the Mummers had, and for about five years—roughly from about 1935 to 1940—they burned like one of Miss Millay's improvident little candles—and then expired. Yes, there was about them that kind of excessive romanticism which is youth and which is the best and purest part of life.

And so we do gather that this once lonely misfit was truly, at last, enjoying his life in St. Louis.

One day the Mummers' director, Willard Holland, phoned Tom to ask how he felt about militarism, and when Tom told him he'd left Missouri U. partially because he couldn't pass R.O.T.C.,

Holland said, "Then, you're the the guy I'm looking for." He needed a brief curtain raiser for Irwin Shaw's *Bury the Dead*, so Williams wrote a pacifist sketch which—presented on Armistice Day—was praised, both by the first-night audience and the local press.

In college that winter he entered the drama department's playwriting contest with *Me, Vashya!*, a play about a double-dealing World War I munitions maker, and, when he lost out in the contest, reacted with a fine display of that violence of which he is still capable when thwarted by individuals, circumstances, or fate. He has never at any time been a good loser, so when he learned that the college contest prize had gone to someone else, he charged up to the office of Professor William G. B. Carson, the head of the drama department, and delivered himself of a tirade.

In speaking of this whole incident, Tennessee has said, "It was a terrible shock and humiliation . . . a crushing blow to me. I had always thought I was shy, but I discarded all humility. I stormed into Carson's office (he was a good professor) and I screamed at him. I forget what my parting shot was, but it was quite a shot. I surprised myself."

Altogether now, he began to behave in erratic ways—and there were reasons behind this pattern of action. Suddenly he lost all interest in fraternity life, became generally apathetic toward his studies, failed in Greek, wrote a cantankerous letter to the dean about a relatively unimportant issue, and finally succeeded in being dropped by the school—all because of problems at home where his parents were growing more and more bitterly estranged.

Because of C.C.'s reluctance to provide her with enough household money or sufficient funds to clothe herself and the children, Edwina (humiliated at being forced to scrimp, make do, merely exist in a drab middle-class environment foreign to the strata of gentility she had enjoyed in Mississippi) was giving her husband a rough time. And whatever may be generally said in Cornelius' defense, it is easy to understand Edwina's reactions in those days, since, already sick of the man's stinginess, she could not help being outraged by his lavishing upon Dakin a warmth of affection, manifested in ample pocket money and the use of the family car, while

Tom received from him only a contemptuous neglect and disapproval.

Here, grown to manhood, was the beautiful boy she had slept beside for nine nights when he had diphtheria, prayerfully willing him to live—this child of her heart, paralyzed by that sickness, later by incarceration in a warehouse—still being mistreated by Cornelius (maybe to spite her) while she, unable to change the maddening situation, must stand by, enraged and helpless.

Edwina seems never to have been as close to Rose as she might have wished to be, and though I have observed that she tries hard to be impartial about her offspring, I have not been deceived for a moment. The casual listener, hearing her speak up in praise of Dakin, might mistakenly conclude that he is her favorite. Seemingly, she feels impelled to speak with pride of her younger son, who, though a fine lawyer and an upstanding citizen, must nonetheless walk in the shadow of his famous brother—but the undeniable truth is this: it is Thomas Lanier who has always been the chick most tender to the hen. Tom, the prodigal, the indifferent one who often forgets Mother's Day, who once failed to write to her for a whole summer, from Rome—he it is who remains the eye's apple, the strong right hand, in brief, the firstborn son with whom she is well pleased.

Tennessee knows and appreciates this fact. And since he cannot help loving Edwina for such unswerving devotion, it is both touching and confusing to hear him say, struggling to defend Cornelius: "It's true Dad never seemed greatly concerned about Rose and me, but in my case, I can't help feeling it wasn't all his fault. If Mother hadn't held me so fiercely close to her, the situation might not have got so bad between us that I froze when he entered the house. I might even have got to know him as a man—and you know, I sometimes feel he wanted to know me, but the trouble lay in the fact that, knowing I was afraid of him, he resented that knowledge so much he turned against me. But then again, who knows?"

He tries hard now, Tenn does, to find good things to say about this lonely, unhappy, cruel man, and though this is admirable, somehow I must always remember that he once wrote of himself

and Edwina in the suburban house which Cornelius had finally
bought:

> Cold, cold, cold
> was the merciless blood of your father.
>
> By the halo of his breath
> your mother knew him;
>
> By January she knew him
> and dreaded the knowledge.
>
> His winter breath
> made tears impossible for her.

Yes, things were intolerably sad in Clayton in those days, but
the worst was yet to be realized—for now, to the anguish of the
entire Williams-Dakin family, the long-feared, hopefully ignored
symptoms of schizophrenia were manifested in Rose. Since her
change from puberty to young womanhood, the girl had grown
more and more withdrawn; and though the whole story of this
withdrawal appears, partially fictionalized, in *The Glass Menagerie*, here are some excerpts from an unpublished story of Tennessee's called "The Four-Leaf Clover," which are poignantly
revealing as to the true happenings in the Williams' house at this
time of tragic realization.

> She was seated on the lawn in a white dress. It was five o'clock
> and the sun was directly behind her so that it was barely possible
> to tell where the light ended and the translucent edges of her
> figure began. She had washed her hair that afternoon. It still had
> a prismatic dampness in the sun. Her bare throat and arms were
> like the inner surface of a shell. She was as lovely and insubstan-
> tial as something remembered, something not actually seen.
> As he came toward the swing where he usually read for a while
> before dinner, she looked up at him and smiled.
> "Look! I've found a four-leaf clover!"
> Her smile was like a delicate web upon his face and hands that
> he had to break away from.

He rose quickly and went toward the house.

The downstairs was empty. From above he heard the now-familiar sound of his mother's weeping. He had climbed half-way up the stairs before he noticed a strangeness about it. This time it was wild and hysterical to a degree that it had never been before and it frightened him so that he could climb no further but stood on the landing in helpless foreknowledge of some unbearable hurt.

The door came open on his mother's passionate sobbing.

"Don't, Margaret, don't!"

"It's no use, it's no use!"

"But, darling, it isn't hopeless!"

Cousin Amelia's voice, hoarse from tears, offering a comfort which she herself rejected.

"They have such marvellous sanitariums, new treatments and—"

"No, no, no, no!"

The door slammed shut and the hard silence of the house clamped down on their strangled voices.

Arthur went slowly downstairs. The hall was flooded with a misty brightness which had its center in the swinging pendulum of the grandfather clock. All of the afternoon's fading brilliance was concentrated in that metal disk as it swung leisurely from side to side in the glass cabinet. Arthur watched it in merciful suspension of thought till the hypnotic gold had drained out and left only the dull brass and the sound that came from its motion was the repetition of one meaningless phrase.

The room was tired and full of shadows.

He moved thirstily toward the window's diminishing brightness. He looked out across the wide lawn and saw that she was still there in the one remaining portion of sunlit earth. Her head was inclined slightly forward and the last and purest light of the afternoon made a luminous cloud of her hair. She was looking at something, something that she held in the cup of her palm, and even from this distance he could see that she was smiling.

He recalled the troubled look in her eyes as he had gone by without speaking and then her voice which now had in his memory the persistently haunting sweetness of a child's:

"Look! I've found a four-leaf clover!—It means good luck!"

The story, except for the quoted passages, is fictitious as to p
but Tennessee once said to me: "The doctors told my parents that
a companionate marriage should be arranged for my sister during
the period in which she was turning from girl to woman. They also
said that under no circumstances should she go through the strain
and excitement of a debut. But in a ministerial family the idea of
companionate marriage was unthinkable, and furthermore, they
paid no attention to the warning about the debut—so Rose went
through with it, and, shortly afterward, began to lose her mind."

In a beautiful story called "The Resemblance Between a Violin
Case and a Coffin" Tennessee has written about his own reactions
to his sister's becoming a young woman, telling how, being still a
child himself, he suddenly felt alone in the country of childhood
which Rose had so abruptly abandoned.

Later, he was to suffer a further, more desperate sense of isola-
tion, when—after Rose's pitiful morning subterfuge of leaving
home ostensibly for secretarial school only to wander through the
downtown streets, museums, and parks of St. Louis was discovered—Rose retreated deeper into herself. She would spend long
hours in her room with the white curtains drawn, strangely remote
even from her worshipful brother—and so, what Cornelius' indifferent cruelty, Edwina's sadly fretful complaining, the Rotarian
blight of St. Louis had never been able to do to Tom Williams
was now finally accomplished: the loneliness and loss of that
summer of 1937 drove him far from the St. Louis suburbs at last.
He would never return again except in those times when hunger
and lack of shelter forced him to recognize the truth of Robert
Frost's conclusion that "Home is the place where, when you have
to go there, they have to take you in."

In September, with Grandmother Dakin again paying his tuition, he enrolled at the University of Iowa. There, for room and
board, he handed out trays in the hospital cafeteria, drummed up
some student coaching in English, and earned himself a little
liquor and cigarette money selling university theater tickets on
commission.

Just after Tom left for Iowa, Rose's condition became more
acutely threatening, and Cornelius committed her to a state

mental hospital where the doctors announced that only a pre-
frontal lobotomy could bring her permanent peace. The family
conferred and consented; the operation was performed, and Rose
emerged from it passive, apathetic, less trouble to the staff of the
asylum where she was confined, lucid, no longer violent on her
visits home—but forever unable to return entirely whole of mind
to the real world from which, without self-choice, she had been
compelled to retreat.

Cornelius and Edwina did not consult Tom before making their
drastic decision in regard to his sister, and when the news reached
him at Iowa, his anguish was scarcely to be endured.

He has never forgiven anyone connected with the operation—
nor even himself for being away from home when the decision was
made. This irrevocable wresting of Rose from him without his
consent has always seemed to him an act of deliberate cruelty, as
well as a mistaken gesture of mercy, which he can never condone,
forgive or forget.

At Iowa, lost in despair at the year's end, he plunged headlong
into study, physical labor, and exercise, but most of all into the
compulsive work of creation which from now on would be his sole
refuge from a growing grief for his lost sister that he dared not
fully admit, even to his own lost self.

He wrote two new plays and revised *The Fugitive Kind*, a piece
about flophouse derelicts which he had begun in Clark Mills' basement workshop after several exploratory night walks through the
slum streets of St. Louis. The revisions were made in correspondence with the Mummers' director, Willard Holland, who has said
of Tom at this time:

> There was an immersion in his work that was staggering . . .
> but I couldn't get warmed up to Tom as a friend. There was
> something of an iron curtain—perhaps it had to do with the
> difficulties he was having with his family—he drew between him-
> self and other people and it was hard to get through to him.

Mr. Holland was right. The curtain had descended with the loss
of Rose, and from this time forth it would be down to everyone

except a few persistent friends who would hammer against it, time and again, with tenderness, sympathy, cajolery—even angry accusations of callous self-centeredness—until he was forced to raise it.

The two other Iowa plays were written for a seminar conducted by Professor E. C. Mabie—the first, *Spring Storm*, being a play about love. Tom read it aloud one spring morning to Mabie's class and of this experience he has stated:

> When I had finished reading, the good professor's eyes had a glassy look as though he had drifted into a state of trance. There was a long and all but unendurable silence. Everyone seemed more or less embarrassed. At last the professor pushed back his chair, thus dismissing the seminar, and remarked casually and kindly, "Well, we all have to paint our nudes!"

Nobody else in the class said anything, but a graduate student at the school named Lemuel Ayers read the play and praised its dialogue and atmosphere, thereby rescuing its author from temporary despair. Professor Mabie is gone now, but one wonders, since he was still teaching at Iowa after *Menagerie*'s opening, whether or not he ever mentioned to his students the incident of that morning when he dismissed *Spring Storm* with a flippancy calculated to transfix a budding talent, while, at the same time, furthering his own reputation as a full-blown, professorial wit.

The second play, *Not About Nightingales*—based on a prison riot in which a group of convicts were actually roasted alive in a disciplinary hot room—fared no better than *Spring Storm*. When he returned to St. Louis in 1938 after receiving his B.A. from Iowa, Williams finished the piece and offered it to the Mummers, but since the depression had driven that small, valiant group to "the end of their economic tether," they were unable to raise funds to stage it.

The Mummers soon disbanded. Clark Mills McBurney was no longer in town. Home was more than ever a place of dissension and sorrow, and so Tom scraped up railroad fare to Chicago where he tried desperately to ally himself with the W.P.A. Writers'

Project as an editor or even a field worker on the *Chicago Guide*.
Of this experience he said:

> My work lacked "social content" or "protest" and I couldn't
> prove that my family was destitute and I still had, in those days, a
> touch of refinement in my social behavior which made me seem
> frivolous . . . to the conscientiously rough-hewn pillars of the
> Chicago Project.

By this time, however, St. Louis represented to him a kind of
spiritual-creative quagmire, so when he returned to the city he had
already made up his mind to take off at once for New Orleans.

There he tried again to be taken on by both the Writers' Project
and the Theatre Project, and was again refused, largely because of
his family's relative affluence. While at Iowa he had offered
Candles to the Sun and *The Fugitive Kind* to the Federal Theatre
in New York, and now he was revising the latter play for the
W.P.A. group in New Orleans, but nothing came of these efforts.
It is interesting to speculate about what might have happened if
the W.P.A. project heads had been farsighted enough to accept
him, in some capacity.

It would seem probable that the Writers' Project, which thrust
Richard Wright into the forefront, or the Theatre Project, which
partially served to launch Orson Welles, might also have helped to
release the light of Tom Williams' talent—otherwise destined to
stay hid beneath a circumstantial bushel for another six years
before it blazed forth, on a Chicago theater marquee, in *The Glass
Menagerie*.

No one can do more than guess at what might have been;
however, I do know that Benjamin Nelson is only half right when
he says of Tom Williams' actual experiences during this crucial
time when he was waiting on tables in a Bourbon Street restaurant:

> Not even the people he knew in the Mummers reacted on his
> personality like these shadow people of New Orleans. . . . In
> New Orleans Williams recognized that loneliness and despair
> were not just his private griefs. And with this growing realization

he came to know that a world existed which was permeated with individuals who would do anything, experience anything, just not to be lonely. He saw and experienced an explosive, wild, frenzied life that overwhelmed him with its excesses. New Orleans became for him a kaleidoscope of drink, sex and revelry, and his companions were prostitutes, procurers, homosexuals and any other of the broken but unbowed night people who through quirks in Fate—or in themselves—were living in a fringe-area of life fraught with desperation and wild despair.*

The truth is that if young Massa Tom was whooping it up with prostitutes, procurers, and homos, he was also, as a young man of gentle birth and old Su'thun family connections, consorting with the likes of Richard Orme, a charming, intelligent man, Joelle Harris Lawrence, a lady of impeccable birth, and such talented writers as William March, Lyle Saxon, and Roark Bradford, who were also among the night people who foregathered at Lafitte's and Pat O'Brien's. Homosexuals he must have known among the casual, amiable habitués of the French Quarter, who are at least no more concerned with what's going on in an individual's bed than what's happening in his mind. He may also have sat at tables and bars with certain male hustlers who were interesting characters, but I doubt that he had more than a nodding acquaintance with a great many ladies of the evening, or their check-vested fancy men. For alas, even in nonchalant New Orleans, female whores and their pimps are usually too busy promoting a "trick" to idle out the lucrative night hours with writers, well-bred Bohemians, or any other group of citizens who are not, in a literal sense, broad-minded.

As to New Orleans' becoming for Williams a "kaleidoscope of drink, sex and revelry," it would be my guess that, while sex and revelry may have been the order of the night for our St. Louis blue boy, excessive drinking was not. In those days he drank no more than three highballs in an evening, having neither the money nor the urge for further liquid indulgence.

---

* Benjamin Nelson, *Tennessee Williams: The Man and His Work* (New York: Ivan Obolensky, Inc., 1961), pp. 38–9.

Suffice it to say that though he was poverty-ridden, and hocked most of his possessions to exist, T.W. was also happy in the Vieux Carré. He stayed at 722 Rue Toulouse in an old house owned by three aristocratic ladies who lived on its second floor. He persuaded the trio to open a restaurant on the first floor of the house, dreamed up the slogan, "Meals for a Quarter in the Quarter," and doubled in brass as waiter and cashier. The eatery was a great success until one night of disaster, which he has described in a letter to his mother:

. . . we've had a very hectic time at 722 Rue Toulouse. As I've probably mentioned, the landlady has had a hard time adjusting herself to the Bohemian spirit of the Vieux Carré. Things came to a climax this past week when a Jewish society photographer in the first floor studio gave a party and Mrs. Anderson expressed her indignation at their revelry by pouring a bucket of water through her kitchen floor which is directly over the studio and caused a near-riot among her guests. They called a patrol-wagon and Mrs. Anderson was driven to the Third Precinct on charges of Malicious Mischief and disturbing the peace. The following night we went to court—I was compelled to testify as one of the witnesses. Mrs. Anderson said she did not pour the water but I, being under oath, could not perjure myself—the best I could do was say I thought it highly improbable that any lady would do such a thing! The judge fined her fifteen dollars.

He goes on to say that he hopes Lyle Saxon will be able to put him on at the Writers' Project and speaks of Saxon's concern for his welfare, closing the letter with the following paragraph, which would seem to indicate that his chief landlady had been sadly shattered by her ride in the paddy wagon and her session at the Third Precinct.

Mrs. Anderson's unpopularity has wrecked the Eat Shop—I don't think she can ever reopen it. But Mrs. Nesbit plans to start a new one when she returns from Florida. Mrs. Anderson plans to sell the place for a $350-lease on the house and out-right sale of the complete furnishings, many of which are valuable antiques.

Yes, it is evident that he was having himself a time in these months in New Orleans, but since Saxon could not wangle the W.P.A. guidebook job, and he was now out of funds, he decided to drive out to Los Angeles with a friend.

He was less afraid of everything at this time, as in the early forties when I first knew him, than he was to become in 1945, faced with his "catastrophe of success." Before *Menagerie* he was preoccupied with actual survival in order to get out of himself two plays of autobiographical origin that he alone knew were crying inside him to be released. He needed money to exist, and he was human enough to dream of fame, but he was more concerned with public recognition of himself as a creative artist than with commercial success, which thus far seemed to him no more than a remote, perhaps unattainable, mirage.

Still he was already enough of a showman to decide that "Lanier," a name which must evoke the image of a great Southern poet, even when attached to "Thomas," was also something less than an ear-and-eye-catching cognomen for an *avant-garde* playwright. The name he'd take for himself that might be a name to help make him, had to be one which would elicit at least a wry curiosity, if not amused consternation. And so one day he wrote on a script, "Tennessee Williams," and smiled, perhaps slyly and pridefully, to himself.

Asked, many times, why he chose to become "Tennessee," he has come up with a number of reasons, but I think he has given no more plausible answer than he gave to my own query: "At Iowa— I don't know why, unless they got mixed up as to the state I came from—somebody started calling me Tennessee and the nickname just seemed to stick."

"Mississippi Williams" he could not be. "Tennessee" he could and would become, and so "Tennessee" he is to me and to all of us who met him after New Orleans. He is as well to us all, "Tenn" and "T.W."; to Don Windham alone, whimsically, "Te-ness-y"; and again to some of us at the end of a rare letter, "10," though he may also at times nostalgically sign a note or a wire to me, "Your ever-lovin' Tom." And while I'm about it, I may as well say that he has never been seriously troubled by the popularity of a certain singer of hillbilly songs, for once in a Miami restaurant when a friend said, "What'll you have, Tennessee?" and the waitress cried, "TENNESSEE ERNIE!" he merely sighed, "No baby, I'm the one who writes all those dirty plays."

2

IN THE WINTER OF 1936 I LEFT NEW YORK FOR ATLANTA WHERE, as yet unaware of Tennessee Williams' existence, I was to acquire several friends who, within three years' time, would enter his life to become a definite, influential part of it.

Since graduating from high school in 1929 I had worked in Atlanta for my father, a former newspaperman who owned some grocery stores, as an usher in a Peachtree movie house, and as general flunky for an outdoor advertising sign company.

In New York from 1931 to 1936 I had been employed by an art gallery, Bloomingdale's department store, the Town Hall Club, a model agency, and, finally, a swank 54th Street speak-easy where Helen Morgan sang. My poems had appeared in most of the quality magazines when my first book of poems was published in

1933 by Dodd, Mead. On the strength of the book's reviews I was given a scholarship to Rollins College, where I majored in creative writing and dramatics, and, in 1935, suffered a nervous break-down—like Tom Williams in St. Louis—as a result of overwork and an unhappy love affair.

Early in 1936 I published a second book of poems, finished off a temporary part-time job of reading manuscripts at the Viking Press, and took off for Atlanta to serve as a non-relief editor on the W.P.A. Writers' Project.

By the end of 1936 I had spent ten months on the Project, in which I had edited, written, and rewritten certain sections of the *Guide to Georgia*, part of a nostalgic novel, and a few new poems. The year had passed pleasantly, highlighted by a magical week spent backstage with my old friend Tallulah Bankhead, who, with *Reflected Glory*, had broken box-office records at the Erlanger. In January, 1937, the Federal Theatre took over the old Atlanta with three companies—one local, one from New York, one from Ala-bama. I transferred to the Theater Project, helped set up its office filing system, trained its green ushers, and, with the first produc-tion, began to write publicity for Atlanta's three daily newspapers. In that first season, I again played the second lead in Merton Hodges' *The Wind and the Rain* as I had, first at Rollins' Annie Russell Theatre, later in stock, with Glenn Hunter; the juvenile in *Fly Away Home*; the musician, Morris Rosenberg, in a première of Robert Nathan's *One More Spring*; and the boy in *Boy Meets Girl*.

I also rented with Jack Barefield, another writer-actor from Birmingham, a small house with a stone terrace over a garage for twenty-five dollars a month, and set about redecorating it. Through an actor, I'd met a young artist and sign-painter named Fred Melton, who not only helped me choose blue Linene drapes, a rag rug, and an India print bedspread (total expenditure eight dollars), but also painted my walls and floors and acted as joint host with Barefield and me at our housewarming.

The little garage place became a hang-out for most of the three theatrical companies, as well as a motley group of would-be Bo-hemians, and one spring afternoon someone brought over a kid fresh out of high school named Donald Windham. He'd brought along a copy of my second book, *Stranger's Garment,* to be autographed, and since he will soon be darting in and out of this book as a close friend of T.W.'s, I shall give my impression of him on this first day when he sat on my terrace glider talking to me about my work and about his current idol, William Saroyan.

Don was a modest youngster with a fresh-skinned, boyish face, curly dark hair, clear shortsighted eyes behind rimless glasses, and a laugh which usually doubled him up with glee at the sheer, exultant joy of being alive.

Almost at once he became a member of my heterogeneous circle which centered on the Theatre Project, and, as time went on, he and I could have been found, Saturday afternoons, heading for the movies downtown or hoofing it out to a Tenth Street delicatessen where everyone drank beer or called for setups with which to mix a communal bottle of gin.

Donnie had a quality then that could be described, in the best sense, as a kind of natural sweetness. There was about him an air of beguiling innocence. He did not drink liquor, swear, or use four-letter words, and sometimes he made up little poems that had something memorable about them. I remember one written about James Reese, a whimsical character actor with our W.P.A. company who would one day appear in more than one Williams' play:

> Jimmy is a little boy
> who comes skipping home from school
> careful not to step on even one pavement crack,
> hoping, expecting to find
> three crisp pungent cherry pies
> cooling on the window sill.

This, as I recall him, was Windham at eighteen. He would become a constant companion and a one-time collaborator of Tennessee's, a novelist, and, later, the author of a volume of short stories with a foreword by E. M. Forster, as well as a book of Atlanta memoirs. But in the spring and summer of 1937, he was simply a quiet-voiced member of a group of young people who gathered, weekend nights, on our terrace for as long as Barefield and I kept the cottage above the garage.

In the winter of 1939 the Federal Theatre began to fold and I was transferred to a W.P.A. State Parks project with offices at the capital. My work took me downtown to the Carnegie Library—and there I met a man destined to function constructively in the uncertain, chaotic years of Tennessee Williams' life between 1940 and 1945.

In the library reading-room one afternoon, I took a copy of *Poetry* magazine from a shelf near the librarian's desk. I was just asking what she thought of a seemingly contradictory use of the word *espada* in a poem of Millay's, when a cultured British voice behind me answered, "It's not really contradictory at all. You see, *espada* in Spanish means two things. the bull-fighter himself *and* the sword with which he slays the bull."

I whirled around, staring into the bright, birdlike eyes of a narrow-faced small man with tight-curled black hair, even as the librarian said quickly, "Mr. Maxwell, this is Mr. Paul Bigelow."

Mr. Bigelow and I shook hands. He promptly asked me what I was doing at the library, and when I told him he said briskly, "I'm sure the W.P.A. wouldn't mind your taking a few moments off for a beer, so let us repair to the nearest pub."

I agreed and we crossed the street to a bar where I listened, for more than an hour, to fascinating tales about the many literary people Bigelow had known in New York and Hollywood. That same afternoon at five-thirty I met Bigelow by appointment again; he came out to my new apartment on Peachtree—a huge, ranch-like, two-room, two-level place in a converted barn with a field-stone fireplace, and, after taking a look around, he decided to accept my impulsive invitation to join me and share the apartment expenses.

He stayed with me three months, in which time we had a number of parties at the ranch-barn apartment where Don Windham came with Fred Melton and Jimmy Reese, and where, as time passed, a joyous crowd of kids I'd met in Macon came on alternate weekends. This Macon gang consisted of six boys and girls, interested in art and writing, among them a young man

named Jordan Massee with whom Paul Bigelow struck up a
friendship.

We'd have a party one weekend at our place, the next at
someone's Macon house, and before the summer was out, Bigelow
had gone to stay with a friend of Jordan's and mine in Macon
where he began to collaborate with Jordan on a novel.

Meanwhile, Paul and I had grown to know each other quite well
on the surface and though his stay with me was financially a time
of trial for both of us, I cannot remember a more entertaining
period in my life. Paul could tell marvelous stories about the world
of arts and letters in which he apparently knew almost everyone—
but somehow there was about him, personally, an air of reticence,
even of mystery, which I found fascinating. I knew that he had
been educated in England, had lived in Greenwich Village in the
twenties, in Hollywood (where he'd been a newspaper reporter),
as well as in Mexico, in the thirties, that he had a sister and
stepmother in California, that he'd been married—and that was
all. His stories, I thought, sometimes bordered upon the incredible, but I was to learn that when Bigelow told me a story that
seemed most incredible, that one—of all his stories—was likely to
prove most factual.

I recall a girl friend of mine, sitting in her garden one evening,
saying thoughtfully, "I like Paul, but there's one thing I can't
quite figure out and that is, how he could have managed to be in
Paris and in Washington, D.C., on the day the Coliseum roof fell
in"—but we both agreed that it scarcely mattered if he did occasionally get his dates and localities mixed, since most of his stories,
like this one, were highly diverting.

Recently, at his small house in Connecticut, Paul came charging
out of his bedroom where he'd been reading a rough draft of this
manuscript and announced, "I don't see, Mr. Maxwell, why you
insist upon trying to present me as a mysterious figure in this
book—and anyhow, why do you say you've never known much
about me?"

"Because it's true," I told him. "For instance, I don't even know
where you were born."

"Why, of course you do," he said. "I must have told you—in

Maine—but only, as my aunt, who raised me, used to say, *because
it was in the summer."*

He nodded with brisk finality, as if to say he was pleased to have
finally settled for me the matter of his origin and past life before I
knew him, and returned to his bedroom—leaving me no more
enlightened than I have been for the last twenty-five years.

But anyway, he is our Paul—and, as Audrey Wood once said,
more often than not a joy to all of us whom he considers his
friends.

He has a wit that flashes on the darkest day as keenly as on the
sunniest, and I remember certain occasions when in defense of one
or the other of us, he has applied his rapier thrusts to the considerable public discomfort of some mischief-maker.

There was, for instance, the evening in Atlanta on which some
prankish friends of mine brought a woman from a New York
publishing house to my place when I was slightly squiffed. Paul
took in the situation, called me aside and whispered, "Don't say
one off-color thing in front of that woman. She's a tiresome bore
and the absolute bitch of the book business." Later the party
moved on to the house of a poet friend of mine, and there,
on his sixth drink, momentarily forgetful, Bigelow, seated on a sofa
beside the book bitch, caught himself up and said, "No, I don't
think I'll tell that story. It's just a trifle too blue." At that
moment, our host, one of the pranksters who'd tried to get me
drunk enough to upset the square old girl—chirped from his
sprawled position in the doorway, "Aw, go ahead, Paul, I'm only
twelve," whereupon Bigelow answered. "We were not referring to
your I.Q. Mr. H."

This is a slight cameo portrait of the man who came along in
1940 when Tennessee Williams was struggling with *The Glass
Menagerie,* and who became for a time a sort of combination
guardian angel and stout man Friday for our youthful, just-about-
to-burgeon playwright.

After Bigelow's departure from my place in the summer of 1939,
the pedantic drag, red tape, and utter uselessness of my W.P.A.
work with the State Parks Department (writing inscriptions for
roadside markers and a radio play about Hernando De Soto, never

to be produced) became unendurable, so I began casting about for some means of escape from Atlanta. One day at the library I found a three-week-old ad in the personal column of the *Saturday Review of Literature* which read:

WANTED: Amanuensis for writer on Long Island. Must be personable, educated, socially acceptable, with preferably an Irish wit. I am seeking an asset, not a liability. PO Box 1234.

I wrote promptly saying that while I was not of the Ould Sod in origin, I was also not of that class of Southerner that leapt up from a front-stoop rocker, bawling, "Fo' Gawd, ef it ain't Sister Bessie," whenever company came. I stated further that I was a college man with two published books, that it was not my habit to squirt tobacco juice between the toes of dowagers who wore openwork summer slippers, and that I had once existed in New York for a year largely by making myself agreeable socially.

In no time I received a letter from Long Island, in which the gentleman of the ad replied that he'd be delighted if I *would* spit between the toes of certain dowagers he knew, and that if I should be coming to New York, he would like to talk to me. He signed himself, "F. H. Markoe."

I showed the letter to my friend James Reese, who promptly cried, "Why, I met him at a party last year in New York. He's a real nice, amusing man," and that was all I needed. I borrowed seventy-five dollars from three friends, stored most of my belongings, and boarded a train.

On the following Saturday afternoon, Mr. Markoe, a fiftyish, stocky, short-statured gentleman with light-blue eyes, a ruddy face, and Mephistophelian eyebrows, met me at the Southampton, Long Island, station with his liveried chauffeur. Twenty minutes later we rolled through a tall Oriental gateway and stopped before a two-story red stucco house, the decor of which proved to be a combination of Chinese Renaissance, ancient Greek, late Malayan, and mid-Victorian. The prim guest room to which the chauffeur carried my bags was connected by a black-and-silverfixtured bathroom adorned with red, Chinese-monogrammed towels to a larger chamber featuring bamboo murals of monkeys, parrots, and cranes—and when I apprehensively stole downstairs for cocktails I had not as yet unpacked.

Over drinks, however, Mr. Markoe and I found we had mutual friends in New York and Atlanta, and after dinner we came to an agreement whereby I would receive a weekly stipend, board and room for handling his correspondence and working with him on a verse novel until early September when he would be going West.

Harold Vinal, the editor of *Voices* magazine, was offering a vacation that year to an American poet to be spent at his ancestral house on the island of Vinal Haven, Maine, which he'd turned into a summer inn catering to writers. To my surprise he gave me the award, so, after this summer, in which with Markoe I had met the fine folk of Southampton, I took a boat up to Maine, stayed three weeks at Harold's, then traveled back down to Boston to visit the John Ritcheys. John was managing editor of the *Christian Science Monitor*; he'd recently done a feature article for the paper's Sunday magazine in which he'd spoken well of me, along with Millay, Frost, Sandburg, MacLeish, Louise Bogan, John Hall Wheelock, and John Holmes—and because of this I was lavishly wined and dined in Boston. I met John Holmes, and Margaret Lee Runbeck, the short story writer and novelist who was to become my good friend, read my poems to Ritchey's evening class at Harvard, and recorded fifteen of them for the Harvard Record Library.

Then, one day, as I was crossing the Common, some lines flared like a dazzling light in my head. I charged up to Ritchey's office at the *Monitor*, and, in forty-five minutes, wrote a forty-line poem called "Go Looking," which, after its publication in the *Saturday Review*, was later plagiarized in a popular song. It also became the one poem of mine which Tennessee Williams learned by heart and which he referred to in his foreword to my selected volume of poems in 1954 as "one of the few great modern poems."

Back in New York that fall and winter, I lived on a loan from an optimistic friend who believed in my future, occasional poetry honorariums from magazines, and from small checks for some prose pieces which appeared in the *Monitor*.

I was living in a hall bedroom on Lexington Avenue when I met Tennessee in the winter of 1940, but my next vivid memory of him is of an April evening and morning in a room I'd taken with a young Irishman (a research vassal at *Time*) in the George Washington Hotel.

The hotel was managed by an impish, lively Londoner named Donald Neville-Willing, who felt an empathy for writers. W. H. Auden had just moved out a week before the Irishman and I moved in; Cecil Roberts, the novelist, and Keith Winter, a young novelist-playwright who would later write a hit play, *The Shining Hour*, were still there, and mine and the Mick's room, which Neville-Willing called "Poet's Corner," shortly became a convivial gathering place.

Tennessee was certainly present at several informal parties the Mick and I gave—including a lively affair where he met Nancy Cushman with whom I'd trod the boards at Rollins and who would later replace Mildred Dunnock on Broadway as Big Mama in *Cat on a Hot Tin Roof*—but only one occasion involving him stands out clear to me now.

He had come one evening with Don Windham and Fred Melton to a party in Poet's Corner and had stayed on with them after all the less durable night birds had flown. We had three-quarter twin beds in the room, so, around four in the morning Don and Fred announced that they were not about to attempt a hazardous homeward journey to Swing Street at such an hour.

Tennessee then cried out that he certainly had no desire to travel back uptown alone, and when I objected to the prospect of the five of us occupying two beds, he said, "Oh, hell, Gil, I don't have to sleep in a bed. All I need is a blanket."

I got the blanket; he spread it on the floor, rolled himself up in it like the lone Indian, and went to sleep. He was up and bathed before the rest of us next morning, and I woke to find him pacing restlessly about the room. He asked if he might borrow my typewriter, and while the rest of us were showering, using electric razors, shouting back and forth from bedroom to bath above a raucous radio, he sat typing ninety words a minute, plainly deaf and blind to all the bedlam. After half an hour he whisked a last sheet from the typewriter, sat back and sighed, and when I asked, "What on earth were you typing, Tenn?" he answered quietly, "Oh—just the new scene for *Battle of Angels.*"

I marveled that morning at his powers of concentration, as well as at his philosophical acceptance of the floor and the blanket the night before—and I have since come to think of these qualities in him as being symbolic, as well as significant, in relation to his ultimate success. For I can see now that among all of us young hopefuls in those days, he was best equipped in certain ways to succeed. By 1940 he had already grown used to not knowing, some mornings, where he'd sleep the following night. And though this must have scared him, it is my belief that his constant obsession with the people and plots of two plays that danced in his head not only deadened his fears but caused him, as well, to exist, for hours at a time, numbed to such imminent dangers as going supperless or riding all night in the subway.

A great many things of importance had been happening to him since the past winter in New Orleans, and because I could never begin to tell about his recent journey West in the touchingly nostalgic way he has done in his preface to the script of his play, *Orpheus Descending,* I shall now quote him, verbatim.

And then there was a wild and wonderful trip to California with a young clarinet player. We ran out of gas in El Paso, also out of cash, and it seemed for days that we would never go farther, but my grandmother was an "easy touch" and I got a letter with a $10 bill stitched neatly to one of the pages, and we continued westward.

In the Los Angeles area, in the summer of 1939, I worked for a while at Clark's Bootery in Culver City, within sight of the M-G-M studio and I lived on a pigeon ranch, and I rode between the two, a distance of ten miles, on a secondhand bicycle that I bought for $5.

Then a most wonderful thing happened. While in New Orleans I had heard about a play contest being conducted by the Group Theatre of New York. I submitted all four of the long plays I have mentioned that preceded *Battle of Angels,* plus a group of one-acts called *American Blues.* One fine day I received, when I returned to the ranch on my bike, a telegram saying that I had won a special award of $100 for the one-acts and it was signed by Harold Clurman, Molly Day Thacher, who is the present Mrs. Elia Kazan, and that fine writer, Irwin Shaw, the judges of the contest.

I retired from Clark's Bootery and from picking squabs at the pigeon ranch. And the clarinet player and I hopped on our bicycles and rode all the way down to Tijuana and back as far as Laguna Beach, where we obtained, rent free, a small cabin on a small ranch in return for taking care of the poultry.

We lived all that summer on the $100 from the Group Theatre and I think it was the happiest summer of my life. All the days were pure gold, the nights were starry, and I looked so young, or carefree, that they would sometimes refuse to sell me a drink because I did not appear to have reached 21. But toward the end of the summer, maybe only because it was the end of the summer as well as the end of the $100, the clarinet player became very moody and disappeared without warning into the San Bernardino Mountains to commune with his soul in solitude, and there was nothing left in the cabin in the canyon but a bag of dried peas.

I lived on stolen eggs and avocados and dried peas for a week, and also on a faint hope stirred by a letter from a lady in New York whose name was Audrey Wood, who had taken hold of all those plays that I had submitted to the Group Theatre contest, and told me that it might be possible to get me one of the Rockefeller Fellowships, or grants, of $1,000 which were being passed out to gifted young writers at that time. And I began to write *Battle of Angels*, a lyrical play about memories and the loneliness of them.

Note how lightly he speaks of subsisting for seven days on his fantastic diet, and how casually he mentions the entrance into his life of Audrey Wood. Actually, alone in that cabin, the clarinet player gone, he must have been no more sustained by those scanty rations than by the "faint hope" stirred by Miss Wood—yet there he was, starting work on a three-act play.

Meanwhile, in New York, though he had no inkling of it, the stage was about to be set for the curtain's rise on a real-life drama involving himself and Miss Wood, which would eventually awe not only the two of them but the whole world of the theater.

Audrey had written him at the insistence of Molly Day
Thatcher, saying she was interested in his work. Williams replied
by air-mail post card telling her he had also heard from another
agent, Frieda Fishbein, and that he had not yet been able to
decide between them. He suggested she read his work; then, after
she'd read it, if she still felt inclined to have him as a client, he
would make a decision.

Audrey Wood read the one-acts from *American Blues* and also
The Fugitive Kind. She did not care much for the long play but
she was sufficiently impressed by the short ones to write that her
offer to him was still open and that she thought him "highly
promising, but not a finished playwright." Williams wrote back
accepting her as his representative. Miss Wood immediately went
to work for him and wrote him again in June, enclosing with her
letter a Rockefeller Fellowship application form as well as a twenty-
five-dollar check from *Story Magazine* for his short story "The
Field of Blue Children." Tennessee replied with thanks telling her
that he would be using the check for typewriter repairs and "a trip
to San Francisco to see William Saroyan and the World's Fair."

He evidently carried out these intentions, for his *Orpheus*
preface continues:

> Although my beloved grandmother was living on the pension of a
> retired minister (I believe it was only $85 a month in those days),
> and her meager earnings as a piano instructor, she once again
> stitched some bills to a page of a letter, and I took a bus to St.
> Louis. *Battle of Angels* was finished late that fall and sent to Miss
> Wood.

He now journeyed to New York to meet Audrey Wood, and
Audrey remembers thinking as he sat in her Rockefeller Plaza
office, slim, smooth-faced, casually dressed, that he looked like a
country boy not yet out of his teens.

She was impressed, however, with his gentleness of manner, his
humility, his obvious sweetness of nature—and though he left her
office feeling "profoundly discouraged" that she hadn't yet got so
much as a nibble on *Battle of Angels,* she has since stated, concern-

ing this meeting, that never before in her life had she felt such a hunch about anybody.

Tennessee stayed in town for several weeks; then he went home to St. Louis where he continued writing and sold a few stories and poems to the arty, small magazines. But home now seemed to him, after the freedom of New Orleans and California, more than ever a stultifying, lonesome place, and only a short time before, he had written Miss Wood, "All optimism has departed. I expect and suspect the worst."

But again, let him tell it, in his own exultant way:

One day the phone rang and, in a terrified tone, my mother told me that it was long distance, for me. The voice was Audrey Wood's. Mother waited, shakily, in the doorway. When I hung up I said, quietly, "Rockefeller has given me a $1,000 grant and they want me to come to New York." For the first time since I had known her, my mother burst into tears. "I am so happy," she said. It was all she could say.

So, in the early winter of 1940, he came back to New York and enrolled for a seminar in advanced playwriting which Theresa Helburn and John Gassner of the Theatre Guild were conducting at the New School for Social Research. Through Harold Vinal he met, and began to pal around with, Don Windham and Fred Melton, who in turn introduced him first to me, then to Paul Bigelow, now ensconced at the King's College Club, near Columbia.

In the spring, just after he'd banged out his new scene for *Battle of Angels* on my typewriter, Tenn completed a fresh draft of his play and submitted it to John Gassner who, with great excitement, turned it over to Lawrence Langner, another Guild director, and before the close of the New School's spring session, the Guild had optioned the play.

Tenn was living at the West Side Y.M.C.A. where I remember Bigelow, swimming with me at some distance from him in the pool one afternoon, wondering mildly if he'd be wearing a necktie when he went down to accept the Rockefeller check, and just where he'd be off to as soon as he got his hands on it.

In those days there was a constant, restless urge in him to be in some place other than where he was. I recall his standing with me one night at a Broadway curb, saying, "I hate New York. After I've been here a while, I always feel as if I'm being false to my friends."

I said bromidically, "Well, one thing's sure, no matter where you go, you've got to take Tenn Williams with you."

He looked at me as though in surprise and said, "Why, yes, that's true, isn't it?"

That was the last time I saw him before he left town. Quite late in the spring he went to Taos, New Mexico, where he had stopped off the year before, en route from Laguna Beach to St. Louis, to call on Frieda Lawrence and to talk to her about a play he wished to write about D.H. In Taos he did a last revision of *Battle of Angels* and came back to New York at the summer's end to start rehearsals with the Theatre Guild.

Throughout the spring and summer, with paste pot, shears, and determination, I pieced together, rewrote, and reconstructed a historical novel for a Kentucky lady who'd been working ten years on her manuscript. When my roommate took off on vacation I moved into the lady's apartment where I finished the book, receiving room and board as part of my pay.

Summer's end found me broke and homeless and it was then that a young woman whom I shall call Gladys (because that was her name) called me and said, "I'm taking a forty-five-dollar-a-month cold-water flat in an East Side remodeled tenement. There's room in it for you, so pack up your gear and move in next Friday. If anybody wants to think we're living in sin, then let them. We'll know we're not and that's all that matters, isn't it?"

Gladys was a handsome girl who'd been one of the Poet's Corner gang that spring. She hailed from the West, where she'd been a trick rider in rodeos; she was now a Powers model, and in her generous heart compassionate friendship took precedence over all her fears of Mrs. Grundy.

Fred Melton and Don Windham helped us move into the new

place, took one look at the layout, and promptly rented the flat below.

We four had some fine times in the east seventies that fall, but I was in a state of frenzy, job hunting and trying to recover from a recent love affair gone sour, so the chief thing I remember—in addition to certain convivial evenings—is being unable emotionally to read more than a few pages at a time of a first book by a first cousin of Jordan Massee's, which had astounded the critics. The book was *The Heart Is a Lonely Hunter*, and the cousin was a twenty-two-year-old Georgia girl named Carson McCullers, who would later become a close friend of Tennessee's.

Tenn came back to town early that fall for rehearsals of *Battle of Angels*, alternately cheerful and moody, and maybe pregnant with premonition, for I recall his saying to Don and me, "Here I am about to have a play done by the Theatre Guild with no less a director than Margaret Webster, yet somehow I've never in my life felt less happy or more uncertain."

In October I worked one "trial" day for a white-haired lady who ran a cluttered midtown bookstore. Tenn revealed to me later that he also put in a "trial" day in her shop that autumn. As an example of how tough things still were in New York in 1940, a trial day in the shop of Miss S. carried no guarantee of remuneration; and since Tenn pleased her no more as a wrapper of books than I did as a general stock man, neither of us received one cent for our single-day stints of eight hours in which the lady's voice never ceased (out of customer earshot) in its loud complaints against her economically hogtied help.

In November I went to work as a holiday section manager at Gimbel's and moved into a maid's room at a nearby hotel. I was laid off Christmas Eve. Melton, as a free-lance commercial artist, was also temporarily jobless, as was Donald Windham, so, none of us having been present in Boston for the opening of *Battle*, I must fall back on Tenn's account of that historic fiasco:

One icy bright winter morning in the last week of 1940, my brave representative, Audrey Wood, and I were crossing the Common in Boston, from an undistinguished hotel on one side to the

grandeur of the Ritz-Carlton on the other. We had just read the
morning notices of *Battle of Angels* which had opened at the
Wilbur the evening before. As we crossed the Common there was
a series of loud reports like gunfire from the street that we were
approaching and one of us said, "My God, they're shooting at
us!"

We were still laughing a bit hysterically, as we entered the Ritz-
Carlton suite in which the big brass of the Theatre Guild and
director Margaret Webster were waiting for us with that special
air of gentle gravity that hangs over the demise of a play so much
like the atmosphere that hangs over a home from which a living
soul has been snatched by the Reaper.

Not present was little Miriam Hopkins, who was understandably shattered and cloistered after the events of the evening
before, in which a simulated on-stage fire had erupted clouds of
smoke so realistically over both stage and auditorium that a lot of
Theatre Guild firstnighters had fled choking from the Wilbur
before the choking star could take her bows, which were about
the quickest and most distracted that I have seen in a theatre.

It was not that morning that I was informed that the show
must close. That morning I was only told that the play must be
cut to the bone. I came with a rewrite of the final scene and I
remember saying, heroically, "I will crawl on my belly through
brimstone if you will substitute this!" The response was gently
evasive. It was a few mornings later that I received the *coup de
grace*, the announcement that the play would close at the completion of its run in Boston. On that occasion I made an equally
damatic statement, on a note of anguish, "You don't seem to see
that I put my heart into this play!"

It was Miss Webster who answered with a remark that I have
never forgotten and yet never heeded. She said, "You must not
wear your heart on your sleeve for daws to peck at!" Someone else
said, "At least you are not out of pocket." I don't think I had any
answer for that one, any more than I had anything in my pocket
to be out of.

In a recent *Life* article, Edwin Bronner, speaking of the unpredictable reception of new playwrights each year, reminisces as
follows in regard to *Battle*'s demise:

"*One of the most incredible dramas ever presented . . .*" Boston first-nighters were stunned and horrified by the bluntness and candor of its dialogue. The young, unknown playwright didn't mince his words.

Neither did Boston's City Councillor. He labeled the exhibit "putrid" and demanded it be closed immediately, adding: "The police should arrest the persons responsible for bringing shows of this type to Boston." (Meaning the Theatre Guild, the director Margaret Webster and Star Miriam Hopkins.) "The play was more of a disappointment to us than to you," the Guild admitted in an unprecedented letter to its Boston subscribers. The show turned out badly, the letter concluded, "but who knows whether the next one by the same author may not prove a success?"*

It is amusing to recall that a play which today would seem shiny-clean in comparison to Williams' later productions should have created such a furor in 1941. Furthermore, it is interesting to speculate as to just what might have happened to the American theater if Williams had been so crushed by the hostile reaction to his play as to have ceased writing for a period of years.

Actually, he was not crushed at all, as will be evident from this wryly reticent paragraph of the *Orpheus Descending* preface:

Well, in the end, when the Boston run was finished, I was given a check for $200 and told to get off somewhere and rewrite the play. I squandered half of this subsidy on the first of four operations performed on a cataracted left eye, and the other half took me to Key West for the rewrite.

The quotation does not tell us that he was chagrined, amused, angry and doggedly determined to rise on spirited wings from the ashes of his defeat. It does reveal that, scared as he must have been of the surgeon's scalpel (he hates even to go to the dentist's alone), he nonetheless considered his eye operation a thing of minor importance compared to the task that lay before him in Key West, Florida.

There he was lucky enough to rent a servant's cabin in the back-

---

* *Life,* August 31, 1962, p. 11.

yard of the Trade Winds, a tourist home owned and managed by an Episcopal minister's widow. This lady was Mrs. Clara Black, who with her son George and her daughter Marion, had existed like Tenn in various rectories, plagued by the small economies incumbent upon a preacher's family. From the start of his winter in Key West, there was a bond between the impecunious playwright pounding his typewriter in the backyard cabin, and the folk in the big house. Sometimes Mrs. Black sent out a tray to him at mealtimes and he went often to the Trade Winds for cocktails or dinner, thus entering upon a lasting friendship with all the Blacks.

In March he wrote to his mother that he had met a "record number" of celebrities, whose names he proceeded to tick off, adding, "They are all busy entertaining each other and having political quarrels. I prefer my writing-desk or the beach to this type of social activity which I got enough of in New York."

Before the month was out Audrey Wood wired him that she had persuaded the Rockefeller committee to grant him another $500 on which to write a new play, and he returned to New York with his revised script of *Battle of Angels*. The Theatre Guild, however, was not sufficiently impressed with the revision to risk a new production, so he moved into the West Side Y.M.C.A., optimistically hoping to live on the five monthly allotments of $100 from the Committee.

He could never quite get by on the hundred, though, and in the last week of each month he was quite as badly off as Don, Fred, and I, who were all either unemployed or, at best, working sporadically. In fact, looking back over 1941 as I find it revealed in letters I wrote to my mother, I marvel that any one of us who was trying to create and survive in New York that year managed to get through it at all.

I went back to Gimbel's for the months of January and February as a floorwalker, got laid off again, and managed to exist till June by working part-time for a vanity publisher.

Jordan Massee had moved in below Gladys with Don and Fred, and Bigelow, who'd been out of town on some family business, turned up at the apartment house around April, vibrant as always, with glittering hopes and plans for us all.

Windham, excited about a story of D. H. Lawrence's called "You Touched Me" which he felt might make a play, showed the story to Tenn, who read it and said, "Okay, let's dramatize it."

T. W. must have been concerned about his precarious financial position in the closing week of each month, but I'm sure he was never as neurotically frightened as I was of having no money, for I recall a revealing visit he paid me one afternoon at the Wolcott Hotel.

I'd been doing some housecleaning and when he saw on a chair an old gray suit I was about to present to the maid, he cried, "Why, what on earth do you mean giving away a real good suit?"

"It's not real good," I said. "It's a relic of my last year at Rollins and you can read the book of Job—which paraphrases my own life—right through its goddam seat."

Nevertheless he skinned out of his clothes, tried on the suit, pulling the too-long pants up high, and turning before the mirror, purred softly, "Why, I love this suit, Gil. Can I have it?"

"Of course," I told him, "providing you'll come on out with me while I go through a foul experience I've never had before."

Out on the street, carrying a paper sack of hockable items, including an electric razor, I said dourly, "I don't know how most people feel about this three-brass-balls thing, but frankly, the very idea of it makes me a little sick."

Tenn shifted the bundle containing my old suit from his left arm to his right.

"Don't be silly," he said. "Last time I left New Orleans, I pawned everything I owned—typewriter, phonograph, everything. Never felt half so free in my whole life."

He glanced sideways at me; we both burst out laughing and all my trepidation regarding the mission on which I was bent completely vanished.

Late in this spring he moved into a nice apartment which Bigelow had rented for himself, Jordan, Don, and Fred, after the latter three occupants had gone home to Georgia to see their folks.

As for me, both the spring and the summer were a nightmare in which I retrograded from an occasional day's work at Saks 34th to several unspeakable weeks, first as a cafeteria bus boy, then as a floorwalker in Woolworth's, so I remember seeing precious little of anyone during this time.

I do recall, though, being downtown with Bigelow one day when he said plaintively, "Tenn's so completely preoccupied right now with something he's working on, he's just not here, and I am so weary of telling him all day long, 'Get up, go wash your hands for lunch, eat, Tennessee. Pick up your shirt off the floor, Tennessee,' I don't think I can go on much longer."

One day in the next week, after I'd left Woolworth's for a few days' sales work at Saks, Bigelow came down to the hotel and told me, glinty-eyed, over a beer, "Now, I am at the end of my tether, believe me. Yesterday I asked, 'Tenn, where are those two checks you got last week from Audrey?' He said, 'Why, I don't know, Paul'; and then, 'Oh, yes, I'm afraid I sent 'em out in the laundry.' Well, naturally I lit out like a comet for the Chinaman's where, thank God, the laundry bundle hadn't yet reached the tubs, pawed madly through all the clothes and found the checks . . . but, really, I am exhausted so I've just told that young man I'm making arrangements for his going to Provincetown this weekend."

I took a sip of beer. "And what did Tenn say to that?"

Bigelow looked nonplussed. "Nothing much. He just looked up glassily from the typewriter and sort of grunted."

I laughed, and Bigelow said, "Yes, I know it's funny, but honestly, Gil, do you realize how difficult it is sometimes to communicate with that man?"

"What do you mean exactly?" I asked—knowing what he meant exactly, but wanting Paul to go on.

"I mean," he said, "you'll, for instance, be sitting with Tenn Williams in Central Park. You'll have told him a long, diverting story of which you will shortly learn he hasn't heard one single word. You will then remark, simply because you can no longer endure the silence and that lonely sense of his just not-being-with-you, 'I saw a most unusual bird this morning,' whereupon he will jump up, shouting, 'Bird? What bird? Where?' Now, precisely what explanation—if any—do you think there may be for that?"

I was laughing so hard I had to set down my beer.

"I don't know, of course," I said, "but I wouldn't be surprised if he was thinking about some play he's planning that's got a bird in it somewhere."

This was in the first week of June. On the following Friday, having packed Tenn's bags, got him shaved, bathed, and into his good suit, Bigelow led him to Grand Central Station.

Tennessee had been submissive and quiet throughout this whole procedure, but now on the train platform as Paul spoke glibly of Provincetown's joys and advantages, he suddenly cried out, "*Provincetown?* Why, what do you mean? I don't want to go to Provincetown, I want to stay right here."

"Be that as it may," said Bigelow, "you are going to Provincetown."

He grasped Tenn's arm, bounced him into the train and sat firmly beside him, with Tenn next to the window. When the conductor came along he said, "This gentleman's going to Provincetown, so please don't let him off till he gets there."

Then, with the train under way, he swung out of the coach and down to the station platform.

"It was pitiful," Paul told me later, over a drink. "He just sat there with his nose pressed to the pane, looking lost and forlorn all the time I was waving good-by to him, but I tell you, Gilbert, this simply *had* to be. He and I were both in most desperate need of a brief vacation."

Tenn had been gone a week when Paul called me and said, "Come over tonight. I want you to read his first letter."

The letter said that our boy was enjoying the sun and sea, writing verse, working on short stories and plays—and it closed with the following paragraph:

Nevertheless, your sins are on your head. I *told* you not to send me here, and here I am, living in a broken down rooming house filled with faggots and lesbians—not to mention a very strange girl named Rachel who each night washes my feet and dries them with her hair.

He really had a good summer, though, at Provincetown, for he finished a play there which I have come to think of as his best one-acter. It was the play about D. H. Lawrence for which Frieda had given him material on his last visit to Taos, and he called it *I Rise in Flame, Cried the Phoenix.*

He came back to Bigelow in late August, and one night I rang the apartment bell, simply because I happened to be in the neighborhood.

When I got upstairs Tenn met me at the door, very brown, muscular, a little high, his cigarette in its amber holder clutched between stubby fingers, and gave me a big hug crying, "Gil! Come on *in* . . . Paul will be here soon."

The living room was full of young men and women, all casually dressed, and he introduced me around. After that, while the music blared and the dancing continued, we sat down on the studio couch to compare notes on our separate summers. We sat there, gossiping, drinking, laughing; then suddenly he looked out at the crowd made up mostly of his summer companions in Provincetown, and said, turning again to face me, "You know, I hate to think of your being here with these people, Gil. You should never be in the company of people like this. . . ."

I was astounded, since the people appeared to be no worse than the usual run of casual, shallow people one meets at New York parties—but even as I assured him that they seemed all right to me, I felt touched and proud because of what he had just said. Proud and humble and grateful, for it is not often any one of us says a thing like this to a friend.

But then it is true of Tennessee that one of his most endearing characteristics is his sometimes exaggerated admiration for his friends as well as the depth of feeling he has for them.

It was much easier for him to care for people in the summer of 1941 than it is today, because he knew in his own heart then that his true friends felt a real affection for him—himself—alone. Nobody he knew back there had an ax to grind in showing affection for him, since he had nothing to give anyone in return, except his own heartfelt affection.

September found Tennessee back in New Orleans at work on his three-act play, *Stairs to the Roof.* In October he bought himself a bicycle and set off along the Gulf Coast on a sightseeing trip which he enjoyed immensely, right up to the moment on a bright, sultry morning when he ran smack into a brindle cow and wrecked the bike's front wheel.

A letter from Edwina that fall brought the sorrowful news that his grandmother was slowly dying of cancer, so he left New Orleans for a few weeks' visit to St. Louis. Upon his return he told me, "You know, Gil, I had it kind of rough down there this time. I'd hardly got in the house when Mother said, 'Son, your father's in the back yard, so go out there and greet him nicely.' I went out and asked, 'How are you, Dad?' He said, 'Just fine, Tom, how are you?' and then, 'You see that firewood on the other side of the yard? Well, I want you to move the whole pile over to this side in the morning.'"

I stared at Tenn and whistled. "Lord, what a homecoming."

He nodded. "Yes, but that wasn't all. You know how I get preoccupied sometimes when I'm eating, and start making those smacking noises? Well, I must've been pretty bad the first night at supper, because next morning when I came down to breakfast, Mother called to me brightly from somewhere, 'Turn left at the foot of the stairs, son Thomas. There's a trough for you in the kitchen.'"

He told me all this laughing and I laughed with him, but it seemed to me I sensed a sadness beneath his laughter, and of course as I later learned, I was right, for it was on this visit that he had found his adored "Grand" wasted by her malady to a skeletal eighty-three pounds.

And so, driven from home once again by the unendurable presence of hopeless illness, he returned, forlorn, to New Orleans.

That autumn in New York, I, as the only member of our small group who had regular employment, moved from a hideous clerical job in a West Side hotel to a sinecure as mail and information clerk at the Fifth Avenue Hotel, receiving, as part of my stipend, two sumptuous meals daily.

Don and Fred sometimes dropped in to see me there, and one day I introduced them to an amiable, modest, blond-bearded giant who often stopped at the desk to chat with me before going back to the rear reception-rooms where he was rehearsing some play, scheduled to open cold in town before Christmas.

The giant's name was Vincent Price, and the play, which would shortly establish him as a Broadway star, was *Angel Street*.

This little story of Price and his play made an amusing bit of main-stem news for one or the other of us to impart to Tenn in a late December letter, but the item was overshadowed by a more personal one involving our Mr. Melton who had surprised us all by taking unto himself as bride Miss Sarah Marshall, the youngest, prettiest member of our Macon contingent.

Tenn received the letter in the French Quarter, where he was a cashier in a restaurant by day and was working, by night, on *Stairs to the Roof* and *I Rise in Flame, Cried the Phoenix*; and I suspect Christmas that year was a rather lean season for him. It was a lavish, gay holiday in my case, for Sarah and Fred had chosen to spend their honeymoon at the Fifth Avenue—and when I sat down with them to the wedding supper I was aglow not only with wine, but a self-assurance engendered of having in my wallet $250 cash which represented only a part of the gifts I had received from the hotel's generous guests.

These years, 1940–1941, had been precarious but creative for Williams and all of us, and since writing this chapter, I have been ironically amused to recall the outcome of the various projects on which we were all so feverishly working. I feel that any reader prone to envy the life of the man of letters may find the following summation instructive. We have already learned what happened to Tenn and *Battle of Angels*. Well, his fantasy, *Stairs to the Roof*, would finally achieve its one and only production under Margo Jones' direction at the Pasadena Playhouse, where it ran for a fortnight in the spring of 1947. The wonderfully wrought one-act *I Rise in Flame, Cried the Phoenix* would not be seen until a winter morning in 1959, when it was staged by ANTA for an invited audience. That crazy-quilt manuscript of the Kentucky lady's novel, which I had pieced together with scissors and paste, fell into the hands of Maxwell Perkins, who, laboring long with the author, shaped it into something Scribners had the mistaken temerity to publish in the fall of 1942. A short story, on which

Margaret Lee Runbeck collaborated with me, was never sold. Part
of a novel of mine that Bigelow had liked—laid aside after several
enthusiastic, confusing letters of rejection from publishers—has
lately formed the nucleus for a novel I hope to complete, and only
a few of my poems written at this time appeared in the quality
magazines.

In the early winter of 1942 the Messrs. Williams and Windham
were plugging away at *You Touched Me,* Bigelow and Massee at
their lengthy, untitled novel. I had been taking my third book of
poems, *The Dark Rain Falling,* around to commercial houses with
no success, and now I was carrying on a private campaign for its
publication. Working with my old friend Jack Barefield I got out a
form letter with an order blank, which I not only mailed, but
stuffed into the letter boxes of those guests at the Fifth Avenue
who I thought might be interested, so by late January I was already sending checks to an out-of-town press to cover the book's
publication costs.

In those days everyone in our group was in a state of apprehen-
sion regarding his draft status except Tenn and Bigelow, who had
already been rejected as physically unfit.

Tennessee, never having gotten over being frightened by his
heart's behavior at the time of his St. Louis breakdown, was now
terrified by the draft doctor's skeptical report. He went at once to
another physician, who told him his palpitations were caused by
unstable nerves. Tenn then came to a typically enigmatic decision,
which brought Bigelow to my hotel one spring morning, wearing
an indescribable look on his face.

He said, "Well, you may or may not be astonished to hear that
Tenn went down to the eye doctor's office yesterday and had his
second operation for cataracts."

I stared, incredulous, at Bigelow. Here was this hypochondriacal
being who lived in dread of physical and mental illness, trekking
off alone to have a knife taken to his left eye without anesthesia.
We agreed that day that it didn't make much sense, but now,
twenty-odd years later, I have decided it did. Williams is morbidly,

pathologically frightened of illness, but he would endure any amount of pain rather than risk the slightest possibility of making an entrance into that nebulous land from whence no traveler has yet returned. He is determinedly set on living, and so, that spring, despite the draft doctor's dolorous report and his operation, he managed almost to complete, with Don, the first full draft of *You Touched Me.*

He then went south to visit Bigelow and Jordan Massee in Macon, Georgia.

Jordan was with his family, so Tennessee and Paul took a room in a boarding house—and that was the start of a summer in the South which Bigelow has long remembered. It would be autumn before I would hear in detail from him about one of its astounding events:

"As you know, Tenn was just submerged in his second draft of the Lawrence play—absolutely withdrawn from all present reality—and that led to some real hijinks, believe me. One evening as we went walking out to take the magnolia-scented air a policeman stopped us and asked to see our draft cards. I whisked mine out briskly, of course, and while the law was looking at it, Tenn began fumbling in his pockets for his. Then, as the cop handed mine back, he stated calmly that he didn't seem to have it. I said, 'Why of course you do, Tennessee,' but he just looked at me blankly and said, 'No, I don't. I think it's in the pocket of some pants I left in St. Louis, last time I was there.' Well, I could see the prison gates yawning, so I began to talk fast, explaining that Mr. Williams was a writer who simply lived in a world of his own. Nevertheless, we were taken down to the precinct and kept there three hours while those stupid minions of the law interrogated us. When a cousin of Jordan's had finally come to our rescue, I asked the officer timidly why he'd stopped us. He said that Tenn answered the description of a German spy reported to have been seen in the downtown area that afternoon."

Paul stopped to wet his dry throat with a swig of beer and continued. "Well, the answer to all this is something you'd never believe if it hadn't been an incident involving Tennessee Williams. He's been wearing his hair in a brushcut, you know—and

that afternoon before the cop stopped us, he'd been seen
heard at a drugstore counter downtown with his raincoat slung
cape-like about his shoulders, smoking a cigarette in a holder, and
singing a small song in German."

This whole experience had given Paul a severe turn, so he was
only too glad when Tennessee's currently avid interest in Chekhov
led to a number of evening readings of *The Seagull* at Jordan
Massee's house, with himself, Jordan, and Tenn alternating in
various roles.

"It was the only way I had of keeping him indoors at night until
the draft card arrived from Mrs. Williams," Paul said. "He was
always brooding or banging away at the typewriter by day, but
those evenings, minus Chekhov, would certainly have been a
problem."

Paul's memories of the summer are largely hilarious and light-
hearted. Certain passages of the diary Tenn kept during those hot
months, however, reveal a zigzag emotional graph, ranging from
his enjoyment of a country picnic, to worry about his heart, and,
on one black Tuesday this despairing notation regarding a
"wooden" short story he had just finished, "Yes, of course, I am
hopeless, hopeless, HOPELESS!!"

When he returned to New York in August, my book of poems
The Dark Rain Falling had just come out. He and Donnie
Windham dropped by my room in the Village one day and I
autographed their copies, saying flatly, "The lousy publisher made
sixteen line errors in this first edition. I've been through hell getting this thing out at all, and now, if the reviews aren't good, I
swear I'm going to give up."

Actually, I was feeling pretty low in mind, body, and spirit at
the time, because I was working ten hours a day at a small hotel on
Long Island where I'd been lured from the plush Fifth Avenue by
an increase in pay and prestige. I was now functioning as a combination desk clerk and assistant manager—driven half insane by
the infliction upon me in the wartime man shortage of one
incompetent night clerk after another.

Tenn was having his troubles too, due to a shortage of funds
and Audrey Wood's inability to interest anyone in either the revised

script of *Battle* or *Stairs to the Roof*. A group of his one-acts had been optioned to Hume Cronyn, but the relatively small sum he had received from this was spent in a short time—so, once again he fled the hopeless New York scene for Florida, where he arrived with $1.70 in his worn pants pockets.

In St. Augustine, desperate, literally starving the first few days of his stay, he heard of a job in Jacksonville, so he hitched a ride to that near-by city. He got himself hired by the United States Engineer Corps as a teletype operator, working an eight-hour night shift for $120 a month—an experience of which he has told me, "You see, I had to make it at writing because as that Jax job taught me, I'd never have been much good at anything else. I worked side by side with a man who'd been in an asylum. He used to tell me the most fascinating stories, and thus entertained, I turned out such poor work the boss practically used to get down on his knees, begging, 'Please, Williams, don't make me fire you in times like these when there just aren't any men.' The poor guy finally had to, though—and since there weren't any other jobs for me in Jacksonville, I came on back to New York."

Meanwhile, in the Long Island hotel, my own problem with impossible night men had driven me to such desperation that I persuaded my boss to bring Paul Bigelow out to work with me.

Paul had never set foot behind a hotel desk; nevertheless, he came to work one evening, learned how to operate the switchboard in five minutes flat and took over the desk like a veteran. When I arrived at eight next morning, I found him, daisy-fresh, drinking his coffee, having polished off each task to perfection—including the room transcript which no other clerk I'd hired had ever once been able to do correctly.

A few weeks later the hotel was sold; my amiable manager boss was fired, and I was gradually so sickened by what the new owners were doing to the place that I lost interest in the whole *enchilada*. Room rates were boosted, the prices of meals in the impeccable, small dining room soared while their quality and quantity descended, and I complained to Bigelow night and day. He begged me simply to go on with my job and keep my mouth shut, as he was doing, but I found this procedure impossible. One day, Paul

not being on hand to restrain me, I settled things for
losing my patience and my temper justifiably with the manage.,
and when he suggested that since I was displeased with the way
things were going under his aegis I might better leave, I heartily
agreed with him.

I departed that afternoon—but not before I'd told him in tones
that pervaded the lobby, the dining room, and the kitchen, precisely what I thought of him for ruining one of the most charming
hotels on the Island.

Stanley Paul Bigelow remained behind the desk; the new owner
eventually resold the hotel; another owner took over and Paul
became, in six months, the hotel's efficient manager.

Shortly before leaving the Island I read from my new book at
the Poetry Society of America, and, shortly after, went to work
behind the desk at the Hotel Fourteen on East 60th Street, Manhattan. As I recall it, Tenn and the rest of our small group were all
present at Jack Barefield's Christmas party—but the outstanding
event of this holiday season for me concerns a day at the Hotel
Fourteen when a small white hand slid across the marble-topped
desk a check signed Laurette Taylor Manners. I looked up into the
white face of a small, somehow overwhelming woman, whose
burning eyes looked piercingly into my own beneath a sort of gray
tam. The eyes and the full mouth smiled almost imperceptibly and
then she plodded on out through the lobby in heavy walking-shoes
with her gray cape billowing sail-like behind her. I was still standing there staring when the manager, also new at the Fourteen,
came up to the desk, asking, "Who was *that?*" I said, "Laurette
Taylor," and he gasped, "*That* woman. Why, my God, when I
saw her in *Peg O' My Heart* she was the loveliest creature in the
world."

I left the Fourteen in a couple of weeks and late January found
me behind the desk of another hotel on East 60th Street. In no
time at all we lost our elevator man who'd also worked the switchboard behind the desk, and suddenly I thought of my friend Williams who was ushering at the Strand Theater. The manager was
desperate, so I phoned Tenn, falsely describing the hotel as a
haven of pleasant association and short hours, and he came around

for an interview. He was hired—and there now began for us one of
the most memorable experiences of both our lives.

The hotel was filled with elderly ladies from old New York
families, one of whom, younger than the rest, I'd met at the
Southampton Yacht Club in 1939. She and the most imperious
dowager of all were at swords' points and I distinctly recall the
look of bewilderment on Tenn's face when he was first treated to
the regular evening altercation which occurred between these two
ladies in the lobby.

Tenn brought down my Southampton friend, Mrs. M., in the
elevator; she stepped out with her Pekingese and was instantly
greeted by the voice of the dowager, Mrs. B., booming, "Don't
speak to her. She's not in the Register."

Mrs. M. sailed out of the lobby, nose in air, replying, "Who the
hell wants to speak to you, Madam," and Tenn moved toward the
desk with dropped jaw. I said softly, "Now you know. And that's
not half—but anyway, as of this moment you're initiated."

Choking, he sat down at the switchboard, lit a cigarette, stuck
the holder in his mouth, then looked up in mild astonishment as
Miss Cora Witherspoon approached me, saying thoughtfully,
"Mr. Maxwell, do let me read you the lyrics to a song I have to do
in this musical I'm about to go into." She did so; we discussed the
possible change of a word or two she had in mind, and, shouting
her thanks for my opinion, Cora lunged toward the door, pulled
headlong by Lucky, her leashed rambunctious poodle.

A peaceful hour passed in which Tenn hopped up several times
to take the dowagers up on the elevator. Then the lobby doors
banged open and Mrs. M. trotted up to the desk carrying a paper
bag sideways. "Here, take it," she whispered, and I promptly
popped the beef pie she'd brought me, dish and all, from the
Automat, under the desk.

Late that evening she drifted down again with several other nice
ladies, including Miss Witherspoon, to join Tenn and me in a
small sitting room off the lobby where we all sat around an electric
heater, swapping theater stories and listening enthralled to one
very Continental guest who had visited Somerset Maugham on the
Riviera.

This was the usual pattern of the night, and Tenn and I thoroughly enjoyed our work at the old hostelry. However, I do recall a quiet evening when he startled me by whirling round from the switchboard, shouting like a suddenly wakened Marxist, "Great God, what *is* this? What in hell are we doing here, working for slave wages in the richest goddamned country on earth? What do they mean, letting a thing like this happen? Why, hell's fire and damnation, we're *artists*—don't the goddamned sons-of-bitches know that?"

I doubled up, laughing—but somehow I now recall this incident as the beginning of the end for us at the hotel.

For a long time the exasperated little manager had been struggling with me over the room transcript, which, with my absolute allergy for figures, I could never quite bring to a balance. Already upset about this, he became even more unhappy with both Tenn and me the morning some tattletale relayed to him an incident of the previous evening when Miss Witherspoon and Lucky had landed, spread-eagled, out on the sidewalk because of our having failed to switch on the portico lights. Cora was much too good a sport to have snitched on us, but there were busybody guests in the hotel, and this was the anticlimactic event before an impending holocaust which caused the manager to dispense with our services.

The evening of disaster was one on which Jack Barefield, heeding my plaintive phone call, had come to help me work out the bloody transcript. We were all busy back of the desk when the two daughters of our dowager Mrs. B. reeled in and got into a drunken brawl with the old lady right before our eyes. Appalled, and losing control, I yelled that if they didn't cease hostilities immediately I'd call the police, and Tenn sprang manfully forward, urging all the combatants to enter the elevator. They did, but before he could get them up to the dowager's floor they were at it again, and when he came down he staggered toward me, white-faced, crying, "Oh *Lord*, Gil, you don't know what I've been through. Those two women started beating up that old lady again, and when I jumped between them I got two awful whacks on my head."

"Where are they now?" I asked glumly.

T.W. shuddered. "In their rooms—but, my God, I thought those drunken bitches would surely kill that old mother of theirs before I got her away from them."

He sank weakly into his chair at the switchboard, and when a new guest entered the lobby, Jack Barefield promptly rose to handle the elevator.

Tennessee had gone to the basement to complete his night watchman's rounds when Jack came back down and said to me firmly, "Maxwell, old boy, you're on your last go-round here. On the fifteenth floor, I found Tennessee had left the doors to the shaft wide open. Just wait till your manager hears about *that* from some big blab-mouth."

He did hear about it, as well as about my threat to summon the cops, and two days later I was jobless.

Tennessee, not waiting to be fired, quietly returned to the Strand Theater aisle, while I went wearily on to another thankless job at a Lexington Avenue hostelry.

It remained, however, for Cora Witherspoon to provide the climactic line to our little drama. When Donald Windham ran into her on Madison just after our contretemps, she told him, "Oh, Mr. Windham, we all miss Mr. Williams and Mr. Maxwell terribly—but somehow the hotel seems a so much *safer* place to be in, now that they've gone."

Not long after we left, the old hotel changed its name—and T.W. insists to this day that this came about as a direct result of our brief, unsettling sojourn there.

3

ONCE, LONG AGO, IN A STATIC NEW YORK SUMMER, I WROTE TO
a friend, "I'm bored and tired because nothing's happening in any
way as it should," and he replied, "Remember, all things are
subject to change."

This was a wise, true assurance and as the years have passed I've
found the one thing we can count on in a life of frustration,
uncertainty, and disappointment is the absolute certainty of
change.

Change was imminent for Tennessee Williams and me, in the
spring of 1943, and it came about for us both in amazing ways.

While Tenn was patiently trudging the aisles of the Strand
Theater, I was winding up my career in the hotel business by
being fired from three hostelries in a row for having become as

bitter and tart-tongued to European refugees and pampered rich residents as they constantly were to me. It was a time of duress in which Management's trite, all-too-frequent excuse, "There's a war on, you know," elicited furious replies from long-suffering guests. It was a time, too, when a five-dollar bill slipped into the itching palm of a clerk who'd just told a desperate traveler, "Impossible, sir, there's not a room in the house," would produce a long study of the room rack, a sudden brightening of the clerk's spuriously earnest face, and the gentle purr, "We-ll now, you are in luck, Mr. Smith, sir—I see we do have one cancellation. . . ."

It was all this and more, too ugly to mention, causing me time and again to say what I thought to management and guests alike that finished me with front desk work in New York hotels. I took my moral scruples, as well as the nervous rash I'd developed because of them, and once more entered the limbo ranks of the unemployed. Through a friend I managed to get seventy-five dollars from an organization that sometimes secretly aided indigent poets, and once more began to seek some kind of work—any kind—that would keep me alive.

The best I could find, in answer to a *Times* ad, was a job as camera assistant to a guy who went around shooting shop windows, and I was ready to take it when my friend Jack Barefield shook his curly head at my news and told me, "No, Gilbert, you can't do that. I think maybe I can do something for you."

He was moving up from his post in the National Broadcasting Company's Information Division, so he made an appointment for me with his boss. She was a woman with an air of serene dignity, and the day I entered her office, I knew, looking into her dark, doelike eyes, that I'd be hired. I had some background for the work, but there was more than that between this lady and me, as time would prove. It is a character trait in both our natures which is less rare in this ugly-magnificent world than most middle-roaders suppose, and since it became a link that held me and Anita Barnard together for years, I call it here by its name, *integrity*.

So much, then, for me: at last, though the starting salary was scarcely a living wage, I'd found a certain security in the desperately needed balance of a nine-to-five business day.

This sort of situation would have been the last thing Tennessee wanted no matter how great his need, so, fortunately for him, the wheel of fortune now made some revolutions, coming to a stop at numbers that stood for success.

That spring the indomitable Audrey Wood secured for her talented, struggling client an assignment as script writer at Metro-Goldwyn-Mayer, in Hollywood. She called to tell him the news, and she remembers his exclamations of delight that any organization should be so charitable as to pay him $250 a month, for writing.

When Audrey quickly told him the sum was $250 a week, there was a long, breathless silence before he said in awe, "Why, Audrey, that's dishonest."

This ultra-naive remark of Tennessee's was spontaneous for the very good reason that, having been reared by honorable parents and grandparents, he'd grown up to be a most honest man.

I remember one election day years later in Miami when all the bars were closed and Tenn and I had called on Muryal Bernstein, a charming lady, who made us martinis.

Muryal, a great admirer of *Cat on a Hot Tin Roof* which contains a constant argument concerning truth and mendacity, remarked that after seeing the play she had gone home and been strictly truthful about a situation she had earlier decided to deal with in terms of a half-lie. Tennessee told her that she was the kind of person he wrote for; then he said, "You know, in the past few years I've never lied about anything except my age, and I even stopped doing that three years ago." He looked thoughtful and added, "Actually, I think you can be truthful about almost but not quite everything. How can you, for instance, go backstage and tell an actor he's given a lousy performance? You have to lie sometimes to keep from hurting people."

I said, "True, except that I recently met an old character actress who's found a fine solution for that backstage problem. She just goes up, starry-eyed, grasps her actor friend's hand, and whispers, 'Ah, my darling—*what* a performance!'"

It was an amusing afternoon, half serious, half light. The conclusion we finally reached was that evasion needn't in all cases constitute even a half-lie, and actually, I think that evasion is a recourse Tennessee has practiced for years, since I have often observed him, back to the wall, resorting to either an ambiguous grunt or an embarrassed, discomfited silence. Yet, the fact remains that he is fundamentally the soul of honesty, as is evident, I think, in the following quote from his first Hollywood letter to Bigelow: "I was sent out here to help write *The Sun Is My Undoing*, but so far I've only been asked to assist in the construction of Lana Turner's latest celluloid brassiere."

It was also perhaps because of his love of honesty, as well as his contempt for ostentation, that he chose to buy himself a motor scooter on which he chugged up to the M–G–M gates cheerfully immune to the chilly stares of producers, haughty stars, and chauffeurs arriving in Isotta-Fraschinis, Rolls-Royces, and Cadillacs.

When Bigelow learned that he was tootling along the dangerously crowded California highways he called Miss Wood and cried in real alarm, "Audrey, you must phone the Hollywood authorities. He will kill himself." But Bigelow needn't have worried, for, as T.W. told it to me: "On my way to the studio one day, a tire blew out. I went to a filling station and had it fixed. Then, about a mile farther on, the other tire went flat, so I wheeled the scooter to the roadside, propped it in a ditch, caught a ride to M–G–M, and phoned the people who'd sold me the damned contraption where to come pick it up."

The breakdown of the scooter seems to have constituted an omen, for I next learned, through a second letter Paul Bigelow received, that Tenn was indeed no more M–G–M's tankard of tea than they were his. The front office sent him a memo, asking, "What shall we do with our new child star, Margaret O'Brien?" and he answered formally, "I have a suggestion but I do not think you would like it."

A frigid silence went into effect between the front office and that of the non-conforming, upstart writer in the screenwriters' building—probably on that highest floor reserved for lesser scribes whence, leaning wildly out a window, Dorothy Parker once cried to all below, "Lemme out of here! I'm just as sane as you are!"

Be that as it may, Tenn was summarily dropped by M–G–M, and since his contract called for the continuance of his salary, he retired in relief to a Malibu Beach cottage.

Edwina recalls that his suspension followed a call Tenn had requested Miss Wood to make to the studio heads, asking if he might travel East to see a production of one of his plays. The bigwigs replied that he could, indeed—on condition he never set foot on the M–G–M lot again.

This may or may not be factual but it is certain he did take himself off gleefully to Malibu, where, living on a small stipend Audrey doled out to him from his salary, he began to work for himself. He concocted an amusing story about a Communist-whore landlady called "The Mattress by the Tomato Patch," and also an original screen play entitled *The Gentleman Caller*. This script he submitted to M–G–M, with a sassy note that said, "First of all, please understand that this script is going to run twice as long as *Gone With the Wind*," to which the studio heads, apparently serious, replied that since Selznick had already produced G.W.T.W., they were not interested in a second Southern epic.

And so, having dealt fairly with his employers, Mr. Williams now settled down with a clear conscience to making the *Caller* into a stage drama. This play later became *The Glass Menagerie*—the screen rights to which were bought by a Hollywood studio for a cool five hundred thousand.

Tenn had a great time at Malibu, writing, sunning, sleeping, until the black day when Edwina wrote that Mrs. Dakin, his beloved Grand, long ill with cancer, was rapidly failing.

He flew at once to Mississippi, where, his mother has said, "He had just about walked into the house when she (his grandmother) died, literally in his arms. . . . It was as though she had hung on until he arrived." And though this sounds dramatic, it is not at all surprising, since, as we have seen, Tom and Grand had shared a mutual devotion all his life.

It was the first time that Tenn had seen anyone die or had attended a loved one's funeral, and the effect of these experiences was the genesis, I'm sure, of Blanche's speech to her sister Stella, in the first act of *Streetcar*.

I, I, I, took the blows in my face and my body! All of those deaths! The long parade to the graveyard! Father, mother! Margaret, that dreadful way! So big with it, it couldn't be put in a coffin! But had to be burned like rubbish! You just came home in time for the funerals, Stella. And funerals are pretty compared to deaths. Funerals are quiet, but deaths—not always. Sometimes their breathing is hoarse, and sometimes it rattles, and sometimes they even cry out to you, "Don't let me go!" Even the old, sometimes, say, "Don't let me go." As if you were able to stop them! But funerals are quiet, with pretty flowers. And oh, what gorgeous boxes they pack them away in! Unless you were there at the bed when they cried out, "Hold me!" you'd never never suspect there was the struggle for breath and bleeding! You didn't dream, but I saw! *Saw! Saw!*

Grand's death was not so violent as the deaths described by Blanche, since Edwina recalls that even on the day of her going she had practiced three hours on the piano; but here, nevertheless, is an anguished, horrified outcry from the depths of a young man's being.

It is no accident—the result of no merely fortuitous imagination—that the dialogue of Williams' characters often rings with unmistakable truth, for as Thomas Wolfe once wrote to Scott Fitzgerald, "A writer must use what he's got; he can't use what he hasn't got," and this playwright is capable, to a marked degree, of using much that he has got from people and situations in the skillful creation of drama.

When he got back to Malibu he turned at once to the partial anodyne of creative work; then, with the coming of autumn he was able to journey East with his new playscript, feeling somewhat shielded by the money Audrey had banked for him out of his studio salary. He went again to Provincetown and there received word that the National Institute of Arts and Letters had granted him a thousand-dollar award, with this citation:

To Tennessee Williams, born in Mississippi, in recognition of his dramatic works which reveal a poetic imagination and a gift for characterization that are rare in the contemporary theatre.

Prior to this event, *Mooney's Kid Don't Cry* had been included in *The Best One Act Plays of 1940*, and a substantial group of his poems had appeared in the New Directions volume, *Five American Poets, 1944*, so he could hardly help observing, as he did, that this was indeed a time pregnant with change for him.

He sent his play to Audrey and when he came on to New York to see her, she told him that she was impressed, also warning him, "It's not going to be easy to sell, but we'll have it typed up and try."

She thought a great deal about the person to whom she should offer *The Glass Menagerie* and finally came up with Eddie Dowling, ex-song-and-dance man, actor, producer, and director.

Dowling has told me that from the moment he finished reading the script he had no doubt of the play's intrinsic worth, so he optioned it at once and looked about for an angel. He found one in the person of a banker, Louis J. Singer, who put up $75,000; then because George Jean Nathan had suggested Laurette Taylor as *Menagerie's* star, he took Tennessee to the Hotel Fourteen to hear the actress read for the role of the valiant mother, of whom the playscript says, "She is not paranoiac, but her life is paranoia."

This description might well have seemed to Miss Taylor suggestive of herself, since as she once publicly stated, she had gone, after the death of her playwright husband, Hartley Manners, "on the longest wake in history."

Dowling recalls that she warned him he might be running a risk in hiring her for the play, as no producer in recent years had been willing to take a chance on her sobriety. But Dowling was determined to have no other star, and he assured Tenn, who had some scruples about Miss Taylor's being able to mimic a Mississippi drawl, that he need have no fears regarding this actress, whom both he and Nathan knew to be magnificent.

Recently, in talking with Dowling, I asked, "Eddie, whom do you consider the greatest actresses you ever saw?"

He answered thoughtfully, "Well, first of all, Duse. Then— though you might not believe it—my wife, Ray Dooley, who's been long retired—and, of course, Laurette."

We went on talking for a while about *Menagerie;* then suddenly he looked up at me and said, "No, Gilbert—I want to rephrase that statement about actresses. I think it takes just one performance, and this being so, I'm forced to say Laurette Taylor was truly the greatest actress I've ever seen."

I have mentioned this conversation because so much has been told about the feud between Eddie Dowling and Miss Taylor throughout the rehearsals and run of the play, and because there is no doubt in my mind that Dowling, despite these differences, has treasured down the years a vast admiration for this complex woman who was first and last an uncannily gifted artist.

The Glass Menagerie, as most readers must know, has just four characters: Amanda, the mother; Tom, the poetic dreamer son who works in a warehouse; the crippled daughter, Laura; and Jim O'Conner, a young man from the warehouse, whom Tom, at his mother's request, brings home to dinner one evening as Laura's first (and pitiably final) gentleman caller.

Dowling, having already directed the ethereal blonde actress, Julie Haydon, in O'Casey's *Shadow and Substance* and Saroyan's *The Time of Your Life*, felt she would be exactly right as Laura, while he himself would play Tom, with Anthony Ross as Jim O'Conner.

The play swung into rehearsal, but there was trouble, straight from the start. Dowling and Miss Taylor were not compatible, and everyone concerned with the show became alarmed by Miss Taylor's apparent inability to learn her lines.

What the company did not know was that Miss Taylor had never been in a great hurry to learn her lines or her business. In the parlance of performers, she was the sort of actress who "saved it" for opening night, and apropos of this her daughter, Marguerite Courtney, says in her biography *Laurette*:

> Although she took the most energetic interest in rehearsals, in everything and everybody that had anything to do with the play, and warmed the nervous author's heart with her understanding and respect for his work, Laurette gave little indication of what she was going to do with the part of Amanda. She was up to her old trick of watching the others, seemingly much more interested

in them than her own part, neither learning her lines nor her business. Tony Ross tried to pump heart into the others by re-calling how magnificent she was, but as time went on he began to worry along with the rest. As Laurette sat hunched over her script, peering nearsightedly at the lines through a large magnify-ing glass, murmuring through her speeches, or walking about like one achieving a hesitant, tactile familiarity with a world and people not yet clearly seen, Dowling was heard to mutter more than once, "That woman is crucifying me!"*

True, no doubt, nor was this all Mr. Dowling was heard to mutter at rehearsals. For instance, standing gloomily with Tenn in the wings one day while the star fumbled, forgot, and skipped, he remarked to the fledgling playwright, "You'll notice the old booger never forgets any good lines," forthwith throwing Tenn into fits of choked guffaws.

Nevertheless, before the company left New York for Chicago, Tenn, inordinately shy by nature, had made a certain contact with Miss Taylor. Of this period he has remarked, "I cannot say I ever got over the awkwardness and the awe that were originally present, but she would not allow that to stand between us. The great warmth of her heart burned through and we became close friends." He has also written the following impression he had of Laurette as he swung down from the train platform on a freezing December morning into Chicago's Union Station:

It is a short and nearly square figure in a peculiar costume, like something rooted from the bottom of an old wardrobe trunk. The coat is grey muskrat, but the many small pelts of which it is composed, are not enjoying the most pacific relation. Discord threatening disunion is at work amongst them. Almost down the upturned collar of this coat is a very broad brimmed hat of the type that is worn by cinema buccaneers. Between these two de-fensive perimeters is a pair of eyes that are much too bright to be described as brown and a cloudy profusion of hair that is lighter than auburn. This is the figure of a star. Her name has been

---

* Marguerite Courtney, *Laurette* (New York: Rinehart & Co., Inc., 1955), p. 398.

famous. It is still a legend, but the face in the station passes
without recognition. The figure passes without assurance among
the jostling swarm. The brightness of the eyes has bravery but not
certainty. The motion of the figure is hesitant; for a moment it
even appears to be lost. One hand which does not wear a glove is
clutching a very large purse as if it contained a more secure world
than that of a teeming station. . . .

"Laurette!" I called her name and she turned and cried out
mine. Then and there we joined forces. The station diminished to
a comfortable size; the bitter cold thawed a little; we moved off
together with a feeling of union deeper than physical, more than
accidental, to find a taxi.*

Still, there was trouble ahead in Chicago as Laurette continued
seemingly to be more concerned with the parts of the other cast
members than with her own. Working especially with Julie Haydon on their scenes together, fretting because the thin, delicate-
boned young actress appeared to be eating too little, she also took
the girl out to shop for a hat against the Windy City's cold.

Julie has told me: "You should have been with us the day we
went after that hat. I'd tried to tell Laurette I never wore hats
simply because no hat ever looked good on me, but she wouldn't
listen, so down we went to Marshall Fields and there in the
millinery department while a crowd assembled—they'd recognized
Laurette, you see—she planted hat after hat on my head. We tried
dozens and each looked worse than the one before, so on we went
to more shops until we were both exhausted and she was finally
forced to admit the hat had never been made that would suit my
face."

It is typical of Julie's self-effacing personality that she does not
suggest part of the crowd may have gathered, recognizing her as
well, since they must have previously seen her either on the stage
or with Noel Coward in the motion picture, *The Scoundrel*. Be
that as it may, Miss Taylor had obviously taken Julie under her
wing, to scold, reprimand, and protect, so no one was surprised at
the star's "turning dressmaker just before the final rehearsal when

---

* *Ibid.*, p. 399.

she found Laura's second act dress too 'bosomy' for the character."*

Miss Taylor also, while conceding that he was "a fine and sensitive director," had "decided reservations as to Dowling's interpretation of his part, finding it, as she had Julie's Laura, unreal and bloodless, and it irked her not a little that an actor of fifty-three should be undertaking the role of her son."†

Between the star and her playwright, however, there was no friction and this must have been partly due to the deference and compassion Tenn had come to feel for this woman.

He told her gently that her Southern accent was too thick. She suggested copying *his*, and when he cheerfully agreed she proceeded to do so. It was another thing when she approached him about cutting a speech in which the word *jonquils* appeared ten times.

> "It's just a few too many jonquils, Tennessee," Laurette said. "Can't you cut a few?"
>
> "Laurette," he answered solemnly, "it's got rhythm. Ah need all those jonquils."
>
> I took the lines home and sort of sang them to myself. Tennessee was right. Not a jonquil came out.‡

This is amusing because of what is not revealed, I think, in Miss Courtney's anecdote. Laurette, being Celtic, having poetry in her own soul, doubtless discovered in singing those lines that since Tenn is innately a poet his dialogue cannot be easily changed. What she did not know was that she could have argued till doomsday and got nowhere with Tenn about his clipping those jonquils. Williams' rhythms and his idiom are uniquely his. It would be impossible for anyone but himself to change his speeches, and I say "impossible" advisedly since I know that if anyone should try to tinker with a Williams speech, he'd come up against a soft-voiced, steel-eyed adamance calculated to wither him completely.

---

* *Ibid.*, p. 400.
† *Ibid.*, p. 401.
‡ *Ibid.*, p. 398.

Apropos of this I digress a moment to quote Tennessee, describing his experience with the *New Yorker's* editors in regard to the publication of his novella, "Three Players of a Summer Game."

"When they sent me the galleys I found they'd changed my punctuation and cut and edited all through the story, so I sat right down and put everything back precisely the way it was when I sent it to 'em."

Amused, he went on to tell me how the editors had been victorious, since with no further argument they sent the story to press as they had edited it, but I'm certain this was the only time anyone, anywhere, ever won out fooling around with a work of Williams'.

All of which brings us to the creation of a new scene in *Menagerie* in Chicago, of which there are some conflicting versions.

Julie Haydon, for instance, recalls the whole thing in one way and Tenn in another, but I shall give Tenn's version since I've found out in talks with him that he is well-nigh infallible in recalling events of his past life.

The whole incident has to do with the evolution of a scene in the play in which Tom comes home drunk, fishes for his key, drops it through a crack and, before he can retrieve it, looks up to face his sister, come to open the door.

LAURA: Where have you been all this time?

TOM: I have been to the movies.

LAURA: All this time at the movies?

TOM: There was a very long program. There was a Garbo picture and a Mickey Mouse and a travelogue and a newsreel and a preview of coming attractions. And there was an organ solo and a collection for the milk-fund—simultaneously—which ended up in a terrible fight between a fat lady and an usher!

LAURA (*innocently*):   Did you have to stay through everything?

TOM: Of course! And, oh, I forgot! There was a big stage show! The headliner on this stage show was Malvolio the Magician. He performed wonderful tricks, many of them, such as pouring water back and forth between pitchers. First it turned to wine and then it turned to beer and then it turned to whiskey. I

knew it was whiskey it finally turned into because he needed
somebody to come up out of the audience to help him, and I
came up—both shows! It was Kentucky Straight Bourbon. A very
generous fellow, he gave souvenirs. (*He pulls from his back
pocket a shimmering rainbow-colored scarf.*) He gave me this.
This is his magic scarf. You can have it, Laura. . . .

Now, it is Julie Haydon's impression that she and Dowling started
improvising this scene with a scarf; also that George Jean Nathan
(after hearing Tenn had a drunk scene in mind for Tom on his
return home, late at night after a quarrel with his mother), finally,
in Chicago, thought up the rudiments of the magician scene and
told it to Eddie Dowling.

Mrs. Williams, in her book, gives this report:

I arrived [in Chicago] in time to see a rehearsal and witness the
friction that seems part of the birth pangs of every play. Mr.
Dowling wanted to sing the bawdiest verse of "St. Louis Blues" in
the scene where the son staggers home drunk. Tom objected,
saying to me, "He's trying to make it funny, Mother. I've got to
stop him." Mr. Dowling gave in to Tom.*

As for Eddie, when I asked him how the drunk scene evolved he
gave me a whimsical gnomelike look, and said, "I'm not going to
talk about that." So here we finally are, with Tennessee's forthright statement.

"The truth is, I didn't want that scene at all. However, Nathan
and Eddie Dowling did start cooking up something between them.
One day Eddie began to ad lib it, so, in self-defense, I had to go
ahead and write the scene as I felt it should be written."

All of which adds up to no more than a teapot tempest as far as
any of the *Menagerie* principals are concerned, but it does prove
that two people can remember an incident of eighteen years past
in amazingly different ways.

The important thing is, no matter who thought of what, the
fourth scene turned out to be one of the most poignant episodes in
the play.

---

* Williams, *Remember Me to Tom*, p. 145.

Incidentally, I find that the published playscript does not include a moment when Eddie Dowling, always a graceful dancer, executed a swaying step or two holding the magician's scarf above his head, intoning sadly, "I wish it would cover this ugly world"— and I'd rather like to ask about that if I weren't scared I'd come up again with more than a surfeit of bewildering accounts regarding this bit which so charmed me at the Playhouse.

But again I digress, for here we suddenly are on Forty-eighth Street in New York, when we ought to be in Chicago where rehearsals went on in the lounge of the Civic Theatre because of the need for working out a complex lighting system. The company did not get onstage in the Mielziner set, with Paul Bowles's incidental music, until the night of dress rehearsal. There had been other troubles, too, including an altercation between Julie Haydon and Miss Taylor. Always self-abnegating, Miss Haydon, having cast herself one evening at the feet of the star to protest her admiration, her debt of gratitude for the help bestowed upon her by a genius, encountered a stare of disbelief on the lady's face, followed by a resounding four-letter expletive. Legend has it Miss Haydon fell back aghast, and that it took some doing on Eddie Dowling's part to restore harmony between his stage mother and sister. However, despite this diverting incident and other minor mishaps dear to the hearts of many who still delight in talking of life backstage with Laurette in those cold Chicago days, *The Glass Menagerie* did arrive, without a major misfortune, at its dress rehearsal, December 25.

The show played that night to the four hundred uniformed cast members of *Winged Victory*, which was currently running in Chicago; and it was on this night that the audience, the cast, and the transfixed backstage crew of *Menagerie* saw Laurette Taylor give a performance of such scope and depth as none of them had seen before, anywhere.

Tennessee has said of that night, "She brought everything together and gave a performance for the first time and the impact of it was stunning! I could never have imagined it. I never saw anything like it in all my life."

He has also told me—as have several others present on opening night—how stage manager Randolph Echols, giving his last call, found Laurette dyeing the dressing gown she was to wear in the first act's second scene, because she felt the color was wrong. She laid the soggy garment in Randy's hands, bade him dry it, walked onstage, and proceeded, as on the previous night, to make theatrical history.

Fired by the brilliance of her art, the rest of the cast also gave great performances, and most of Chicago's reviewers raced to their typewriters to record in superlatives the phenomenon they had witnessed.

Nevertheless, the public for some reason stayed away the first week, and it was then the critics went into action.

Returning time and again to see the play they began in their daily columns—Ashton Stevens, Claudia Cassidy, Henry T. Murdock, and others—to flay the Chicago public for neglecting a work of art, and as a result the receipts at the box office soared beyond capacity during the last six weeks.

Toward the end of the run hundreds were turned away at each performance. Williams' exquisite play became the talk of the toddlin' town—and Laurette Taylor, the toast of it.

Yet again there was trouble as the forthright, sharp-tongued actress continued her criticism of Eddie Dowling's handling of his part and began to feud with him not only backstage but in public.

When Ashton Stevens, Taylor's old friend, warned her that public fighting, recorded by the Chicago columnists and already being picked up by columnists in New York, was hurting the play, she went like a dutiful child to Eddie's dressing room to apologize—but Eddie, having taken considerable abuse, was not to be easily appeased.

Miss Taylor, on the other hand, being Irish and a scrapper by nature, could not understand why Eddie should be seriously upset by her critical outbursts, and again, in *Laurette*, Miss Courtney briskly sums up the situation.

To share stellar honors and not share equally in all the adulation does not smooth out backstage tension between feuding stars. Dowling received unstinted praise both as producer and director

but to Laurette, unquestionably, had gone the lion's share of the
acting honors. In his testier moments her co-star was heard to
murmur, "That old woman should kiss my feet for what I've
done for her!" But instead of showing a seemly gratitude for the
opportunity he had provided she was going around saying what a
lousy actor he was. It was hardly conducive to a beautiful accord
between the two.*

At any rate, it does seem certain that Miss Taylor, great actress,
lovable, blunt-spoken lady that she was, could be an occasional
trial, not just to Eddie but to others as well, for Tenn recalls an
evening when she shook him to the roots of his hospitable Southern being. He had invited her for cocktails with an urbane, charming publisher friend of his, to whom she had been equally charming. However, when the trio ventured out on the street and Tenn
got a cab to take them all to a party, La Taylor turned on the
running board to say firmly, "Oh no, this man is not invited"—
leaving the embarrassed gentleman to retreat with as much
aplomb as he could summon.

And so it went through the last triumphant weeks in Chicago,
while the playwright and all the company looked forward, by turns
elated and frightened, to the uncertain gamble of Broadway.

Now, it would be easy for me personally to stretch the truth and
state that I, as a friend of Tennessee's, was beside myself with
excitement when *The Glass Menagerie* made its successful bow at
the Playhouse on the day before Easter, 1945.

In retrospect however, I find the situation astonishingly different. I did not see *Menagerie* on its opening night in Manhattan.
Furthermore, the only plays of Williams' I'd seen at this time
were a pair of short pieces given in a small auditorium on Ninth
Avenue in 1942. I sat on a plank bench then and watched an
actress laboring under the fatal handicap of no talent, in *The Lady
of Larkspur Lotion*, and a slightly more able cast in *The Long
Goodbye*. I thought the latter piece well written, and I also sensed

---

* Courtney, *Laurette*, p. 406.

something intriguingly new in its offbeat construction, but if I were to say I was greatly impressed that night by Tennessee's talent, I would be lying.

I had not kept up with what was happening to him and *Menagerie* in Chicago, so I suppose I was more affected by Tenn's personality at this time than by his gifts as a playwright. Anyhow, the first pertinent thing I remember clearly about the play occurred on the Saturday of *Menagerie's* opening.

Paul Bigelow and I were having lunch at the English Tea Room, that long-gone, delightful spot with old playbills on its walls, when Tenn walked in, looking decidedly dazed. He said, "Why, hello, Paul, hello, Gil," and hailed a passing waitress, telling her he'd like a container of coffee to go. The waitress tried to tell him the place never sent out orders, whereupon Tenn looked at her and said firmly, "But it's for Miss Laurette Taylor." The statement was made in gently polite consternation, with no fear of the waitress's possible refusal, and that young woman promptly took her cue, heading out to the kitchen.

Tennessee turned to Paul and me and said, "The poor old lady's in a terrible state of nerves. She's really very sick." The waitress came back with a cup of coffee and a saucer. Tenn thanked her, said good-by to us and left the restaurant carrying the coffee carefully in both hands.

Paul and I finished our lunch, unaware of the near-tragic events in progress half a block down at the Playhouse.

Eddie Dowling has since told me of what had been going on there since Laurette's arrival at ten-thirty in the morning, exhausted from apprehensive nights of insomnia—and of his own fears for her, the playwright, and the company.

He said, "You must understand I was mortally afraid (in fact, I felt sure) if I let Taylor out of the theater she'd get drunk, so I determined to keep her there all day. Tennessee, Randy Echols, and my own wife kept calling me inhuman, but I didn't yield one inch till five-thirty when I finally gave in to their pleas and threats and dismissed the company."

In all those hours when she was not onstage, Miss Taylor was retching or vomiting into a bucket set in the wings. At the supper

break she could not eat, and she was so weak just before the
opening scene that Julie Haydon and Anthony Ross's wife had to
help her to the dining table.

Dowling further recalls that she started in, as the curtain rose,
on the opening speech of the second act—then suddenly, as
though by a miracle, rallied and launched strongly into Amanda's
correct first-act speech, "Honey, don't push with your fingers.
. . . And chew—chew!" He says, shrugging, "After that I knew
she was safe so I stopped praying—and Christ Almighty, what a
performance she gave that night!"

The rest has often been told in print. Before the final curtain
could rise again the audience stood up, clapped, shouted, whistled,
and shrieked.

On the twenty-sixth call Dowling stepped down to the foot-
lights to help Tennessee Williams, thirty-four years old, with a
short haircut, wearing a gray flannel suit with a missing jacket
button, up to the shimmering stage. He made a few quick little
bows to the cast with his backside to the wildly applauding
house—and the memorable evening was rounded out.

Next day all the critics in town joined in an ecstatic chorus of
praise for Laurette's Amanda, and nearly all of them spoke glow-
ingly of America's new, fresh-voiced playwright.

And so—at long last—Tennessee Williams had triumphed over
all the anguish of St. Louis, failure in Boston, years of eking out an
existence at humble jobs, of going hungry, and often wandering
sick with the fear of no roof at night above his head.

But this was not all the story, for there would still be with him,
no matter where he went about the wide, beckoning world, a
haunting loneliness, unresting, achingly sad—but let him tell it, in
Tom's last narrator's speech, after the poet has fled the drab
Wingfield flat, with his mother's voice echoing back of him down
the alley, "Go, then! Then go to the moon—you selfish dreamer."

Tom: I didn't go to the moon, I went much further—for time is
the longest distance between two places—Not long after that I
was fired for writing a poem on the lid of a shoe-box. I left St.
Louis. I descended the steps of this fire-escape for a last time and

followed, from then on, in my father's footsteps, attempting to find in motion what was lost in space—I traveled around a great deal. The cities swept about me like dead leaves, leaves that were brightly colored but torn away from the branches. I would have stopped, but I was pursued by something. It always came upon me unawares, taking me altogether by surprise. Perhaps it was a familiar bit of music. Perhaps it was only a piece of transparent glass—Perhaps I am walking along a street at night, in some strange city, before I have found companions. I pass the lighted window of a shop where perfume is sold. The window is filled with pieces of colored glass, tiny transparent bottles in delicate colors, like bits of a shattered rainbow. Then all at once my sister touches my shoulder. I turn around and look into her eyes . . . Oh, Laura, Laura, I tried to leave you behind me, but I am more faithful than I intended to be! I reach for a cigarette. I cross the street, I run into the movies or a bar, I buy a drink, I speak to the nearest stranger—anything that can blow your candles out . . .—for nowadays the world is lit by lightning! Blow out your candles, Laura—and so goodbye. . . .

It was Easter eve when Julie Haydon, as Laura, blew out his candles; and though Tennessee did not know it on that night of heady triumph, there was not only for him no saying good-by to the haunting past and to his sister: there were new, undreamed-of problems to come, as he stood at the edge of a world that was lit by lightning.

I find it difficult to reconstruct the days between *Menagerie's* opening and the Friday of April 27, 1945, when I attended Tenn's party for his mother and Laurette Taylor.

The truth is that all through that past winter and early spring I had been so madly, five-sensually in love that I was only half aware of the outer world of events and people whirling about me.

In the Information Division at NBC, I listened to the war news, worked at my program correspondence, played back European newscast records of the *Army Hour*—sometimes, for a frantic parent, locating a son reported missing—and waited numbly, 2A in the draft, for the small card that would say 1A, all in a vacuum

daze behind which this obsessive passion burned with a vehement
flame.

I was living next door to the Harvard Club in an apartment
with William Hughes, an actor friend, who, as I came in one
evening, turned from his work at the living-room desk to tell me,
"I think you'd better see *The Glass Menagerie*. I saw it last night,
and I can't get it out of my mind. There's something about this
play that haunts you."

"Oh?" I said. "Then I'll see it after next pay day."

I went on into the next room, poured myself a stiff drink, and
sat down, haunted by no play but by my own life drama. I'd been
writing a first novel, but I couldn't even work on that in these
days, having recently quarreled with my girl.

It was in the middle of this same week, I think, that Tenn,
Laurette, and Eddie Dowling appeared on an NBC program.

The staff of the Information Division monitored all the shows,
and on this day we heard Mary Margaret McBride proudly an-
nounce her guests. The discussion program went on, after the
usual flub-a-dub of inane commercials, and I listened a while,
then, toward the program's end, went out of the office briefly. I
came back to find my cohorts oh'ing and ah'ing over the scandal of
Laurette Taylor's having said *damn*, loud and clear, on a program
sacred to countless sponsors and several million Moms. So far,
however, we'd not suffered the verbal attack of semimoronic
housewives on our phones which usually followed any untoward
event, so I felt free to run down to Mary Margaret's studio.

I'd expected, at least, an atmosphere of fixed-smiling strain in
the small studio, but strange to say, all was sweetness and light
there. Miss McBride was talking to Eddie; Tennessee, just rising
from the discussion table with Laurette, cried out, "Oh, Gil, how
nice to see you. Miss Taylor—Laurette—this is my poet friend,
Gilbert Maxwell."

Laurette greeted me warmly, nodding bright-eyed from under a
shovel-like hat.

I said, "What's this I hear about you corrupting our air waves
with a vile cuss word?" and she answered, "Oh, go on, man, you

know *damn* don' mean a thing to us Suth'ners. Down home we don' call that cussin', it's just sweah'in'."

Tennessee and I laughed, and I suddenly realized that La Taylor had achieved the impossible by charming everyone, including the live studio onlookers and that sacred cow, the enormous ether-audience, entirely out of any desire to attack. It was a triumph of personality over puerility, and I told Miss Taylor so, adding that I was now more eager than ever to see her in the play, whereupon the incredible eyes lit up as she replied, "Oh, yes, you must. You really should, you know. I mean, *if* you can get a seat."

That's all there was to this brief encounter. However, it strikes me today as strange that Tenn, always generous with tickets, didn't offer that minute to get me a house seat, so I can only conclude that he must have thought I wasn't really interested in seeing his play. And certainly I can understand this, since, as I've said, I was in those days afflicted with the aforementioned malady of possessive, self-centered, jealous love to an incredible degree.

On the afternoon of Tenn's party, still depressed and in a numb state, I bathed, dressed, and headed up Fifth Avenue toward Sherry's. When I arrived I moved down the receiving line, all smiles and amiable murmurs.

Tenn was there beside his tiny mother, who stood in turn by her rector father—and the instant I shook hands with this lady who would one day become, permanently, *Miss Edwina* to me, I sensed that I'd met a personality as powerful in its way as Laurette Taylor's Amanda. Mr. Dakin was then—as he would be until his death at ninety-seven—an arresting personality, and it is true, as his daughter has always said, the white-haired, patrician-faced little padre in his clerical vest and collar did steal the Sherry's show that day from her and *The Glass Menagerie's* star.

But as for me, in my lovelorn condition (to say nothing of a perpetual stagestruck state), I was out for booze and stars and glamour, so I clasped Mr. Dakin's hand and moved eagerly on to greet the portrayers of Amanda and Laura Wingfield.

La Belle Laurette had on another of her face-shading hats. Miss Haydon looked lovely in a green suit with hat to match (Laurette having got one on her head at last), and when I told her how becoming the outfit was she said, "Yes, Miss Taylor chose it for me," and looked a bit rueful. (Recently, when I read this account of the party to her, the gentle Julie laughed and told me, "I *hated* that costume, Gilbert.")

When I'd gotten myself a martini I returned to the ladies, and asked Miss Taylor if, as Noel Coward had said in his autobiography, the characters in *Hay Fever* were drawn from her and her family.

She stood up to her full five-four and answered, "Cer-tainly not. I'll never forgive Noel Coward for coming into my house and writing those ridiculous things about us."

I recall this remark distinctly, since I was later beguiled by a chance excerpt from her daughter's book:

> Laurette adored Noel's gift for words.
> "He never had to search for the right one. They came effortlessly to his obvious delight as well as to his listener's."
> Later when Noel was back in England and word drifted across the Atlantic that his new play "Hay Fever" was supposed to be an intimate picture of the Manners family, Laurette was hurt. After seeing the play in New York she found it hard to forgive him; the addlepated group of rugged individualists whom he depicted were not her family at all. "None of us," she declared emphatically, "is ever unintentionally rude."*

Now I've no idea as to the date in time when Miss Taylor arrived at the above unanswerably wicked rebuttal to Mr. Coward (incidentally, it's just the sort of thing the actress Judith Bliss, whom she's supposed to be in *Hay Fever*, might have said); but I do know, recalling the flash of fire in her great eyes at Sherry's, that she was still put out with him in 1945.

Being in a mood to get high I recall little more of this party of Tenn's, except that he seemed somehow to fade willingly into the background, surrounded there by his home- and stage-families and friends. I still think it's sad, though, that his father wasn't present at this first big success party Tenn had so proudly given for his mother and his star.

---

* Courtney, *Laurette*, p. 261.

In her book Mrs. Williams tells how her husband, refusing to accompany her to the play's Chicago opening, "went on by himself a few weeks later to see *Menagerie* and found it sold out." She continues:

> They put a chair in the aisle for Cornelius because he was the playwright's father. He did not believe I was Amanda; he was a very literal man and he had not left home, nor did the lives portrayed on the stage resemble ours in any way, he thought.*

Later, she states that her son asked her to the New York opening, saying, "I would like to give you the trip as a much-delayed present." And she adds, "But I did not get to the New York première . . . because Cornelius said since we had both seen the play, it would be a waste of money."

It is hard to understand why Edwina paid any mind to Cornelius, not only since the railroad fare would be coming out of Tenn's pocket, but because she *did* come up two weeks later, and I do think it's too bad, that Tenn could not have had both of his parents at his Chicago opening, his New York opening, and his charming party at Sherry's.

It may have been, having done so little for his son financially and nothing at all to help him in his career, that Cornelius Williams felt he had no right to take part in any of the above-mentioned events. Still, one senses pathos in Edwina's account of their putting a chair in the aisle for him in Chicago, as well as in his stalwart reaction to the play, which sounds rigidly loyal to her. And saddest of all, I think, there is the incontrovertible fact that Cornelius could not stay away from Chicago. For whatever reason it is plain that this poker-playing, heavy-boozing, man's man, shoe-company executive, *did* have to go to Chicago to see for himself what his sensitive, talented son had wrought in his first successful play.

I like to recall a little story Eddie Dowling told me of going with Tenn, Laurette, and Cornelius to the College Inn after Cornelius had seen the performance.

---

* Williams, *Remember Me to Tom*, p. 151.

"The old boy was a riot," said Eddie. "He took one look at the Inn's wine list, whisked out a bottle from his pocket, set it on the table and said, 'Now, anyone who likes can share this with me, but I'll have no part of these prices.' It was a convivial evening in which Laurette and Cornelius got into some lusty arguments about a number of things, and my only regret was, feeling that I had to be host, I couldn't let go properly, but had to wait and get drunk later, all by myself."

There is really so much nostalgia over the whole *Menagerie* period—such a mist of sentiment rises before the eyes of all who were connected with it—I find it truly hard to reconstruct this time in which, as I've said, I was also bemused by the misery of an obsessive love affair. And yet I finally did see the play, and when I saw it I was overcome not only by the acting but by the shimmering, fragile vehicle itself; for having grown up in that hell so often inadequately called "a broken home," I could vouch for the truth of the tragic events unfolding before my eyes on the stage of the Playhouse.

I did not see the play until fall, and in the spring of 1945 I saw Tennessee just twice. One day he dropped by the Harvard Annex apartment, heard the story of my recent disillusionment with an *amour* whom I had caught *in flagrante* with an actor I had always thought of as my friend, and asked, "Did you introduce these two young things?"

"Why, yes," I said. "How could I help it, since the two of them turned up here on the same evening once?"

He looked at me and sadly shook his head. "What did you think would happen when you'd brought two beautiful, very young people together? Frankly, I envy you—being still naive enough to expect faithfulness from anyone twenty years old."

I was impressed by the things he said, but I'm afraid it did nothing to alleviate my hurt pride and fearful new torments of distrust.

On Tenn's second visit to the walk-up in the Annex, I was down with a slight illness. He sat on the foot of my bed and showed me a copy of *Harper's Bazaar* in which his story "The Malediction" had just appeared. Later, I read to him an opening scene of the novel I'd been trying for months to get right. The scene had to do with a spinster waking in the morning and traveling, in her mind, all through an old Southern house, into her sister's room, across the street into the rooms of her twin brother and his wife, and, finally into a bedroom in the manse of the Episcopal rector whom she loved.

Tennessee listened without comment; then asked, "Why have you introduced your characters in this way?"

I shrugged. "It's just a device to introduce most of them as they are on waking. It seems legitimate to me, especially since all the action of the book occurs in a single day."

"Devices are not necessary," T.W. said—and promptly dropped the subject of this chapter on which I'd been laboring.

I know now that he thought of me, in those days, primarily as a poet. He had no faith in my being able to write a professional novel, and if the truth were known, I had damned little faith in my own ability to do so at that moment.

After he'd gone, I began to think about the differences between him and me and came up with some baffling conclusions. Here I was, unable to get on with this novel, mainly because of my frenzied preoccupation with a love affair. In my life I'd suffered through three such major catastrophes, as well as a number of minor liaisons, and while they lasted I'd not been able even to write good poetry. It was only after I'd won—and lost—that the poetry had come. Some of my better poems *had* been eventually born of such torments, but I was dealing with prose now, and I couldn't think clearly enough, or work long enough at a stretch, to accomplish what I needed to in that medium.

It occurred to me that I'd never seen Tennessee Williams thwarted by any romantic attachment and I recalled a thing that had impressed me.

When I'd lived at the Y.M.C.A., Tenn had a little penthouse in a small hotel nearby. Sunning on the Y roof on weekends, shooting the breeze with casual friends, I could see him over on his roof banging away at his portable, and always I'd marvel at his working consistently there for hours, seemingly immune to loneliness, the need for love, or any other self-disruptive influence.

Depressed, I lay in my bed on this day after he'd left me, recalling his having said that he envied me for still being naive enough to expect faithfulness in a young lover, and I thought, *There is a lesson here, if I could learn it.* The trouble lay in my trying to find some completion of my *self* in someone else that would allow me to work, emotionally satisfied, mentally at peace.

Tennessee had no delusions about achieving such an ideal state and that was one reason why he'd already accomplished a great deal more than I had.

Still, this couldn't be the whole of his story: he had a directed drive toward success the like of which I'd seldom seen, and I wondered about its source and motivations.

It seemed that nothing would ever keep him from his daily stint at the typewriter, and even as I tried to fathom his great singleness of purpose, I deplored my basic lack of such self-discipline.

Ironically, what I did not know was that just at this time something was already happening, deep within my friend's self, that would keep him from pursuing his schedule for the next three months. Even now he was undergoing, in his suite at the Shelton Hotel, a kind of torment of which I knew nothing, and since he has written poignantly of this experience, I quote from an essay of his called "On a Streetcar Named Success," which first appeared in *The New York Times* Drama Section, November 30, 1947.

Some time this month I will observe the third anniversary of the Chicago opening of "The Glass Menagerie," an event which terminated one part of my life and began another about as different in all external circumstances as could be well imagined. I was snatched out of virtual oblivion and thrust into sudden prominence, and from the precarious tenancy of furnished rooms about the country I was removed to a suite in a first-class Manhattan hotel. . . .

The sort of life which I had had previous to this popular success was one that required endurance, a life of clawing and scratching along a sheer surface and holding on tight with raw fingers to every inch of rock higher than the one caught hold of before, but it was a good life because it was the sort of life for which the human organism is created.

I was not aware of how much vital energy had gone into this struggle until the struggle was removed. I was out on a level plateau with my arms still thrashing and my lungs still grabbing at air that no longer resisted. This was security at last.

I sat down and looked about me and was suddenly very depressed. I thought to myself, this is just a period of adjustment. Tomorrow morning I will wake up in this first-class hotel suite above the discreet hum of an East Side boulevard and I will appreciate its elegance and luxuriate in its comforts and know that I have arrived at our American plan of Olympus. Tomorrow morning when I look at the green satin sofa I will fall in love with it. It is only temporarily that the green satin looks like slime on stagnant water.

But in the morning the inoffensive little sofa looked more revolting than the night before and I was already getting too fat for the $125 suit which a fashionable acquaintance had selected for me. . . .

I lived on room-service. But in this, too, there was a disenchantment. Some time between the moment when I ordered dinner over the 'phone and when it was rolled into my living room like a corpse on a rubber-wheeled table, I lost all interest in it. Once I ordered a sirloin steak and a chocolate sundae, but everything was so cunningly disguised on the table that I mistook the chocolate sauce for gravy and poured it over the sirloin steak.

Of course this was all the more trivial aspect of a dislocation that began to manifest itself in far more disturbing ways. I soon found myself becoming indifferent to people. A well of cynicism rose in me. Conversations all sounded like they had been recorded years ago and were being played back on a turntable. Sincerity and kindliness seemed to have gone out of my friends' voices. I suspected them of hypocrisy. I stopped calling them, stopped seeing them. I was impatient of what I took to be inane flattery.

I got so sick of hearing people say, "I loved your play!" that I could not say thank you any more. I choked on the words and turned rudely away from the usually sincere person. I no longer felt any pride in the play itself but began to dislike it, probably because I felt too lifeless inside ever to create another. I was walking around dead in my shoes, and I knew it but there was no

one I knew or trusted sufficiently, at that time, to take him aside
and tell him what was the matter.

This curious condition persisted about three months, till late
spring, when I decided to have another eye operation, mainly
because of the excuse it gave me to withdraw from the world
behind a gauze mask. It was my fourth eye operation, and perhaps I should explain that I had been afflicted for about five years
with a cataract on my left eye which required a series of needling
operations and finally an operation on the muscle of the eye.
(The eye is still in my head. So much for that.)

Well, the gauze mask served a purpose. While I was resting in
the hospital the friends whom I had neglected or affronted in one
way or another began to call on me and now that I was in pain
and darkness, their voices seemed to have changed, or rather that
unpleasant mutation which I had suspected earlier in the season
had now disappeared and they sounded now as they used to sound
in the lamented days of my obscurity. Once more they were
sincere and kindly voices with the ring of truth in them.

Now, after thirteen years of being close to Tenn, I find it impossible to believe that he shouldn't have thought of me in 1945 as a
friend to whom he could say that he was walking around dead in
his shoes. What's more, it seems not only improbable but shameful that I was not one of the friends who visited him in the
hospital after his eye operation. And once again I can explain this
state of affairs only by saying that I must have been so maniacally
involved in my own troubled affairs as to be oblivious to the
serious afflictions and problems besetting someone else.

If I *had* known, though, that Tenn was feeling alone and friend-
less—if *he* himself had not become "indifferent to people" and so
suspicious of his friends' sincerity that he "stopped calling them,
stopped seeing them"—I might have been for him, at this time, at
least a companion in misery, if not a friend who'd have brought
him some comfort.

A few weeks after *Menagerie's* opening Laurette Taylor won the
New York Drama Critics' Award for the year's best dramatic per-

formance by an actress. The play captured this same award as the best play of the season, as well as the *Billboard*-sponsored Donaldson Award, voted upon by two thousand people in show business, and the Sidney Howard Memorial Award of $1,500 for a new playwright who had "brought a vigorous new talent into the theatre."

Nevertheless, as Tennessee reveals in the latter half of his "Streetcar" essay, he'd had it, of late, with *The Glass Menagerie*, and so, in the late spring of 1945, he sailed for Chapala in Mexico.

He worked there on a script with a New Orleans background, called *The Poker Night*, laying it aside temporarily to concentrate on another play with a Delta setting, entitled *Summer and Smoke*.

He'd finished *You Touched Me!* before he left New York, and he returned to the city in time for its opening on September 26.

The play, produced by Lee Shubert and Guthrie McClintic, with Montgomery Clift, Marianne Stevens, and Edmund Gwenn, was destined not to repeat the success of *Menagerie*, still playing to packed houses, but Williams had at least the rare satisfaction of having two plays running on Broadway.

I am not sure about the time when I next saw Tenn, but I think it was in October. He'd asked me for dinner and I'd dropped by his hotel in the late afternoon to have drinks with him beforehand.

He was dressing and I was wandering around the living room, glass in hand, when I paused at the dresser, picked up a framed photograph and asked, "Good Lord, Tenn, who is this lovely girl?"

He stopped buttoning his shirt and said in a small, quiet voice, "Why, I thought you knew. That's my sister, Rose. She's in the asylum."

I could feel his indescribable gaze upon me as I set the photograph down and said only, "No. I didn't know."

I'd had a shock that I didn't know how to cope with, so I looked round at him and said brightly, "Well, ain't you the smart young man-about-town? Where'd you get that beautiful suit?"

He turned to survey himself in the pier glass as he answered, "Oh, this is my hundred-n'-twenty-five-dollar suit I got just after *Menagerie* opened."

I thought quickly, *He's come a long way since he carried that old worn-out flannel suit of mine home under his arm,* and then, *He hasn't changed much, though,* as I said aloud, looking him over, "Hmm-hmnn. Just yo li'l ole hunderd-n'-twen'y-five-dollar suit—and with it you're wearin' your one-dollar Cardinal tie, eh, baby?"

He threw back his head to laugh—as he almost always can—at his own inconsistencies and we went on out to dinner at a small French restaurant.

This was the first time we'd dined together without going Dutch and I felt he was sort of proudly looking ahead to the moment when he'd pick up the check.

We talked, over Vichyssoise, about our friends; then, through the chicken cooked in wine, about his new status and I told him, "I can actually see a new alertness and assurance in you which I suppose does come with sudden success. In the days before *Menagerie*, you used to seem aloof and uncertain sometimes. But then, I guess that was also partly due to your being slightly deaf."

His curly head jerked up. "Deaf? Why, what're you mean, man? I've never been deaf. It's just I was always so preoccupied, keeping myself housed and fed, I never could concentrate on much else around me."

We then finished our meal with brandies and set off to see *You Touched Me!* I enjoyed the comedy (which after a recent reading I'd incidentally decided was underrated by its reviewers) and was completely beguiled by the scene in which Edmund Gwenn as the retired sea captain gave a lurid, outrageous account of his youthful affair with a porpoise.

At intermission I asked Tenn how he'd ever come up with this bit and he said, "I heard it, baby, practically word for word, from the mouth of an old salt one night in a waterfront bar."

We had a fine evening together, but when Tenn had left me at the door of the Harvard Annex I climbed the stairs thinking of the girl in the photograph on his dresser of whom he'd said, *Why, I thought you knew. That's my sister Rose. She's in the asylum.*

The face of Rose Williams and his hush-voiced remark had implanted themselves in my mind.

This was the first time I'd ever known Rose existed, for in all the bull sessions we'd had, sober or drunk, Tenn had never once told me he had a sister.

Shortly after the evening described above he left for St. Louis to visit his family, moving on to spend the winter in Mexico and Texas where he continued to work on *The Poker Night* and *Summer and Smoke*. And finally, in late October, with Howard Griffin, a poet whose work I admired, I saw *Menagerie*.

I had read reviews of the play and heard some firsthand accounts of it, but I can truthfully say I had been in no way prepared for the miraculous thing I was about to witness that night at the Playhouse.

From the moment the curtain rose on the Wingfield trio seated at the small dining table in that squalid St. Louis flat with Amanda's distraught voice nagging Tom, I sat motionless.

When the first curtain fell I turned to Howard, crying, not knowing until then I'd been crying. I asked as I blew my nose, "Is this woman's acting as great as I think it is?" and Howard answered, "Oh, yes. There's nothing to compare it to."

At the end of the play there were many calls, the last of which Laurette took by herself—just as Diana Barrymore has said she did in Chicago after her heartbreaking portrayal of Mrs. Midget in *Outward Bound:*

> She came out, with little, hesitant steps, as if to say, "Who, me? Are you sure it's me you want?" As if to say, in astonishment, almost in bewilderment, "What, are you applauding me? For what? For what . . . ?"*

As the final curtain fell I said to Howard, "Let's go backstage, I must try to speak to her"; and as we made our way back I told him a little incident about her in the show mentioned above.

She had come in one night, drunk, and an old character actor, a long-time friend of hers in the cast, had been sent to the dressing

---

* Diana Barrymore and Gerold Frank, *Too Much, Too Soon* (New York: Henry Holt & Co., Inc.), 1957.

room to speak to her. He found her with her head down on her
arms on the make-up board, apparently beyond revival, but when
he asked gently, "Laurette, dear, you seem so unwell. Should you
really go on tonight?" the touseled head came up slow and the
liquid voice said clearly, "Yes. Just tell 'em to ring up the rag and
I'll make the magic."

"This story," I said, "may not be true, but anyway I know now
what she meant. I didn't know before, but I certainly do know
now."

We found Julie Haydon backstage and congratulated her. Then
I asked, "Do you think we'd dare step in to see Miss Taylor?"

Julie said, "Oh, of course, come on. She'd be so happy to see
you," so we went in with Julie and found her there in Amanda's
ancient flounced ball gown with an open book of cartoons on her
lap and a glass of beer on a small table beside her chair.

She was used by now to superlatives, so she merely thanked us
politely for our compliments and held up the book of cartoons,
asking me, "Look at this thing, will you?"

The book was one of Abner Dean's in which his spindle-
shanked, pot-bellied little egghead wandered through indescribable
nightmares of frustration—and if I'd known then what I know
now, I'd have understood why Laurette Taylor held up the book
to me so eagerly. I have since read and re-read her daughter's
superb biography and in it Marguerite Courtney has said of her
mother's alcohol-crazed, half-cognizant nightmares at Easthamp-
ton in 1927:

> In the rambling frame house the night stillness would be broken
> by sinister mutterings and angry cries from the third floor which
> Laurette had appropriated for her sleeping quarters, and the floor
> boards would creak and groan under a constant restless move-
> ment, undirected and purposeless.*

Miss Courtney goes on, telling how the family, banded together
in the pretense that Laurette was not over-drinking, suffered with
her.

* Courtney, *Laurette*, p. 305.

The nights in the frame house were unspeakable. Each conspirator lay in bed frozen with misery and horror listening to the sounds emanating from the third floor, sounds which seemed to come from hell and under. It was as though one side of Laurette fought to suppress all knowledge of her mounting disintegration, while the other racketed wildly through the hours of the night crying out in loud inhuman voice on the vistas of damnation it had come to know.*

But I knew nothing of these things back in 1945, so I said to Laurette, "Yes, but I don't want to talk about Dean's cartoons, Miss Taylor. The critics have written such wonderful things, nothing I could say would matter, but I still have to tell you I've never seen anything like what you're doing on this stage. And, of course, your accent—did you ever live in the South?"

"Oh, no," she said. "I've never been south of Washington. We always had colored servants, though, and when I first started working on the part, I had them in mind. But I knew something was wrong, so one day I asked Tennessee what it was, and he said, 'Laurette, Ah think you've got a little too much darky in it.'"

She drawled Tennessee's remark and as she did so, I swear I turned around to see if he was behind me as she went on, "So, I just started copying *his* accent, and as you see it came out all right."

I said, "Yes, but what you *do* with this part altogether . . . ?" and she shrugged as she answered, "Oh, well, Amanda almost plays herself. She's so well realized as a character, any good actress could play her. And besides, you have to remember Tennessee wrote me a great play to start with."

She and Howard and I talked on a few minutes about the play as a whole; then she showed us the ragtag, frazzled rosebud detail she'd had made into the blue net ball gown, and I said stupidly, "Yes, but why should you go to all that trouble? The audience can't see these little details from out front."

Her face quite fell under the mad witch's bangs, as she said like a disappointed child, "Oh, *can't* you really see it?" and Howard,

---

* *Ibid.,* p. 207.

bless him, said quickly, "Why, of course you can. You just need glasses, Gil."

She seemed much happier then. We said good-by after more pleasantries, leaving her there with her memories and Abner Dean's little man—and I am glad I did not know that night that I would never be privileged to talk with her again.

I did see her twice more in *Menagerie*, and one night—to my amusement and consternation—I saw that something was radically wrong in her fight scene with Tom. It was plain that Eddie Dowling was doing a staccato ballet, trying to keep up with her movements, and when I asked him recently, "*Had* she actually changed all the business and crosses that night, as I thought she had?" he laughed heartily and answered, "Oh, God, yes. And every damn line she could, too."

But that was a long time ago, and Eddie is long past bitterness. He has forgotten nothing of his long feud with Laurette, but he remembers best how, always, sick or well, happy, ill-humored, angry or sad, she made her indescribable magic each time they rang up the rag.

There's a story extant that on the last night she played Amanda—long after she'd been too ill from high blood pressure and other ailments to have been playing at all—she was carried out of the Playhouse.

Eddie Dowling was walking beside the stretcher as she told him, "I'm dying, Eddie."

He answered, "Oh no, stop that, lass, you know it's not true, you'll be back next week," but she only shook her head and said, "No, I'm dying, and I don't want you to come to my funeral, Eddie, because I know you'd bring the understudy."

Well . . . that is past now, too, but Eddie, like everyone else who saw her Amanda, knows that no understudy ever could have matched Laurette in her greatest role.

True, Amanda is a fine part and I have seen it well played by amateurs, but here, for instance, is an example. Seeing the play done by a little-theater group in Florida, I was impressed by the woman who played the mother, but I also told the director,

"Something's wrong with that fire escape scene where she tells Laura to wish on the moon. Somehow, it just falls flat."

"I know," the director said, "I feel that. Do you know what it is, maybe?"

"We-ll," I said, "when Laura asks, 'What'll I wish for, Mama?' your actress answers only, 'Wish for good fortune.' Laurette Taylor said, 'Oh, wish for good fortune, honey. Anyhow, a little bit of good fortune.'"

The director looked at me, nodding. "Of course," he said. "Of course that would do it. But you see . . . it's not in Mr. Williams' script"

The moment was a revelation. I asked Tennessee about it later, and he said, "No, it wasn't written. She put it in—perhaps for just the one night you heard and remembered it. She did things like that, sometimes."

He said this thing with no resentment of Laurette's having tampered with his lines, and gradually I have come to understand: there was only one Laurette Taylor, and when she was at work on a part there were no restrictive rules. If she felt like ad-libbing she did and it was all right and Tenn has summed it up this way:

> She was continually working on her part, putting in little things and taking them out—almost every night in Chicago there was something new but she never disturbed the central characterization. Everything she did was absolutely in character.

Laurette is long dead now, but the depth and devotion of Tennessee's love for her may be recognized in this incident: she died while he was in New Orleans living above Dick Orme's own apartment in Dick's house, and Tenn told me once that Orme broke the news to him in a heartless, shocking manner just after hearing it over the radio. But when I asked Dick about this he cried out in obvious shock, "Why, that's not true at all. I knew, no matter how he heard it, what it would do to him, and I swear to you I tried to tell him as gently as I could."

The story speaks for itself: no matter how Tenn might have heard these tidings his reaction would have been one of instant, nerve-shattering horror; for it is never easy for him to establish a deep, warm contact with anyone, and with Laurette he had managed to do just that.

Now she is gone, it seems a crime there are no recordings of *Menagerie*. However, one night not long ago at the house of Dick Skinner, who, with Day Tuttle, once presented Laurette in *Candida*, I heard a recording of *Peg O' My Heart*.

Laurette was over sixty when she made the record, yet the voice, running curiously, almost monotonously up and down a few notes of the scale, was incredibly young and vibrant, and even on the recording she overshadowed all the accomplished players around her.

Her loss in the flesh has not been easily borne by those who knew and loved her; least of all, perhaps, by Tennessee, who has said:

> In this unfathomable experience of ours there are sometimes hints of something that lies outside the flesh and its mortality. . . . There was a radiance about her art which I can compare only to the greatest lines of poetry, and which gave me the same shock of revelation as if the air about us had been momentarily broken through by light from some clear space beyond us.*

---

* *New York Times*, December 15, 1946. "An Appreciation" by Tennessee Williams.

4

The winter of 1946 found Tenn in conference with Margo Jones regarding the production of either *The Poker Night* or *Summer and Smoke* in her Arena theater.

He had known Margo for several years. She had directed *You Touched Me!* in the fall of 1943, first at the Cleveland Playhouse, later at Pasadena, and she had also assisted Eddie Dowling in the staging of *Menagerie*. Now, as old friends, playwright and producer discussed the two plays on which he was still working and Margo decided that she would be most successful in handling *Summer and Smoke* when it was finished.

In this winter, too, Tenn heard from a former amusement editor of the St. Louis *Star-Times* who had interviewed him on his short respite visit home the past year, during *Menagerie*'s Chicago rehearsals. This young man, who'd later gone to Chicago in Christmas week to see the play, had asked Williams at that time to look at a play of his, and now he'd sent it on to Mexico. The hopeful dramatist's name was William Inge; the play was called *Farther off from Heaven*, and Inge recollects Tenn's saying, "something like, 'Bill, this is a nice little play'; his statement was in complete proportion to what the play was." Nevertheless, Williams thought enough of the piece to pass it on to Margo Jones, who also thought well enough of it to plan a production in Dallas.

In December, 1957, a revised version of this play appeared on Broadway as *The Dark at the Top of the Stairs*, dedicated to Tennessee Williams, who on one fortunate day had sent Bill Inge to Audrey Wood.

Audrey turned down the first play Inge offered her and she has said in *Esquire* of his reaction to this decision, "He thought I was a stupid dame and was damn mad. I lost him, but I lost him because of my own courage. But somehow, thanks to Tennessee, Bill gave me *Come Back, Little Sheba*." All of which apparently adds up to Tenn's having said to Audrey after reading *Little Sheba* himself, "Here's something you'd better consider carefully"; for this is the way he is. If he likes a thing his enthusiasm is heartwarming to the frequently frustrated writer who is still unsuccessfully struggling.

Tenn came back to New York for a brief time in the spring, but I did not see him before he took off for Nantucket Island, where he'd rented a summer cottage and would shortly be joined by Carson McCullers.

He'd read *Member of the Wedding* and been impressed by it. When he'd discussed it with Carson's cousin, Jordan Massee, Jordan said, "You ought to write to Carson. She'd love to hear from you," and Tenn and she had been corresponding for several years.

Alone now on Nantucket in the summer, obsessed with the notion that he might die as a result of a recent abdominal operation, Williams wrote, expressing a wistful desire to meet McCullers before he should go, all unwilling, to join his ancestors.

Carson journeyed to the Island from her house in Nyack, New

York; almost immediately after her arrival Tenn asked her to spend the summer with him, and the lady accepted the invitation.

Tenn was sure there was a Broadway play in *Member of the Wedding*, so the two writers settled down to work at a long table in the front room of the cottage, one at each end with a portable—she on *Member*; he on *Summer and Smoke*.

Miss McCullers recalls that it was a lovely summer in which, since neither she nor Tenn was culinarily gifted, canned tomato soup was a frequent menu item.

The two of them swam, after the day's work was over; sometimes in the evenings Tenn read aloud from Hart Crane, or Carson played gentle airs on the upright piano—and at the end of August Carson's play went to Audrey, who would finally get it to Broadway for an impressive run in 1950.

In a letter to his mother, Tennessee wrote, "Carson is leaving the island this week and I am accompanying her as far as Martha's Vineyard where we will visit Katharine Cornell, and I may show her part of my play which is being written for her, though it is still very rough." He goes on, "I'm sorry I didn't write you sooner about the X-rays. They told me nothing abnormal was shown in them, which relieves me a great deal." And toward the letter's end, he says:

Menagerie seems to have run its course in New York. A while back Audrey wired me that she had a good and definite offer for the movie rights but I have heard nothing further, since the wire. The road company is now in rehearsal. I may visit New York for a few days to see if the cast is all right. I think the play could have run another year if Laurette and Dowling had stayed on good terms and the show had been properly managed. . . .

"The road company is now in rehearsal." Yes—and in reading over this excerpt, I suddenly recalled an incident relative to its casting.

One day in the late summer a dark-haired, blunt-nosed, attractive young actor named Will Hare, whom I'd admired in Horton Foote's play, *Only the Heart*, called up and asked me to lunch—

again, at the English Tea Room in Forty-eighth Street. He said to
me, "I called to tell you they're casting the road company of
Menagerie this afternoon, and I want to go read for Tom, but I'm
scared to."

I dropped my fork. "What do you mean you're *scared* to?"

Will shrugged. "Oh, well, you know those things. There'll be all
kinds of good actors reading. They'd never in this world choose
me."

I said, "Listen, Hare, I've seen that play three times, each time
feeling convinced that you and no one *but* you should play Tom
Wingfield. This is God's truth, and you have to believe it. You
were made for that part and you'll get it, so as soon as you've
finished this lunch, you take your ass right down to that Playhouse."

Will, who'd been out of work for some time, was so downcast at
the moment he wasn't as sure about any of this as I was, but he did
go down to the theater, and three hours later called me, elated, to
say he'd gotten the part.

I take no credit for this happy turn of the wheel for Will, except
to point out the obvious: if a thing's for you and you're too beat by
circumstances to think you can get it, then it's a damned fine idea
to go and talk to some friend who can see the whole situation more
clearly than you can.

Anyhow, I knew full well how Will Hare felt that day, because I
too was desperately in need of someone to believe in me and in
what I needed to do.

Having signed a contract for my half-finished novel, *The Sleeping Trees*, I'd let my publishers' misguided editors talk me into
writing the last half of it as *they* wanted it written, and these same
editors, plus a new editor in chief, had dropped it cold. If Tenn
had been around he'd have sympathized with me in this situation,
but he wasn't, of course. He was on Nantucket Island with
Carson, and I was not to see him again until the fall of the
following year.

In the autumn of 1946 he took *Summer and Smoke* to Margo
Jones, who, tremendously pleased with the script, put the play on
her production schedule for the summer of 1947.

I was drunk several times through that Christmas of 1946, and I recall an hour at cocktails with Bigelow when he said to me, "Yes, but this week you can't expect to be with anyone, Gilbert—not even someone you love—who has a family." He looked out my window and added softly, "No. This is the time when even the whorehouses all but close their doors—because you see, everyone who has a family is with them."

Paul had no family, so he was here with me in the late, sad afternoon of a winter's day in my sublet apartment, high in the Southgate. Tennessee had a family, but he could not be at home in St. Louis where his parents still were—and Rose was not. I had no one except my mother, in Georgia, a thousand miles away. I was not with her at this holiday season, but shortly after New Year's I was on my way to her—on the train, because she was scared of airplanes and certain that if I flew I'd never get there.

She had influenza, complicated by typhus, and she died at the age of seventy-four, ten days after my arrival at home.

So, lonely and sick, desolated by the loss of my mother, I returned to New York, where I was destined to meet, one twilight, in a bar where the NBC crowd drank, a girl named Nancy. She was so beautiful I was sure she'd have no truck with the like of me and my five o'clock shadow. She did, though, and from that night when I took her to dinner there began between us a thing so understandingly close that I was sometimes able, as the winter months slipped by, to forget my other amorous afflictions and even to bear the cold emptiness of a world in which my mother no longer existed.

From Key West, in February, 1947, Tennessee mailed a copy of *The Poker Night* to Audrey Wood and went again to New Orleans where he rented the flat on St. Peter Street in the house of Richard Orme.

Audrey read the new play and realized that she had something great. She was sure she could get any number of offers from producers, but she had another hunch which she felt inclined to heed. Irene Selznick had produced on Broadway a short-lived

Arthur Laurents drama which Audrey and her husband, Bill Liebling, had liked, so they submitted the script to Miss Selznick.

Meanwhile in the Vieux Carré, Tennessee read the play to Dick Orme under its new title, A Streetcar Named Desire, and apparently (as he often does with friends) misinterpreted Dick's reaction.

Years later, Tenn told me indignantly, "I finished reading and Dick said, 'Now, Tennessee, you can do better than that,' and you certainly know I can't do better, Gil. Streetcar's my best play, for God's sake."

I made a mental note to ask Dick about this incident, when I saw him again; and when I did mention it in New Orleans in 1953, Orme's generous mouth dropped open. He turned pale, and after he'd recovered the power of speech, gasped, "Why, I never did any such thing. I was impressed with the play. All that I said was, I thought Tenn could do better as to a title."

This whole mess was good for a laugh all around, but I must say I can't imagine Dick's having been shortsighted about this play's title—unless it seemed to him, as a New Orleans native, too obvious or commonplace.

Such an explanation seems likely, for when I asked Tenn how he'd ever thought of his marvelous title, he smiled and said, "Well, there the damn thing was, running past my door all day, so wouldn't you think something would occur to me?"

Something fortuitous occurred to him, too, in choosing a name for his play's hero. Some years back I'd introduced him in New York to a young man named Stanley Kowalski and when I asked Tenn why he used Stan's name he answered cheerfully, "It was the one Polish name I knew."

Stan gladly gave Tenn permission to use it, but he has told me that he's had a time since 1947 with new acquaintances, who invariably ask him, "Just who do you think you are, taking the name of the leading man in a play as famous as that?"

Anyhow, there was Tenn reading his play to Dick Orme in the French Quarter, while Irene Selznick was reading it in New York; then Miss Wood phoned, asking him to meet her and Miss Selznick in Charleston, S.C., which she'd decided could serve as a good, halfway meeting place for all concerned. Tennessee came, but since he was apparently wary of planes in those days, his hegira by trains and buses caused him to reach Charleston two days after the ladies' arrival.

Miss Wood suggested that he and Miss Selznick take a walk together through the moss-hung streets of the old, sea-girt town to talk things over, and when the pair returned to the hotel, all was roses. Contracts were signed, and Tennessee, high of heart, returned to New Orleans where he again began to revise *Summer and Smoke.*

In June, 1947, he went to Dallas for Margo Jones's successful production of this play at her Arena theater. And I, on leave of absence from NBC, went to act as publicity director for a summer theater at Great Neck, Long Island.

There in July, in one of those freak accidents that sometimes happen to young people, I broke a bone and stayed walled up, waist to ankle, in a spica cast for eight hot, humid weeks at Parsons Hospital in Flushing. Throughout this time I had forty-three visitors—friends from New York and Long Island, stars, featured players, and backstage folk from the Chapel Theatre in Great Neck, some of whom came to sit with me, first in the ward, later beside my wheelchair under the big tree in the hospital's backyard.

None of these visitors was Tenn, who was again in Provincetown. There, through the composer John LaTouche (as friendly and merry a grig as ever drew breath), he met a young Sicilian veteran of World War II named Frank Merlo. This young man had seen six years' active duty in the Navy as a pharmacist's mate, working intermittently on a construction gang owned by his uncle. He had not been privileged to finish high school, but he was well read and well informed, and he was destined, in 1949, to become Tennessee's secretary, traveling companion, and friend—thus beginning an association of fourteen years.

All through this summer I had no idea where Tennessee was. My Nancy was back from a fruitless screen-test sojourn in Hollywood, after winning a Miss Greenwich Village beauty and talent contest. She came walking up the street one day with her arms full of amusing puppets she'd made, spied me in my chair under the

tree, and rushed toward my outstretched arms with joyous greet-
ings.

At this time, too, in late August, came Donald Windham and
his roommate, Sandy Campbell, neither of whom I'd seen for
quite a while. Don came to give me a short story he'd written
about me and to ask if I minded its being published. It is a cruel,
uncomplimentary story in which the hero materializes as a neurotic young poet with little, close-set eyes, who is something of a
country bumpkin as well, given to wearing cheap, ill-fitting suits
bought off the rack.

In the first half of the piece, the poet returns by bus from his
mother's funeral in a small Georgia town to Atlanta where he
lives, and compulsively tells a kind old lady about the ordeal of
watching beside his mother's bed until she died.

Don had written this account more or less as I'd told it to him
in New York when I was talking to anyone who would listen
about my mother. It was a skillful bit of semifictional reporting,
and though the poet was made to seem an uncontrolled, hysterical
weakling as he rattled out his woes, I thought, "Well, what of it?
The story, for what it is, seems successful."

As a writer I felt disinclined to complain because a fellow writer
had used a legitimate device in twisting the facts of any man's life,
even my own, to suit his needs in creating a work of fiction. I
could ask myself only whether or not Don had done what he set
out to do—and since I felt he had, I told him, "Sure, go ahead."

It was only human of me, I think, to hold a certain hurt resentment about a distorted semiportrait of myself which some of my
friends might recognize. However, I was quite unprepared for a
reaction Tenn had to the story—and for my own violent reaction
when, years later, he brought up the subject in Miami.

I'd said that I couldn't help disliking Don's having used me to
create a shallow, ludicrously pitiful central character who bore no
true resemblance to me, nor his cruelly satirical handling of the
scene in which the character talks about the loss of his mother.

Tenn said, "You shouldn't feel like that, because I don't think
either the character or the situation comes across as you see it." He
paused, then looked at me and asked, half curiously, half as

though he feared the answer I might give, "It's not true, though, is it—as the story seems to imply—that you helped your mother out of this world with consistent shots of morphine?"

I stared at him, numb with shock. Then, as his meaning got through, I leaped from my chair, crying out, "Great God, I never read *that* into the story! Surely you can't be thinking . . ."

"Well, maybe not," Tenn said hastily, "but the poet's account *did seem* . . ."

"Jesus Christ," I said. "If you got that reaction the suggestion *must* be there. Listen, while I tell you the facts, Tennessee: three days before her death, kneeling beside Mother's bed I asked, 'Darling, are you in pain?' and she answered, 'No.' I said, 'I'm glad, but I want you to promise that when you are, you'll tell me.' She said that she would, and the next day, seeing a look of anguish on her face, I leaned down and asked, 'Mama, are you in pain?' She said, 'Yes, son, I ache all over now.' The doctor was there at the foot of the bed. I nodded toward him—and it was then that he prepared a morphine injection. My mother had a horror of narcotics, and even with her eyes closed she must have sensed what was happening, because she said, 'No, don't!' But it was time, and the doctor gave her the shot. He and I had both agreed that she must not go through any needless agony, so she was kept under sedation from that moment until the next night, when she died. That's exactly what happened—and I've never been sorry one minute that our family doctor, who was also Maude Maxwell's childhood friend, was merciful enough to use a drug that would cause her to sleep, peacefully, through to the end."

Tenn said, "Uh-*huh*," and looked thoughtful. A silence fell in which I tried to control my inner shock of outrage, but it was a bad half hour which I was glad to forget as soon as I could.

I had no idea that day that Tenn had any motive in asking me a question so appalling, other than to satisfy himself that I was not guilty of an unethical action. I am still not certain that he had any further motive; however, these are the facts: as a man who works with disturbed characters in high-voltage dramatic situations, he is curious about all kinds of maladies of body and mind as well as all situations involving violence, disease, and death. In his plays the sinner perishes as a result of his own helpless weakness, some twisted evil within him, or at the hands of other weak, twisted, helpless men and women who, out of self-hatred or ignorance, wreak vengeance upon him. Tenn was working on *Orpheus Descending* at the time of which I have spoken, plainly preoccupied with this project twenty-four hours a day, and when he read the finished play to me I had a strange feeling of familiarity about one scene. Later, I read this scene in the playscript, and it was my turn to say, "Uh-huh." In the second half of the scene Lady Torrance (wife of the wicked storekeeper dying of cancer who has destroyed her father and herself) hating her husband, loving her shoe clerk, Val Xavier, has this exchange with the sick man's nurse:

NURSE PORTER: Didn't I hear you shouting to someone just now?

LADY:—Uh-huh. Some drunk tourist made a fuss because I wouldn't sell him no—liquor. . . .

NURSE (*crossing to the door*):   Oh. Mr. Torrance is sleeping under medication.

LADY: That's good. (*She sits in shoe-fitting chair.*)

NURSE: I gave him a hypo at five.

LADY:—Don't all that morphine weaken the heart, Miss Porter?

NURSE: Gradually, yes.

LADY: How long does it usually take for them to let go?

NURSE: It varies according to the age of the patient and the condition his heart's in. Why?

LADY: Miss Porter, don't people sort of help them let go?

NURSE: How do you mean, Mrs. Torrance?

LADY: Shorten their suffering for them?

NURSE: Oh, I see what you mean. (*Snaps her purse shut.*)—I see what you mean, Mrs. Torrance. But killing is killing, regardless of circumstanes.

LADY: Nobody said killing.

NURSE: You said "shorten their suffering."

LADY: Yes, like merciful people shorten an animal's suffering when he's . . .

NURSE: A human being is not the same as an animal, Mrs. Torrance. And I don't hold with what they call—

LADY (*overlapping*): *Don't give me a sermon*, Miss Porter, I just wanted to know if—

NURSE (*overlapping*): I'm not giving a sermon. I just answered your question. If you want to get somebody to shorten your husband's life—

LADY (*jumping up; overlapping*): Why, how dare you say that I—

NURSE: I'll be back at ten-thirty.

LADY: Don't!

NURSE: What?

LADY: (*crossing behind counter*): Don't come back at ten-thirty, don't come back.

So here is the scene, in which Lady, planning to put her man away with morphine, is thwarted by being naive enough to reveal her intentions to the sharp-nosed nurse—and for me it has more than a passing interest.

During this period in Miami, also, while Tenn was working on *Orpheus*, I was doing a pre-Christmas stint in Burdine's book department. He asked me one day if I made a commission, and when I said yes, he asked how much. I said, "One per cent."

He clicked his tongue and sighed, "Isn't that just awful," and I thought how kind he was to sympathize with me for having to work for such a tiny bonus. Later, in *Orpheus*, I found some dialogue between Jabe the storekeeper, Lady, and Val Xavier, the clerk, in which Jabe, learning that Lady is paying Val $22.50 a week, tells her she's getting him cheap, whereupon Val announces that he also gets a commission of "one per cent on all sales."

So much for our playwright's methods of acquiring medical and mercantile facts for *Orpheus Descending*.

The point is that you just can never be sure of what he's up to, or where he actually is or isn't, when he's writing a play or is at work on any production.

In the year 1947 I did not see Tennessee at all until early September, after I'd left the hospital. One afternoon I was sitting in Jack Barefield's car in front of the West Side Y with Nancy, when Tenn, bouncing out of the place after his swim, rushed up to me and cried blithely, "Oh, Gil, I'm so glad to see you. I heard you'd been crippled and confined to a wheel chair for life."

Now, God knows I have no idea what prompted this exuberantly macabre greeting to which I could find no answering sally. However, Tenn being the paradox that he is, I was not too surprised, a few days after this chance meeting, when he rang me up. I was staying at a hotel in the East thirties.

During his early rehearsals of *Streetcar* he came often to see me alone, and once, with someone else, to take me out. Because I hated my crutches I walked through the hotel lobby between the two men, arms about their shoulders, and we taxied over to his place where we passed the evening, drinking and reading poetry before a bright log fire.

At this writing, I have known Tennessee more than a quarter of a century, so I think I understand at last why he hadn't looked me up before that day when he ran headlong into me outside the Y.M.C.A. He was preoccupied with his new play and when he erroneously heard I was crippled for life, he felt a momentary regret, but pigeonholed the unpleasant news mentally, telling himself, like Scarlett O'Hara, "I won't think about that now. I'll think about it tomorrow."

Out of sight, out of mind, I was—a nebulous phantom. But when he saw me again I became once more an entity, a human being, a friend of some years' standing, whose visibly crippled condition affected him.

Anyhow, I do know he was spasmodically thinking about me and my future at this time, because he said to me in my room one Sunday, "The thing you should do at this point is go down South somewhere and teach."

I said, "Good God, what made you think of that? I've got no vocation for teaching; and, besides, why should I leave New York?"

He shrugged, and the subject was dropped by mutual agreement; yet, head south I did before long, to Tampa, Florida, where after Christmas I started teaching. I've wondered since how much Tenn's suggestion affected this eventful change in my life, and more than that, whether it came about through old T.W.'s clairvoyance, or a process of legerdemain in which he simply pulled a random idea from a hat.

That autumn Sunday was the last time I saw him for at least two weeks. Then, making it carefully along the blue-shadowed avenue with a cane one sunny day, I spied him just ahead and he skipped toward me, arms outstretched, joyfully crying, "Gil, how grand to see you walking so well. Whyn't you come on down with me to the theater?"

I needed no extra urging for this, and so it came about, sitting with him in the semidarkness of the New Amsterdam roof theater, that I saw an early rehearsal of *A Streetcar Named Desire*.

A young man named Elia (Gadge) Kazan, a former actor with the Group Theatre who'd distinguished himself in staging Thornton Wilder's *The Skin of Our Teeth*, was directing *Streetcar*. Jessica Tandy was cast as Blanche, Kim Hunter as Stella, Karl Malden as Mitch, and a relatively unknown actor named Marlon Brando as Stanley.

The rehearsal that afternoon began in a relaxed sort of way with Kazan, onstage, almost in the footlight's trough, teetering back in a straight chair. Everything seemed to go smoothly until the first ugly scene between Blanche and Stanley, when Kazan began to work methodically with Brando. He asked the boy to make the same cross no less than eight times, each time saying softly, "No, Marlon. No, not yet," and I (fool that I was) thought that this young man must be either stupid or simple-minded. Actually, Kazan was just waiting for Brando, via the Method, to reach at a perfection in the cross which he knew the actor would arrive at through his own true inner feeling. And this, I think, is as good an example as any of how Kazan works, since Tenn has told me he never once has heard the man's voice raised in anger to a performer.

After this scene came a break. Kazan walked up the aisle, squatted down beside Tenn's aisle seat and half-whispered, "Tennessee, this is your play, Now please tell me what I'm doing wrong here."

Tenn took his cigarette holder out of his mouth. He said,

"Nothing, Mr. Kazan, just absolutely nothing. It's all completely right."

When Kazan had gone on up the aisle he told me, "It's unbelievable. This man hasn't made one single mistake in judgment since these rehearsals started."

At some time in the afternoon Tenn introduced me to Irene Selznick, whom I thought charming. The rehearsal ended with Jessica Tandy as Blanche walking off on the arm of the asylum doctor, speaking that memorable line, "I have always depended upon the kindness of strangers."

Tenn gripped my shoulder and said, "Quick, let's go out by the side door," but we didn't quite make it. Someone called to him, he went to join a huddled conference, and at its end I found myself standing beside him at the elevator with Kazan and a tall, hollow-cheeked man whom Tenn introduced to me as Mr. Miller.

Kazan and Arthur Miller were discussing the play's last scene while Tenn stood apart, hands thrust in his pants pockets, when Kazan turned to ask me, "How do you think this play should end?"

I said in complete surprise, "Why, just as it does. What could possibly happen, except that she goes to a madhouse?"

The two men nodded and we all stepped on the elevator—I, wondering mildly why Tenn hadn't said anything, since who should know better than he how his play should end?

Outside the New Amsterdam he asked me to come home with him and we hailed a taxi. At my suggestion we stopped off at a grocery to get something for supper, but when we got to his place he said that he'd just take some Ovaltine.

I made it. He sipped it, said it was frightful, that I must be a lousy cook, dashed to the bathroom and vomited.

When he'd recovered I asked why he'd gotten sick and he said, "Tensions about the play, I guess."

I think this was the evening he told me he'd given his mother half *Menagerie's* earnings so that she could leave C.C. if she wanted to, and when he also spoke of getting his sister out of a state institution.

It was then, I suppose, that I first realized some part of the impetus behind his extraordinary drive toward success.

He was in an odd state of mind in those days: there was another evening when he sat, depressing me with his somber mood, and moaning, "There's just nothing to do in New York." Then he looked up and said, "Come to think of it, I was asked to dinner tonight at so-and-so's and I guess I can take you, if you'd care to go."

The lady was famous and notorious, so I said sure, I'd like to, whereupon he remembered, "Oh, Lord, no, we can't work it. It's a seated dinner, with place cards."

So he did not go to this actress' formal dinner, nor did he call to make an excuse, and I have since wondered what reason the lady gave for this newly sought-after young lion's last-minute absence.

He was being asked everywhere now, and he didn't care. Sometimes he forgot engagements, or failed to show up for an appointment on time—but this was nothing new. He simply hadn't changed, having always been nonchalant about social doings.

Tenn grew busier with rehearsals, so I didn't see him again before I left town on an impulse.

Meanwhile, I'd heard that a London production was being planned for *Menagerie*, and because I'd fallen in love with Leatrice Joy at the Chapel Theatre in Great Neck, I insisted she go with me to the offices of Liebling-Wood to read for the part of Amanda. I made the arrangement with Audrey by phone, worked with Leatrice, reading Tom's part—and on the appointed day went with her to see Bill and Audrey.

Liebling greeted us and almost at once little Audrey came in, snub-nosed, pert, extremely pretty, to perch on Bill's desk, asking, "Now where are the youthful producers?" One of these young men was Randy Echols, but neither he nor his partner showed, so Leatrice and I read for Miss Wood and Liebling.

When we'd finished Audrey told Miss Joy, "Well, anyway you got the Southern thing, which is more than anyone else has done around here lately"; and as we left, Liebling was kind enough to tell me, "My God, you read Tom beautifully." I said thank you and that I'd always loved the part, not telling him I'd give my eye-teeth to play it.

This was the first time I'd met Audrey and Bill, and I've set down this trivial incident simply to give my first impression of two gracious people.

Nothing was to come of the potential "youthful producers'" plans for taking Menagerie to London, as Miss Joy and I soon learned. And since little of importance seemed to be happening to me in Manhattan, I began to think about visiting some warmer clime where maybe the sun would take the stiffness out of my side, which had been immured in plaster.

One day, during the last rehearsals of Streetcar, I read the manuscript of my novel, hurled it at a wall, took up my cane, and stomped down to the hotel bar. After three martinis I went back upstairs, called Don Windham, and told him I'd obviously slapped together the lousiest novel I'd ever tried to read.

Don said, "Well, that's how I feel sometimes, too, about this one I'm working on, but it's probably not true in either case." We talked a while and hung up; then I retrieved the manuscript from the floor, read it through again and decided it was maybe just impossible in the last half, which the editors had caused me to muck up.

Several days later I got on a bus during a rush hour. I remained on it for thirty minutes before it crawled to Rockefeller Center— and on this day I decided definitely to bid Manhattan good-by. I called a friend in Tampa and asked if I could visit her. She said of course, so as soon as I could get my possessions stored, I took a train for Florida.

I went there to stay two weeks and stayed three years. Shortly after my arrival, as I sat with friends discussing Menagerie and Streetcar, one snobbish young man said, "I never heard of this Tennessee Williams. Who is he?" I smiled like a cat as I told him, "I predict you'll find out before long"; and this was no time at all before the Life spread after Streetcar's opening, which caused our young skeptic's eyes to bug.

After the curtain came down last week on the Broadway opening of *A Streetcar Named Desire*, first-nighters clapped until the actors took a dozen curtain calls. Then the audience began to shout, "Author!" Finally, the stubby little man who wrote the play, Tennessee Williams, came out from the wings, and, in a daze of happy embarrassment, gave a few choppy bows. He wasn't sure whether he should bow to the actors or the audience. But he could be sure of one thing. He had written the season's best new play and had proved he was now a top U.S. dramatist. Next morning the critics called his play "superb," "fascinating," "a terrific adventure."*

More than a year later *Life* told a story about the after-midnight hours that followed the opening, and again I quote, because this excerpt gives a human and touching flash shot of Audrey Wood:

On the night *Streetcar* opened members of the company were invited, together with certain celebrities, to an after-theatre party at "21." They were fairly tense until the late editions of the newspapers appeared; but as the notices began to come in, rave piling on rave, the air filled with elation. Williams wandered easily among the guests, accepting their congratulations with felicity and pleasure. But there came a moment when later on he found himself temporarily alone and as always his thoughts turned inward and his eyes gazed far away. Then someone appeared at his elbow and said, "Tenn, are you really happy?" It was Audrey Wood.

"Of course I am," Williams replied in surprise.

"Are you a completely fulfilled young man?" she asked sternly.

"Completely," said Williams. "Why do you ask me?"

Miss Wood looked at him searchingly. "I just wanted to hear you say it," she said.†

Naturally she wanted to hear him say it. And it is possible that Williams on this night believed it, for a few hours; but the coming of the morning meant another thing. He has never been a completely fulfilled man and he never can be, because, for one reason,

---

* *Life*, December 15, 1947.
† *Life*, Lincoln Barnett, February 16, 1948.

there is The Work which has no end; and so, even after this
night's triumph, compulsion and habit drove him back to his
typewriter. Streetcar had been a great experience, for he had been
an integral part of its production, giving his opinion, when asked
by Selznick and Kazan, on such details as the lighting of Mielziner's set, Paul Bowles's background music, and even the casting
of Kowalski, as well as certain bit parts. But now the fiesta was
over—and New York was once more a place afflicted with mer-
curial weather wherein he found no solace except in the bemused
hours given to writing.

Meanwhile, in the St. Louis house, Cornelius and Edwina had
finally come to the end of their endurance of matrimony as a result
of dissension over Edwina's father. Mr. Dakin, since the death of
his wife in 1943, had made the house on Arundel Place his headquarters between short stays at the Hotel Gayoso, in Memphis,
visits to Tenn in New York and Key West, and to old friends in
Clarksdale, Mississippi. However, since Cornelius was wont to
refer to him either as "the old parson" or "the old buzzard," the
retired rector, while silently pretending not to hear, maintained a
saintly tolerance toward his son-in-law which doubtless drove
Cornelius to demand that Edwina send him away.

His wife replied, "I cannot allow my father to be put out on the
street. You'll have to make up your mind whether you want to go
or stay. The choice is yours." So Cornelius chose to go, giving
Edwina the house and some shares of International Shoe stock
before he departed for Knoxville to live with his sister Ella, who
ran a gift shop.

Edwina wrote all this to Tenn, who in turn wrote Paul Bigelow,
"As for the old man, he has probably suffered more than anyone
and it will be a bitter end to his blind and selfish life," finishing
with the remark that although he, Tennessee, could now "come
home . . . a tragic situation has worked itself out too late."

In her book Mrs. Williams says of Cornelius' stay at Ella's:
"Even she could not cope with him and he lived by himself at a
hotel."

She seems, at this point, to be dealing in understatement since
Tennessee later told me that Ella finally told her brother, "Cor-

nelius, I'm poor and I need your board money, but I'm afraid you'll have to go. I'd rather starve to death than live with you." Which forces me to conclude that C.C., despite his many good qualities, must have been, as the old folks used to say down South, "an outside angel and a home devil."

At any rate, Edwina was now free of marital ties and she has stated flatly, in print, "I was happy to have my freedom—the walls of the house had resounded with wrath for too many years and now there was peace at long last."

There was a new life opening up for her all around, too, for in this January, by the time Tenn had bought himself a new Burberry topcoat and sailed for Europe, he had made up his mind to contribute as much as he could to brightening his mother's life from this time on.

In February, 1948, he took a small apartment in Rome where he began to ready *Summer and Smoke* for Broadway, as well as to work on a new play which he called *The Eclipse of May 29, 1919*. When plans were made in the spring for the British première of *Menagerie* at Brighton, he invited Edwina and Dakin to come over. He had hoped that Mr. Walter Dakin would come also, and his letter of May 17 to the old gentleman is revelatory of his most sincere, generous self:

Dear Grandfather:

Your letter made me feel quite sad for you. I hope you are not more than temporarily depressed, for that is not like you. I am not at all pleased with your apparent decision to stay in America. I would so much rather you came over with Mother and Dakin for I don't think there is anyone in the world who enjoys travelling as much as you do. Please think it over, reconsider, and let me and Audrey know. Audrey has wonderful connections with travel agencies and she can make all the arrangements for your passage by ship or by air. If you are really afraid of an ocean voyage, then why not let Audrey buy you a roundtrip plane ticket which is not more expensive and which only takes about 18 hours. Mother says you are not going because you are "afraid of being buried at sea." Now that is ridiculous! In the first place you would not die. In the second place we would make sure that you were returned to Grand's side in Ohio. So put that silly idea out of your mind and take this holiday which is due you after the long winter in St. Louis. It will make me, personally, ever so much happier to have you there in London. I don't like the English and I am only going out of duty. It is difficult to tear myself away from Italy which is the nearest to heaven I have ever been, the people are so friendly, gentle and gracious and the days so tranquil and sunny. I have an old jeep that I travel around in. Perhaps I shall drive to London. Margo (Jones) is flying to Rome. She will join me here on the 26th and we will go north together, either in the jeep or by train. You and she could have some nice card games as you did in New Orleans while I am at rehearsals. Perhaps we could all get a nice apartment together. So if you feel you really might enjoy the trip, write Audrey a note, or have Mother call her long distance. The trip will be with my compliments, of course, and Audrey will buy the tickets and make the reservations, whichever way you decide.

His grandfather could not be persuaded to cross the Atlantic, but his mother and Dakin did. Helen Hayes was the star of the play and on the opening night in London, Edwina, Dakin, Audrey Wood, and Bill Liebling were present to see her as Amanda, while Tennessee, on a visit to Paris, was not.

His mother went on to an after-theater party given by Lady Sybil Colefax in honor of Miss Hayes and the absent author—there to enjoy the camaraderies of the star, of Charles MacArthur, and such British notables as John Gielgud and Noel Coward. She was driven home to the Savoy in a carriage belonging to Lady Colefax, through the quiet streets of the British capital in the small hours, and when she arrived at the hotel she found a telegram from her elder son, signed with love, suggesting she take a bow for him at the opening if he should not be there. In retelling this incident she concludes, "When Tom finally appeared the next day he gave no excuse, merely said he had been delayed."

Prior to Edwina's arrival in London, she had received a letter from Irene Selznick, from which we learn that Williams was definitely in good spirits around this time, for Irene states, "I saw Tennessee last Wednesday night in London . . . he was looking remarkably well and seems to have lost that little excess weight he had—he looks shockingly young. He seems to be enjoying his experience in England and I am sure that he is eagerly looking forward to your arrival."

He was there for Edwina's arrival and there for the performance at Brighton, but not for the London première or the party afterward, so one is forced to conclude (with a certain awed admiration) that whatever simple pleasures he may have been enjoying in Paris seemed to him more important than the high jinks concurrently going on in London, where his absence must, to say the least, have been conspicuous.

He came back to New York in time for the *Summer and Smoke* rehearsals at the Music Box Theatre, where the play opened October 6 under the direction of Margo Jones.

Edwina, in town for the opening and the party her son gave afterward, was scandalized to learn at the time of the guests' departure that he'd taken off with Marlon Brando on the actor's motorcycle—possibly as an antidote to the appearance of the play's notices, which were mixed.

He also took off shortly for Key West where he settled down with Frank Merlo and his grandfather, to go on writing, each day from early morning to high noon in the white house he'd bought on Duncan Street. The disappointment of *Summer and Smoke*'s reception was now a thing of the past. The *Battle of Angels* fiasco was not; and he was doggedly revising that script as well as writing further drafts of a play he'd worked on in Rome, the title of which he'd changed from *The Eclipse of May 29, 1919* to *Eclipse of the Sun*.

The play went through four drafts, finally emerging as *The Rose Tattoo*. He had created the role of Serafina Delle Rose with Anna Magnani in mind, and when he returned to Europe in the summer of 1950, he was in quest of the brilliant Italian star, whose work in films had impressed him.

He met her in Rome and almost immediately felt for her, as a woman and as an artist, a warm respect and affection which Anna earnestly returned.

She loved *Tattoo* and longed to play Serafina, but she was afraid to tackle the play on Broadway because of her faulty English, so she compromised by promising to act in the picture version if a Hollywood sale should be made. Tenn was disappointed, even cast down by this turn of events, but as usual he had his nimble wits about him. He came back to New York and sought out a young woman named Maureen Stapleton of the Actor's Studio, who, as yet unknown to the general public, had begun to be thought of by her associates as a kind of Magnani—American style. Danny Mann, who would direct the play, was pleased with Miss Stapleton's audition, as were Tennessee and the producer, Cheryl Crawford, who had seen the actress at work on a project at the Actor's Studio. And so, having known, on the closing of one door, how to set about opening another, playwright Williams came up with a winner in the person of his star. With Eli Wallach as Alvaro, the truck-driver lover, Phyllis Love as the daughter, Rosa, and Don Murray as Jack Hunter, Rosa's sailor boy-friend, Maureen gave a fine account of herself as the half-crazed Serafina, obsessed by the death of her adored husband, and *Tattoo* began a successful run on February 3, 1951, at the Martin Beck.

Now, it is not my intention in these informal memoirs to criticize Tennessee's plays nor even to discuss them at length, but since I am dealing with the man and his intricate psyche, I feel I must point out that this play, more than any other, symbolically reveals the playwright's preoccupation with the tragedy of his sister. For there are roses everywhere in *Tattoo*. Serafina's daughter's name is Rosa; the chest of her deceased spouse, Rosario Delle Rose, was adorned with the rose tattoo, and he used oil of roses on his hair. Our heroine flourishes a palm leaf fan embossed with a rose; climbing roses entwine the porch posts of her cottage; she cuts and sews a rose-colored shirt for Alvaro; she believes that on the night of her daughter's conception she felt a burning rose on her breast, and at the play's end, after bedding down with Alvaro, who has had *his* chest tattooed with the immortal flower, she once more feels a burning bloom on her breast and is once more convinced that she has conceived.

It will also be recalled that Tennessee's first play *Cairo! Shanghai! Bombay!* (fantastic as it sounds in the light of ensuing events) was presented in a little theater called the Rose Arbor, owned by a Mrs. Roseboro, and this too, sentimentally, may have something to do with his preoccupation with the flower. However, it is more to the point, I think, to quote from his article in *Vogue*, of March 15, 1951, which is or should be the last word that need be said regarding the play's symbolism.

The Rose Tattoo is the Dionysian element in human life, its mystery, its beauty, its significance. It is that glittering quicksilver. . . . It is the dissatisfaction with empiric evidence that makes the poet and mystic, for it is the lyric as well as Bacchantic impulse, and although the goat is one of its most immemorial symbols, it must not be confused with mere sexuality. The element is higher and more distilled than that. *Its purest form is probably manifested by children and birds in their rhapsodic moments of flight and play . . . the limitless world of the dream.* It is the rosa mystica. . . .

The italics, except for those marking "rosa mystica" are mine, and let us pursue analysis no further—except to note and savor, in passing, the delicate, pristine nostalgia of the lines italicized.

Just after the opening of *Tattoo*, Edwina and Dakin visited Tennessee and his grandfather in Key West. The old gentleman was with his grandson a great deal of the time now, as is evident from this letter:

New York
Dec. 18, 1951

Dear Gilbert,

I have been searching at least a month for that letter you wrote me in order to find your address which Paul Bigelow could not provide. At last it turned up tonight, stuck in my private journal.

This won't be a long letter for I shall be in Florida soon and count on seeing you. I am coming down with that ancient charmer, my grandfather, who will be ninety-five in April! Do you suppose we'll ever achieve that vintage?

My secretary-companion, Frankie Merlo, will drive the car down later, when it gets here. It is now on a freighter somewhere in the Atlantic. Grandfather and I are going first to New Orleans.

But we ought to pass through Miami the first week in January. It's wonderful knowing you will be so close and we can exchange calls across the Keys. Do you know many attractive people in Miami? I'll wire you when I expect to arrive there. We usually stay at the Robert Clay Hotel.

Can't type this as Grandfather is sleeping in the next room and he is only deaf when you don't want him to be.

à bientôt (with love)
Tennessee

Oh, yes! Merry Xmas!

Tenn arrived in Miami early in January, and I remember his delightfully surprising appearance one morning on the catwalk of my small second-story apartment. We fell on each other's necks with gladsome cries and shortly set about catching up on certain highlights of our lives from the time I'd seen him last in Manhattan.

Through the press I'd been able to keep up with his activities over the past four years, but since he'd heard little of mine, I bent his ear for hours while we both bent elbows at my little place.

I told him about going to Tampa where I'd ended up teaching, as he'd said I should—conducting an evening class in creative writing at the University while finishing my novel, *The Sleeping Trees*. The book, issued by Little, Brown in the fall of 1949, had been excitingly reviewed and I'd gone on a successful lecture tour with it, so I was more than a little annoyed to learn that Tenn hadn't read it. I demanded to know why, since I'd read *his* first novel, and he confessed that while Frank Merlo had read and liked it, Paul Bigelow who also had—and disliked it—had given him a rundown of the plot and a somewhat derogatory report on the book as a whole. Upon receiving this information I made a mental note to give Mr. Bigelow what-for when next we met, and poured us another drink while Tenn briskly changed the subject.

He said, "Since you seem to be doing all right these days, teaching, why don't you have a phone so your friends can reach you, man?"

I sat down beside him on the couch and propped my feet on the coffee table.

"Now, there," I said, "you touch on a situation that's not to be believed. You see, just after I began to get around socially in Tampa in 1947, I suddenly found myself fleeing from no less than six tomatoes of various ages, shapes, and sizes with nothing less on their minds than matrimony. When I started my writing classes, I gathered three or four more, ranging in age from twenty-two to fifty-six—and it was then I began to ask myself, rather alarmed, about this new, excessive appeal I seemed to have for the ladies. Ten years ago I might have been fatuous enough to believe I was that attractive, but since I'm now at the age where life begins, I was puzzled as to just what could be . . ."

Tenn cut in. "We–ll, charm's got nothing to do with age, you know. And of course the nicest thing about people who have charm is, they never seem to know it . . ."

"Balls," I said. "Most people I've known with charm have always used it for all it was worth—and anyhow, whatever charm I possess had damn little to do with this whole enchilada. It was simply a matter of mathematics: I found out one day Florida's population ratio is five females to one male, and usually the male's either married or queer as a duck's third leg. Also, the past three years of teaching have totally demolished whatever conceit I might've had, because the unvarnished truth is most women who go to adult education classes are either unmarried and hating it, or married and hating it. So you see, no bachelor instructor who isn't senile or actually deformed has much of a chance retaining his single status in these here parts."

Tenn was laughing now as he said, "Still, you seem to've managed, so far."

"You think so?" I held up my left hand with its thick gold band on the proper finger.

Tenn's blue eyes widened. "Gil! You don't seriously mean you've . . ."

"Hell, no, of course not," I said, turning the ring. "I bought this thing in Woolworth's, and now, each time I start a new season I gesture with my left hand all through my lectures like old Walter

Hampden in *Cyrano*. It works sometimes, but not always, so when some bit of fluff past forty starts getting coy over a third martini, I say I'm divorced. And whenever I see that downright determined gleam in some broad's eye, I give out with the most cornball crap you ever heard about how my former mate, now dead, was the one great love of my life, so there just never can be anyone else for me this side the gracious grave."

Tennessee shook the couch. He said, "You are a funny man, Gil."

"I am a hunted man," I said. "And sometimes it ain't so damn comic, I'll tell you. Because nothing—just nothing—has worked with a couple of middle-aged bags I've been teaching. One of 'em constantly sends me amorous telegrams and notes, and if I don't phone her, she just turns up here, as you did, on my catwalk. Also, last week, one skinny, middle-aged beast, who's the spit'n image of old Katisha without even that greatly admired left shoulder blade, wrote a story about a sex dream she'd had in which she and I were the main characters, if you please—and I'm so dumb, I was half through reading the goddamn thing aloud to the class before I caught wise . . ."

"However," I said, "beside all these harpies, I do have about half-a-dozen dolls in the group right now—so the answer to the question you asked in your letter is, 'Yes, I do know some attractive people, and I shall certainly see that you and they meet up social while you're here.' "

We talked on a while about this and that, and presently I told Tenn my favorite story about the first class I taught at the Lindsey Hopkins Vocational School. "My superintendent told me when I first came to the school, 'All of us here know there's going to be one in every class, and sure enough, before the first session's over, we can usually spot her and say, "Uh huh, you're the one this time . . ."' and this was because I was fit to be tied because of the one I'd just acquired. I'd walked into the class on enrollment day—and there was this white-faced dame in a lavender hat sitting in the front row. I started explaining some technical points of the short story with a blackboard diagram, and every time I'd pause for breath, she'd say, 'Miss Velma Winters didn't tell us to do it that way.' I took this for about an hour and then I told her, 'Since you and this Miss Winters seem to've got along so well—if you want to go back to her class, ma'am, I won't do a thing to stop you.'

"That was the first day, Mr. Williams. On the second she brought you into the act, showing up with *The Roman Spring of Mrs. Stone*, and demanding to know why anybody would ever write such an awful, immoral book, and I said that since the book wasn't on my reading list this term, I felt we might waive that question. Just before the next class I was called down to the superintendent's office and told that old horse-face had reported me for using obscene literature in my class. I told my story to the super, and said I'd handle this biddy. I went up to class and there she was on the front row, with half-a-dozen women around her, discussing *Mrs. Stone*. I sat down, rapped for order and asked how many people had read the book. Six or seven ladies held up their hands; then my old stool pigeon piped up, 'I still want to know why any man would feel it necessary to write such an awful, immoral book.' I fixed her with a cold eye and said, 'Madam, I hadn't planned to discuss *Mrs. Stone* here, but since quite a few class members have read it and apparently want to *talk* about it, I'll answer you by saying first that I don't think the book is awful, and second, that it seems to me not immoral at all but almost a preachment, in that the author has shown us the destructive aftereffects of war in a conquered country. The starving Italians, in order to survive, are forced into thievery, deception, and whoring, and the Americans are pictured as callous, sexually greedy conquerors who take full advantage of the situation, both in the lowest and highest circles of Rome.' I then leaned forward and said, 'Now Miss Blank, since I've answered your question, how about your answering mine: how did a half-dozen ladies in this class manage to read Mr. Williams' novel in such a hurry?'

"There was a dead silence; then she said with a toss of her old gray head under that hideous lavender chapeau, 'Well . . . I passed it around—under the desks.' "

Tenn let out a howl and I joined him, nodding.

"Yes, it is funny, and I was dying to laugh out loud right in class.

That afternoon I went to tell the superintendent, and he said, 'Yeah, I guessed she was the one when she came in here to complain again today, so I told her I'd decided to sanction the use of any literature that had been passed by the postal authorities. However, this thing of her sneaking the book under desks, and accusing you . . .'

" 'Exactly,' I said, 'and while I know you've no right to expel a tax-paying student from a school supported by state taxes, I'm afraid it's got to be either this fool or me.'

"The superintendent frowned and then he grinned, and said, 'Well, I've never done it before, but this time I will. I'll tell this old bird that since she seems to've been happier with her friend Miss Winters, we'll give her back her registration fee and release her.'

"So that," I said to Tenn, "was that, and I hope you're satisfied with what you got me into, writing your first novel, Mr. Williams."

The afternoon had begun to wane so we made plans for dinner, and separated.

That evening we went on a tour of the more exotic and risqué beach clubs where I introduced my famous friend to a number of talented, crazy night-club performers and we closed an after-hours dive right merrily, reminiscing about the old Manhattan days when we'd both lived from hand to mouth.

Next day I lunched with Tenn and his grandfather beside the pool at the Robert Clay Hotel, and David Kraslow of the Miami *Herald* staff came in the afternoon for an interview in which Tenn generously asked me to join him. A picture was taken of Mr. Dakin and us on this day, with Mr. Williams reverently holding *The Sleeping Trees*, a first novel by Mr. Maxwell, which he had not read.

We told the reporter about the old days when we worked the front desk at the hotel in Manhattan; then, when Kraslow asked about his latest work, Tenn said he was writing a fantasy on human existence called *Camino Real*, which he hoped to finish in April, since it was scheduled for an August production. The interview continued. Asked when he would do a play with a South

Florida setting, Williams replied: "Probably never. The people don't seem to belong to Florida. The place has no indigenous character of its own. Key West used to have its own character, but then President Truman arrived."

In the photo Mr. Dakin seems to be looking at his grandson with an air of serenely prideful satisfaction, which indeed was his usual attitude. The truth is, though, that the reverend had cataracts and was almost totally blind.

I began to know the old gentleman on this brief visit and to feel respect and affection for him, as did everyone who ever knew him, I think (except maybe his son-in-law).

Mr. Dakin took a dim view of paper napkins, feeling that any restaurant unable to afford linen must be deficient in the food department, so once when we stopped at an untried Chinese place on the Tamiami trail, I was convulsed as Tennessee whisked away the folded paper square and went into a fast whispering session with the waitress who sped to the kitchen and scooted back with a thick linen serviette—evidently snatched from a stack reserved in that informal eatery for such festive occasions as the Miami Laundrymen's Annual Banquet.

On the third night of this visit, I had Tenn and Grandfather out to my house for fried chicken and hot biscuits, with Lillian Grant, a gifted poet who looks like a Dresden figurine, and Tenn and Lil got along fine. He also liked quite a few more people I knew and there were dinner parties and midnight rides, on one of which a group of us, including a couple of lady versifiers, read from our favorite poets all the way from Miami out to the beach.

There is one incident at this time which stands out in my mind, and it has to do with Tenn, Mr. Dakin, and me at lunch at a downtown restaurant. Tenn was reading *Variety* while his grandfather and I discussed the hereafter, and when I asked the old man if he really felt certain of an afterlife, he answered in his musical, methodically measured voice, "Oh, yes, indeed, yes. I am quite sure that when I go, I shall cross over to the other side and my dear wife will be waiting there to take my hand."

He was a most touching person, this old padre, and when I said once as he sat with us by the hotel pool, quite still, plainly at peace

within himself, "I think it's great of you, Tenn, to take him every-
here with you," Tenn answered, "Oh, no, it's a privilege. You
see, whenever I'm disturbed or discouraged with my work, I just
go and sit near him. Sometimes we don't speak at all, but even as
we sit in silence I seem to get a great spiritual solace from him."

There was one fine afternoon, too, when Tennessee and I sat at
the Hotel McAllister bar and talked quietly of many things.

He asked how well *The Sleeping Trees* had done and when I
said, "Fair. Two editions, about five thousand copies," he said,
"Why, that's very good. I don't believe so-and-so's first book sold
more than three hundred." I asked how he had fared with *Mrs.
Stone*; he said it had done about ten thousand and that he had
never been satisfied with the book.

I said, "I like it—especially the barber-shop chapter. The scene
shimmers and glows there."

He said, "Yes, I like that, too."

A small silence fell; then I said, "I'm pretty discouraged right
now. I'm not yet through with this second novel and it's been
nearly three years since *Trees* came out. I'm a failure, you know—
really."

Tenn's expression seemed to me unreadable. He said gently,
"Some writers take five years on a novel. And anyway, who's to say
who's a failure or who isn't?" He laughed and went on, "You
know, when I was at a party in New York not long ago with lots of
rich people who'd been asked in the hope they'd put some loot
into *Camino Real*, a fat woman rushed up to me and said, 'Oh,
you will never know how much I enjoyed your wonderful play,
The Time of Your Life.' I said, 'I fear you have me confused with
William Saroyan,' and she promptly cried out, 'Oh, of course I
have. You're Tennessee Williams.' Then she grabbed my hand
and drug me across the room, drooling, 'You just *must* come meet
Edna Ferber.' Well . . . of course Ferber had no more wish to
meet me than I had to meet her, so I wasn't surprised at what
happened when this old gal waltzed up to her and cooed, 'Miss
Ferber, TENNESSEE WILLIAMS!' Ferber looked slowly over
her shoulder and drawled, 'Well, the best I can manage is a mild
Yippee.'

"I said, 'I can't even manage that,' and retreated, but I was so damn put out I whirled on this big-busted matron and said, 'You look like you've got money, madam. Whyn't you put some of it into my play?'"

I laughed, happy to realize that with the advent of success Tenn had learned not only to take it with humor, but to dish it out with asperity. I told him as much and we went on talking about ourselves, human behavior, and the relative values of fame and notoriety till dinner time.

Toward the end of the week, Frank Merlo drove into town in Tenn's black Jaguar, having been ill with dysentery all the way down from New York.

When I met him he was lying on a bed in Tenn's hotel suite, pale, small, dark-haired, compact of build. He seemed too ill to give me more than a perfunctory hello, yet when I read aloud a new lyric I'd written called "Duo for Strings," he said, from behind his closed eyelids, "I like that. It's beautiful, concise, and perfectly expressed."

I was seldom with Frank except in the presence of other people at a party somewhere, but I have this picture of him—and one other, which I find diverting. Once when I was in Key West and Tenn was not, Frank asked me over to Duncan Street for cocktails. He was making the drinks and passing them, and when someone in the room made a remark about a friend who, he said, looked like a fox, Frankie said cheerfully, galloping around the room, "Oh, people look like all kinds of animals. Take me, for heaven's sake—I look just like a pony."

He could be very amusing, but he was not feeling well enough on this trip to Miami to be in good spirits. He was also apparently unable to cope with the thought of unpacking the Jaguar and getting the heavy luggage piled in it onto a train, so Tenn called me on the day he was to leave town and asked if I knew anyone with a car who would drive him and Mr. Dakin to Key West.

I phoned Lil Grant, who said that her ancient tires would never make it. So, in the end Frank drove off in the Jaguar leaving Tenn and the old gentleman to come on down by bus.

Mr. Dakin liked a certain kind of English cheese wafer, and I scouted around till I found him a tin of this delicacy; then, leaving Tenn who had a last-minute errand, the old man and I walked slowly over to the Greyhound station.

Mr. Dakin said that he'd like some food, and I'd hardly got him seated at the lunch counter when a man came up to me and said, "He has such a wonderful face. May I have the pleasure of buying his lunch?"

I answered, close to his ear, "Thank you, no. I know what you mean—but I'm afraid the suggestion might offend him. He's not just a poor, retired minister, you see. He happens to be Mr. Tennessee Williams' grandfather."

The man said, "Oh, I see, I'm sorry," and walked away.

He looked slightly abashed, but I hadn't known what else to do, being unprepared for this request from a casual stranger. It seemed an unusual occurrence, to say the least. Yet, on the other hand, perhaps it was not unusual: there was something truly not of this world about that old man which even the most materialistic or shallow person seemed often to recognize.

I recall this whole time of reunion with Tenn as being idyllic. Then, sometime in April, I paid a visit to him in Key West which was not quite as pleasant, since I'd just completed a first draft of my second novel, and was suffering from hypertension. When I swung off the bus in Key West, Tenn was there in the Jaguar to meet me, cheerful despite a steadily streaming nose and teary eyes. We compared physical symptoms and I said, "*Nobody* knows how *I* feel, having just finished this goddamned five-hundred-page book. Even if I tried to tell someone—anyone who doesn't write, that is—he'd never believe me."

"Of course not," Tenn said, "but *I* would. When you've finished a big piece of work, you've torn your guts out, that's all." He was driving slowly, looking everywhere at once, and he said, "I have to be extra careful, driving here, because I don't see too well, and also because these cops would do anything to get me, just to say they had. They grabbed some man for speeding last week and said, 'Uh-huh, Tennessee, we've finally got you,' and the guy said, 'Sorry, I hate to disappoint you boys, but you see, I don't happen to be Tennessee.'"

He went on to ask me what I was doing with poetry and suggested that I ought to get out a selected volume, adding, "I'd be glad to write a foreword, if you like." I said of course that I'd love to have him do it, and he went on, "It's possible we might interest my old friend James Laughlin at New Directions in doing the book, so if you'll assemble the manuscript, I'll speak to him about it." I said I'd like that very much, too, and that I'd get busy on the project soon.

We pulled up at a white fence enclosing the small front yard of a square-pillared, white, two-story house and entered a comfortable living room where Mr. Dakin sat peacefully awaiting us. There were cocktails, and after about half an hour, Leoncia, the housemaid from the Bahamas, came and asked Tenn to run down to the grocery store. She told him what she wanted for supper, making a special point of his getting cream of mushroom soup.

At the grocery, however, Tenn, having characteristically forgotten her admonishment, or maybe not having heard it, said with a dreamy air and a smacking of lips as he paused at the soup shelves, "Ah, navy bean, do let us have navy bean," so that's what we emerged with, along with a few other viands more or less resembling the items on Leoncia's list.

At the check-out counter I picked up a nasal inhaler and told Tenn, "Here, use this. You'll get some fast relief from that drippy nose." He took the inhaler and dutifully sniffed it; then, outside, I said, "You don't know it, baby, but you just got away with a thirty-five-cent inhaler, free. The guy didn't charge you for it."

Tenn cried out, "What? Oh, no," and charged back in the store to lay a quarter and a dime on the counter.

When he bounded out again he told me, "Thirty-five bucks, yes, maybe. Thirty-five cents, never."

Back at the house Leoncia received the navy bean soup with a look of resignation. Then, after a nice dinner, Tenn, the old gentleman, and I sat down for me to read the first two chapters of my novel.

I said, knowing Mr. Dakin was too deaf to hear, "I'm afraid this may be an awful bore for you, sir," but he only answered with a beatific smile, "Oh, no, indeed, Mr. Maxwell. I shall sit here and dream dreams and see visions," and that's just what he did. But Tennessee's face, as I read, took on first the look of one who sits suspended in willing disbelief, then, on chapter two, an expression of bleak disappointment, until suddenly he exploded, "But you can't do this, you know. You can't, Gil."

"Do what?" I asked. "What in hell're you talking about?"

He made a frustrated, desperate gesture. "I mean, these people are so ultra-sophisticated—so unbelievably chic. Why, even Noel Coward couldn't get away with 'em, using all the lights and trappings of the stage. No, sir. You cannot do this, baby."

I looked at him, appalled. Worn out as I was from struggling with the bloody characters, I didn't know what to do except protest feebly that they didn't seem like that kind of people to me.

I refrained from wailing (as I'd told my students they must not do in defense of unrealistic characters), "that's how they were, dammit, they're taken straight from life," but I must say I've never felt so much like giving this illogical excuse—and, actually, not only the evening but most of my visit to Key West was darkened for me by Tenn's reaction to this book.

He is a good host, making no demands of a guest, asking what you'd like to do, trying always to be amiably hospitable—but though we went to some lovely candle-lit restaurants and clubs where I met several charming people, I returned, forlorn, to Miami, feeling that my book was a hopeless failure.

For, of course, writers are not to be believed. They read a thing to a friend and say, "Now I want your honest, completely truthful reaction," when, as any fool knows (or should), they want no such thing. They want you to say, "This is quite perfect, dear friend. I am not only enchanted with it, I feel it is a privilege to have heard you read it aloud. Thank you, oh thank you—and allow me to kiss your hands."

Tennessee knows this as well as I do, but both of us, by God, are honest men and more than once in the past twelve years the air has been temporarily blue-cold with grievance when one of us has said exactly what he thought of something new the other has read aloud.

On this first visit, Tenn took me everywhere in Key West from the charming old Trade Winds bar and restaurant to a final, town-edge dive on Saturday which was simply indescribable. I was pretty high so I remember the place only as a dimly lit barroom in an old ramshackle building.

We came out of it into a sort of yard with trees; I heard someone call, "Tennessee," and looked up as he yelled, "Hey, Mom," to an unmistakable madam leaning out the window of a square frame house.

"Come on," said Tennessee. Mom sped to throw the front door wide and we entered a long, well-furnished living room where the girls, all sitting around in idle fashion, chorused their greeting to Mr. Williams.

Tenn and I sat down and we all began to talk about this and that. The girls weren't drinking; not one of them in the course of conversation uttered a vulgar or blasphemous word; and I had the wondrously baffling feeling of being right back at Rollins College gabbing away with my favorite dolls in the living room of the Theta house.

Suddenly a dark-haired little girl in a diaphanous white negligee came out of the kitchen with a plate of French-fried potatoes, said hello, and sat down on the floor by my chair. She insisted upon sharing her repast with me, now and again popping a hot potato stick between my lips, and presently there was some talk of thee and me which eventually came to nothing—she deciding that I was a little too drunk.

The next day was Easter Sunday and I rose to find Tenn bumbling about the kitchen in Leoncia's absence. I shooed him out, took a straight shot of bourbon and somehow managed to whip up a passable breakfast.

Mr. Dakin wanted to attend eleven-o'clock mass at the High Episcopal church, so I went with him, arriving just before the previous mass ended.

We sat down in an outside patio to wait, and I, emotionally upset by a controversial religious theme I'd tried to handle in my novel—to say nothing of being still half drunk from the night before—found myself silently weeping. Unfortunately I'd told Mr. Dakin that I'd been studying Christian Science of late, and he astonished me now, blind as he was, by saying quietly, "You're very disturbed this morning, Mr. Maxwell."

I said huskily, "Yes, sir, I am. I don't know just why, but I am," and the old man said then, "*I* know why. Your conscience is troubling you, sir, because you've been putting Mary Baker Eddy above Jesus Christ."

There was no answer to that one, so I took Mr. Dakin's arm and led him around to the church door.

He was a hard man to fool, this old gentleman, and I had reason to regret my helpless performance in that patio. He was courteous to me for the rest of the day, but on the following morning he privately instructed Leoncia to keep Mr. Maxwell away from the filled decanters on Tenn's dining-room sideboard.

I left Key West on Monday, having had a great time, but when I'd boarded the bus I found that my candid host had handed me two nagging problems, legitimate, but nonetheless appalling, to brood upon in chagrin, all the way back to Miami. He'd made no bones about loathing the chapters I'd read from my novel—and worse, had cried out in dismay, seeing me on Sunday in swim trunks, "Oh God, what's happened to you? Why, you used to have a beautiful body!"

I'd answered coldly, "I used to be less than forty, too, m'friend," and now as the bus sped over the flat highway toward home, I questioned the value of utter candor between old friends. Criticism could be either a constructive slap or a sadly deflative blow, and at the moment my timorous ego was shattered.

Nevertheless, I started, in the next few days, to revise my first two chapters and I also went on a two-week starvation diet attributed to the Mayo brothers, which consisted largely of hard-boiled eggs, tomatoes, and grapefruit, ad nauseam.

One day as I stood at my kitchen sink in a thin sports shirt and tight pants, making myself a highball, I heard footsteps on the stone of my catwalk.

I looked round to face Tenn on my threshold, and even before he said hello, he paused to gasp, "Oh, Lord, Gil, you really are *something.* What on earth did you do?"

I laughed in pleasurable triumph, made him a drink, and sat down to tell him what I'd gone through as a result of his having looked upon my excess poundage with shocked disappointment.

We laughed and reminisced about my long weekend in Key West—and I concluded that the lively events of my stay at the house on Duncan Street had turned out to have some salubrious results after all.

But alas—I was in for a shock: next day when I stopped in at the hotel, Tenn, standing with his grandfather in the lobby, whirled around, finger on lip, pulled me aside and whispered, "Don't speak till I get him upstairs. He's decided I mustn't see you because you drink too much, and have a bad influence on me. I mentioned you this morning, and he flew into a vile rage. Lord, I've never seen the old boy in such a temper before!"

I stood there with dropped jaw, and Tenn clapped his own hand over his mouth, shaking with helpless glee, but the die had been definitely cast. Mr. Dakin had made up his mind that I, who can't handle one third the amount of sauce Tenn can without collapsing, had been leading his grandson astray.

Tenn was in and out of Miami all that summer and fall; and because I was careful to drink moderately in the old man's presence, he seemed gradually to become grudgingly resigned to my being around.

One day as we sat at a table outside his Robert Clay cabana Tenn suddenly cried out, "Oh look, Gil, Grandfather's right at the edge of the pool. Please go get him, quick, before he falls in."

I dashed over and took the old gentleman's arm, telling him, "You're too close to the pool, sir. Here, let me walk with you a bit."

He reached over then, touched my hand, and said plaintively, "Oh, thank you. I am living much too long, Mr. Maxwell, but there's nothing in this world I can do about it, you know."

I was touched, but when I recently reminded Tenn about the little incident, he laughed softly and said, "Yes, but he didn't mean it. He didn't want to die at all. He wanted to celebrate his hundredth birthday, and I do wish he could have made it."

In January, 1952, Tennessee wrote his mother, "I am working on a play and a film-script, the latter at the command of Audrey

and Kazan and not according to my own wishes." The play was
Camino Real, and he was trying to construct the script from four
short plays in 27 *Wagons Full of Cotton*, his volume of one-
acts.

He also stated in a postscript to Edwina, "*Summer & Smoke*
. . . has been a hit in England and should make money for
Rose's trust fund. *Tattoo* still running in Copenhagen and Nor-
way."

In Miami, while teaching three creative-writing classes and hack-
ing away at my novel, I'd been assembling, as T.W. had suggested,
a selection of poems from my published volumes. He stopped off
to see me on his way north in the spring; we discussed the matter
of his giving the poems to James Laughlin of New Directions, and
I mailed the manuscript to him, in New York, in May.

On May 30, I was surprised and touched to receive this telegram:

DEAR GILBERT MANUSCRIPT NOW HERE. YOUR POEMS RECEIVED
GREAT OVATION AT READING. THANKS AND LOVE—TENNESSEE.

He had told me that he was to read from his works on an
Equity Library evening in New York, but he had characteristically
failed to mention that he planned to include me in his program.

That same summer he sailed for Europe on the *Liberté*, and in
the first week of July, wrote a newsy letter to his grandfather.
Frank Merlo had driven the Jaguar down from Paris to Rome,
whence he himself had proceeded by train, and they were now
back in the old apartment.

He'd stayed a week in Paris, where he'd seen Reeves and Carson
McCullers, spent some French money waiting for him, and gone
out a good deal with Anna Magnani who seemed seriously interested in making a picture of *The Rose Tattoo*. He'd seen her again
in Rome and was about to have a conference with her business
manager. The letter continues:

Carson McCullers' dog, a beautiful prize-winning Boxer, is going
to have puppies this summer and she has promised me one to take

back to America, so we may have a young addition to the family in Key West, next Fall. I do hope that you have gone to the mountains where you will be comfortable and that this letter will be forwarded to you there. I worry about you in the heat of Memphis or Mississippi, as I suspect it may be even hotter than Rome. Frank promises to write you a long letter full of news. I hope he gets around to it soon. He hates writing letters you know, but when he does he thinks of more news than I. I am always wrapped up in my work.

Meanwhile, having heard nothing further about my poems, I'd written, giving Tenn the Miami news, and asking what he might have done with my manuscript in the past two months. After a time, I received this letter:

7/15/52

Dear Gil:

You know me too well to require an apology for my failure to function properly in any sphere of human activity. It will not surprise you to learn that I have your manuscript with me, that I take it out from time to time and peruse it privately to my great solace and joy. I did not get to give it to Laughlin, for he did not return to New York until the very evening before my sailing, and we had a five-minute session in a restaurant before I dashed off to my lawyer's to make certain arrangements in case I should perish at sea. I have been meaning, and wanting, to tell you what a great success your poems were. I only wish my own had been half so well received. "Go Looking" always got a big hand and so did "Forfeits" and "Hand to Mouth!" I limited myself to three or four of them at each reading, as I also had to read from my own works, stories and plays. As you know I read badly, but nevertheless the poems came across through their own indistinguishable merits and made a deep impression on that (Always) minority which comes with anything like a potential sensibility to lyric things. I have, as I said, the manuscript right here with me in Rome, as I thought if I had a chance to, I would start working on a short preface. However, I could mail it directly to Laughlin if you prefer. I am only going to be here a few more weeks, as I have to return some time in late August for a prospective stage production in early Fall. It would be better for me to keep the verse with me, and take it personally to Laughlin and give him the pitch as soon as I get back. Don't you think so? Fortunately good poetry is something that keeps, but I do feel most ashamed of not having let you know about this sooner.

Grandfather is in Monteagle, which is in the mountains of Tennessee, and Tennessee is on the plains of Rome. But leaving tomorrow on a brief visit to Germany. . . . Look forward to seeing you in the early Fall. Be good. Take care of yourself. Don't worry about the novel. You know you can do it, and I know you will!

Love,
Tenn

I wrote back that I'd send the carbon of the poems manuscript on to Robert McGregor at New Directions, who, he'd said, would read it if I decided to send it, in Laughlin's absence. I thanked Tenn for having read my poems at the Young Men's Hebrew Association as well as on the Equity Library program, and told him that his rendition of my things had undoubtedly been more than a little responsible for their reception, because, as I knew, he always read beautifully.

I said that it was wonderful of him to be taking so much interest in my work in this period that might be called the twilight years of lyric poetry—a period in which I would have no chance with editors at any commercial house unless I could first present them with a best-selling novel. I did not tell him I was fit to be tied because of what had been happening with my novel The Long Pursuit since January, and I shall not bore the reader, either, with details about the absurdly contradictory reactions I was getting from my agent and a couple of publishers. Tennessee was to have a great deal to do, later on, with me and this book, so I'll get around in time to all that. For the moment I shall say just this: I have recently been an editor in a New York publishing house, but I am no nearer today than I've ever been to understanding the mind-machinations of agents, editors, and publishers. I had one hell of a time with these madly ambiguous, vague ladies and gentlemen back there, eleven years ago, and my head is still whirling from the conflicting good and evil impressions my book made on the staffs of three major New York houses.

The summer of 1952 passed, and having heard nothing from Tenn since mid-July, I wrote again, to Rome in September, once more asking wistfully about my poems. I also said that, what with three classes, women's club lectures, and the continuous revision and rewriting I was doing on the novel, I'd lately been, and doubtless would be, all Fall, busier than a one-armed cranberry merchant on Thanksgiving Eve. This is his answer to me:

> "Nix on Nixon Club"
> 50 E. 54th Street
> New York, N.Y.
> October 8, 1952

Dear Gil:

I think some day you should write a book in the style of your letters, perhaps a book of letters about bringing culture to Miami in the fifties! (The decade, my dear, not your age!)

I have your poems, safe and sound, but Laughlin is knocking about the Orient for the Ford Foundation which is getting out a journal of which he is editor; it is to be a compendium of world letters, and he is the hatchet man in the Far East at this moment. I read the poems to myself and aloud to guests. "Go Looking," "October Schoolroom," "The Terrapin," are probably my favorites, but so many are lovely it's hard to choose. I can't guarantee that Laughlin, with his very modern bias, will be altogether sympathetic to the traditional lyric tone of most of these poems, but if he doesn't there are other houses. I've only been back two days, and Laughlin doesn't return till late November.

He went on to tell me that Paul Bigelow, acting as play reader for the Theatre Guild, had also had his name on a playbill at the Westport Theatre as coproducer of a popular play. He said that Paul had put on a great deal of weight and continued, referring to my own bout with corpulence in 1951:

You'd better send him the Mayo's diet. I took him to lunch. He had Hungarian goulash with noodles, a side order of French fries, a large salad and a butterscotch meringue pie. I had a lean lamb chop and lettuce with lemon juice, and that is the price we pay for our perennial figures! Are they worth it?

How long I stay here depends on whether or not the play just finished is to be produced this season, and that will not be quite definite till Kazan returns from Europe the end of this month. If it doesn't go on this season, I'll be seeing you about cranberry picking time and we can sell 'em together, with four arms. The old gentleman is enduring St. Louis till we fetch him South again. I have been sending him an allowance of $200 a month to supplement his rather meagre pension from the Episcopal church. Yesterday Mother sent his last check back to me, saying he didn't need it since he was staying with her. I doubt very much that *both* of them are still alive in that house!—Love—10.

I was overjoyed to learn that he might be around for the Christmas season, and highly amused by the reference to Mr. Dakin and his mother.

Edwina has neglected, in *Remember Me to Tom*, to discuss certain lively altercations that occurred from time to time between her and her father. Nevertheless, disagreements did occur in the house on Arundel Place and, according to Tenn, Mr. Dakin, who had a decided will of his own, did not always emerge from these contretemps in defeat.

Tenn arrived in Miami well past cranberry-picking time—in fact just before Christmas, in fine spirits, and shortly after his arrival, despite the trouble I was having with my half-revised book that was still going the rounds of the publishers, I found myself in good spirits, too.

I'd already been somewhat cheered by the surprising appearance in my short-story class of a half-dozen bright young students, and I'd also been enjoying, with a crowd of kindred spirits, some convivial late hours in a soft-lit bar on First Street, run by a beautiful young woman named Kipling Gunther, ex-wife of a German baron. I had a light but unavailing crush on Kip who was not only a joy to look at but something of a wit as well, and Tenn was charmed with her too, so we spent several lively evenings at her place.

It was my annual custom to bring the people from my three classes together for a Christmas party at some student's house, and this year I asked Tenn to join us. He said he'd love to, and I told each class in turn that he'd be with us, asking a favor of them all.

I said, "In spite of his fame, this man is a simple, rather shy human being. I want him to have a good time at our party, so I'm asking you to see that he has it by adhering to these requests: when you're introduced to him, say, 'I'm glad to meet you, Tennessee' (not Mr. Williams), and from there on, treat him as though he were one of you. You may talk to him about anything except his work. He hates to discuss it, anytime, anywhere, and God knows he has a right to get away from it at Christmas, so please don't mention his plays. If you'll just do these things, I assure you he'll be most grateful—and so, incidentally, will I."

We'd drawn names from a hat, including Tenn's and Marion Black Vaccaro's, for an exchange of little nothing gifts from the dime stores. The women, in good old Southern camp-meetin' style, were to bring the solid refreshments, and we'd taken up a collection for the liquids that would fill the punch bowl.

The night arrived and so did everyone who was asked, and more beside. Tenn came early; he met the people, all of whom, to my delighted relief, betrayed no evidence of awe at meeting a celebrity in the flesh—and I had a feeling all would be well.

Tenn asked if he might call Marion Vaccaro, and I said sure, so he did and told her meaningfully, "Yes, it's a lovely party, dear, and they're serving a *delicious rum punch*. Yes, *punch*. Just delightful, dear." He listened a moment, smiling, then told me that Marion would like to speak to me.

I took the phone and Marion asked in her hushed, softly apologetic voice, "Gilbert, darling, would you or the hostess be offended if I brought my *brandy*?"

I said, "No, of course not, slap it on your hip and hurry along, sweetie."

She arrived in a few minutes, and promptly took me aside to tell me, even more apologetically, "As I left the house Mother said,

'Sister, if you can't drink what they're serving at the party, you shouldn't go,' but I wanted to come and I've had some brandy today, so I didn't dare mix things up. Do you really think it's all right, darling?' "

I assured her again that it was and led her out to a bedroom where I found my friend Addie Palmer, a young woman of the Jewish faith, busily wrapping small presents.

I said, "What's this, Miss Addie?" and she said, "Well, honey, just as I thought, several unexpected characters have shown up, so I'm just wrapping a few extra little old knickknacks I bought today."

I was curiously touched, for there were husbands, wives, and lovers of the students, who'd come along at the last minute—and thanks to Addie's thoughtfulness, no one was left out when Santa Claus unburdened the tree.

Certain of my students always especially remembered me, and this year I got the usual light haul. I don't remember what old Mr. Whiskers handed to Marion, but I do recall the trinket he gave Tenn, and precisely what our boy was doing when I found him, high on the rum punch, seated Turkish fashion on the floor: he was ecstatically running the tiny red fire engine over the hostess' carpet.

Luminous-eyed, he glanced up at me and said, "Oh, look, Gil, isn't this *something?* I just love it and I know Frank will, too, so I'm going to take it down to Key West for him."

He looked blissfully happy, and as I smiled down at him I asked, "Are you really having a good time here tonight, Tenn?"

"Good time?" he said. "Why, man, I'm having a marvelous time. I think these're the sweetest people I've met in years."

The evening wore on with much hilarity, jitterbugging, and countless refills of the punch bowl. Toward its close Tenn called me aside and said softly, "Now, I want you to pick a few of your favorite kids from this group and let me take 'em out on the town."

I circulated, choosing two girls and three young guys whom I especially liked; then when I'd told the rest of my gang good-night, Tennessee, Marion, the kids and I took off for Kipling's.

We stayed there till dawn, singing and dancing, celebrating this occasion which I recall with nostalgia as one of the gayest pre-Christmas nights I have ever known.

In his usual last-minute rush for the airport on the day he departed, Tenn called and asked me to pick up a book he'd left for me at the front desk of his hotel. I can't remember the name of the book, but I've never forgotten the note that accompanied it, folded over a bill.

It said, "Dear Gilbert: Santa Claus thought you should have some Christmas loot. Love, Tennessee."

He had taken me out everywhere—to bars, restaurants, night clubs, always insistent upon picking up the checks—but he'd forgotten to get me a present, so here was something I could use to buy myself a bright bauble.

That winter, when Tenn stopped off again in Miami en route to New York for the *Camino Real* rehearsals, we talked at length about the novel and the book of poems.

The Long Pursuit had been turned down after three months' consideration by the third house my agent had sent it to, and I was now rewriting the book in the third person. I'd heard from Bob McGregor at New Directions who said he'd liked the book of poems immensely. He felt that James Laughlin would, too, but Mr. Laughlin was still away and besides, I could not hope for publication with the firm for at least two years since they had contracted for two books of verse ahead of mine.

I said to Tenn, "I don't want to wait two years. My novel came out four years ago, and that's too long between books, baby. I'm going to find me a publisher and get these poems out, so if you're serious about writing that foreword, why not do it while you're here?"

He promised to try, and he did. He wrote several versions of a preface, none of which satisfied either him or me. I said then, in effect, "Look, didn't you once tell me you thought this and that about the poem, 'Go Looking,' and about the body of my work?"

He said, "Yes, of course I did."

"So all right," I said. "Why don't you just write what you've said into this foreword?"

He agreed, and here is what he came up with:

SOME WORDS BEFORE

A poet once asked a playwright who was his friend to compose a foreword to his first volume of verse. The playwright, having enormous admiration for the verse, though he acknowledged an incomplete understanding of it, gladly assented to the request. However time passed and the foreword remained unwritten, although the publication of the poems was waiting only upon the foreword's completion. Poet and publisher began to press the playwright a little; and at last he made his shamed confession. He simply couldn't do it. He didn't know how to. The mere attempt of it made him feel a fool . . .

The poet was Hart Crane. The playwright was Eugene O'Neill. The volume was *White Buildings*.

Happily, the playwright's defection did not, in the end, prevent the poet's first book's coming out.

I find myself understanding Mr. O'Neill's predicament. What makes it so difficult to write a preface to a collection of verse is that it doesn't require one, and that is even truer in the case of Maxwell and Williams than it was in the case of Crane and O'Neill. There were possibly things in the eclectic idiom of Crane that a foreword might helpfully introduce to his first startled readers. But Gilbert Maxwell presents no such difficulties. He rises entirely fresh from the spring of tradition.

When I first suggested to him that he assemble this book, I said, "You are the only major poet I know of who has not yet published a selection of his work." He answered me, "I am not a major poet, and besides, I don't think more than a handful of people now living would care whether or not I brought out another volume."

There is a measure of truth in Gilbert Maxwell's protest against my suggestion. Certainly there is not more than a handful of people who care about the publication of a volume of fine verse. There never has been. But a handful of people may be more important than a thousand boatloads of them—under some circumstances . . .

A poet lives for the few. And as evidence in favor of my

importunities, I cite the title piece of this volume, *Go Looking,* which I believe to be one of the few great modern poems.

Now, emotional, or even intellectual, reaction to poetry is a personal thing. But I believe that you will find in this collection, as I have, more than a handful of poems which will strike you as being the work of a lyric talent of the first magnitude.

Tennessee Williams

Altogether, this visit of Tenn's was quite pleasant, except for a single incident which enraged me. I had in my short-story class a young student with talent. He had much to learn about plot, but he could create live characters, and since he also seemed unable to write a poor sentence, I thought Tennessee might be able to interest Audrey Wood in his work. I asked him to go out with Tenn and me one evening and Tenn took us to the lounge of the Biscayne Terrace Hotel.

Everything went smoothly until the end of the second drink when this young jackass fixed Tenn with an agate eye and said coolly, "Mr. Williams, I didn't like your *Roman Spring of Mrs. Stone.*"

There was a static second in which I held my breath; then Williams exploded: "I don't give a goddamn what you thought about *Mrs. Stone.* Who the hell are you to tell me a thing like that? *I* know there's something wrong with that book—I've never been satisfied with it—but it's certainly no business of yours to criticize my novel to me."

I tightened my jaw and did what I could to clear the air, but the party broke up almost immediately, and when we'd left the kid outside, Tenn started raging, "Why did you bring that boy to meet me? My God, he must hate me if he could say a thing like that to my face."

We went to the McAllister Hotel for a nightcap so that he could calm down. I said, "I know how you feel about this little nowhere character's rudeness, but it shouldn't affect you for the simple reason that he *is* nowhere and because of course he pulled that stunt to make himself seem important."

I might as well have saved my breath. T.W. paid not the

slightest attention to anything I said, and as he looked at me, his blue eyes dark with resentment and grievance, I thought, *Oh, Lord, now I'm going to get it*, which I did, as he snorted, "You should talk. You told me, sitting right here at this bar, you didn't like anything in that book except the barber-shop chapter."

I whirled on the bar stool then and let him have it. I said, "That's an absolute lie and you know it. By God, you always hear just what you want to hear and half the time it's something that has not been said. I told you I *especially* liked the barber-shop chapter, and I said other nice things about the book as a whole. I've not only read your novel—which is more than you can say about *Trees*—I've used it in my Contemporary Lit. course. I've analyzed it for my classes, page by page, paragraph by paragraph, and there's nothing I don't know about *Mrs. Stone*. I know exactly what's wrong with it, and I still think it's a good book, so I'll be damned if I'll let you accuse me of something I never said, just because you're mad with this snot-nosed kid."

Tenn took all this, gradually breaking into chuckles; then he asked, irresistibly curious, "Well—if you know what's wrong with the book, why don't you tell me?"

I said, "Well, actually, I think it's near the end, and the flaw seems incredible. You're a skilled dramatist, yet in your penultimate scene you violate the first rule of dramatic fiction by *telling* the reader what's happening as Mrs. Stone throws out her parasitic guests. You don't *show* her, or the guests, in violent action, with the sort of unexpected, yet inevitably right dialogue you always have in your plays."

Williams, the playwright—not the man—looked hard at me for a moment; then he said slowly, "I think you may be right."

This was a day or so before he left. When my story class met again I peremptorily called my wicked little student up to the professorial desk and asked him, "Since you knew I'd taken you out with us hoping to persuade Mr. Williams to read your stories and help you to get an agent in New York, why did you choose to hang yourself by being so damned rude?"

The kid said stubbornly, "I don't know. I just felt like saying that thing to him."

He'd brought a brief piece he'd written about the incident, making himself a sort of enigmatic hero and Williams a tired, irascible, famous older man, and I made short shrift of it indeed, after I'd read it aloud.

I was outraged with this stupid boy for having made such a fool of himself, but that wasn't the half of my over-all reaction.

The thing was, I could not (as I never can) understand why anyone would wish to be nasty to Tennessee Williams without cause. This man is usually the soul of courtesy and kindness to anyone, great or small, whom he happens to meet. I have often seen him (especially around the Robert Clay pool) being Job-like in patience with the kinds of illiterate bores I wouldn't put up with five minutes. I have seldom seen him react with indignation toward anyone, except on some occasion when he actually has been affronted or has mistakenly taken an innocent remark for a jibe. Yet time and again since he has become world famous, many people, especially less successful writers, have gone out of their way in public to be cruelly rude to him.

This is the sort of pitiably shameful behavior, engendered of jealousy and envy, which sometimes causes distinguished people to turn into serpent-tongued monsters around Williams—a man guilty of no offense other than being famous and rich, who often seems pathetically eager to be pleasant to everyone, asking nothing except to be treated with the common courtesy and respect that is any decent man's due.

5

TENN STAYED IN NEW YORK UNTIL AFTER "CAMINO'S" OPENING. THE first-night audience applauded the play, but somehow he had an ominous feeling and he went home after the performance, hoping to be alone.

When he came down to Miami he told me about what happened after that. He said, "I was in a dreadful state. I'd told Kazan I didn't want to see anyone, and when he and his wife arrived with the John Steinbecks, I was so mad I kicked the inside of the front door as I opened it. It was a foul evening and I was lousy company, but you know, that Steinbeck was marvelous. He asked me to lunch next day and was so completely understanding, so tactful and kind I could hardly believe it. He's a wonderful man, John Steinbeck, simply wonderful."

I had been keenly interested in Camino Real, having read its opening scene in the script. A friend in New York who'd seen the play sent me a few clippings, and Marion Vaccaro's brother, George Black, who'd saved them all, gave them to Tennessee. They were on the table by Tenn's bed at the hotel, and one night when I picked them up, he began to pace the bedroom, restless, asking, "Now, just why do you want to read those hideous notices?"

"They're not all hideous," I said. "As usual, you're dwelling just on the ugly things these boys have said."

I skimmed the reviews, reading aloud excerpts of genuine praise, especially stressing Brooks Atkinson's thoughtful, discerning comments, but old T.W. would not be consoled. Laughing, yet plainly annoyed, he kept right on repeating, "I cannot see why you'd want to read them. I simply can't."

"I'm reading them because I'm interested in you both as my friend and as a playwright," I told him. "Also to remind you that you ought to concentrate on some of the good things these guys have to say. These are my only reasons, and you might as well believe me, because it's true."

It is possible I may have half-convinced him on this night that my intentions were good and sincere, but I frankly doubt it. When a play of Williams' receives anything less than rave reviews, he always suspects his friends of sitting round with the dry grins, invisible pitchforks and tails, rejoicing in his misfortune.

Actually I have always been disappointed that I could not see this play, so excitingly staged at the Morosco by Elia Kazan. Many people were impressed by both the play and the production, as was Jimmy Reese, an actor of intelligence and discernment, who once told me, "I was crazy about it. Went to see it five times."

I used Camino in my poetry-playwriting class and when I read aloud the speech of Esmeralda, the Gypsy's prostitute daughter, my students were as moved as I was by its sad, colorful, compassionate content. Tenn likes this speech too, and so I quote it here for my own and the reader's pleasure:

God bless all con men and hustlers and pitch-men who hawk their hearts on the street, all two-time losers who're likely to lose once more, the courtesan who made the mistake of love, the greatest of

lovers crowned with the longest horns, the poet who wandered far
from his heart's green country and possibly will and possibly
won't be able to find his way back, look down with a smile
tonight on the last cavaliers, the ones with the rusty armor and
soiled white plumes, and visit with understanding and something
that's almost tender those fading legends that come and go in this
plaza like songs not clearly remembered, oh sometime and somewhere, let there be something to mean the word *honor* again!

I think time has already proved the critics wrong in flaying
Camino Real, for certainly it is a fast-moving, colorful play of great
scope, humor, and imagination, which is as well deeply moving at
times.

Tennessee was stunned for the moment in the spring of 1953 by
Camino's reception, but he could take no vacation from creative
writing. He began to deal with several projects at once, integrating
the material for the movie script Elia Kazan would direct, con-
tinuing his dogged revisions of *Battle of Angels*, tinkering with a
one-act play that had as a working title, *The Enemy: Time*, and
even beginning a new play.

The New Yorker had published his novella, *Three Players of a
Summer Game*, in which two of the players were Brick and
Margaret Pollitt. He began to write this new play including them
as considerably altered characters, and as the piece took form,
Margaret, an unsympathetic, shadowy figure in the novella, gradually got under his skin. He began to like her so much that she grew
and changed within him—emerging at last as the willful, indomitable Maggie of *Cat on a Hot Tin Roof*.

All through this spring and summer I taught, and hammered
away at my novel. I bought up the last four hundred copies of the
second edition of *The Sleeping Trees*, which I'd always used as a
textbook in my novel course, and was now getting a little unexpected return from that book. In September I sailed for a weekend
in Nassau on an ancient vessel staffed by an insolent crew and with
a dull assortment of passengers. The food was tasteless; the rain

fell daily and nightly upon the Atlantic and Nassau, and as I set foot on the Miami docks after a dismal return trip, I cursed the old boat—which, I am pleased to state, deservedly foundered and sank some six months later.

In October the house of Harper rejected a more than half-finished second version of *The Long Pursuit*. The editor wrote that the book had been greatly improved by revision, that the story now followed a logical course, that the writing showed new cleanness and strength and that the editor had much admiration for me as a writer, but . . . they were not going to publish the book.

I longed to call Tenn in Key West, but since I'd neither heard from him nor seen him since March, I feared he might be having a tough time himself and would not welcome a wail from me via long distance.

Instead, I read and reread the baffling letter, got drunk, and gave several loyal friends who came to console me a thoroughly appalling evening.

In the fall I wrote to the publishing house of Bruce Humphries in Boston and sent them my poems manuscript. I had a fine letter from the editor-in-chief who said the firm would gladly publish the book, standing a substantial part of the costs, if I could sell five hundred copies in advance. I said that I could, and began a campaign, sending out mimeographed letters to all my friends.

Christmas came and went, and still I'd had no word from Tennessee, who'd apparently forgotten my existence both as a poet and a person. Nevertheless, at New Year's, I made one firm resolution: if I could not sell my novel, nothing on God's earth was going to keep me from publishing my poems in 1954—and I needed some help, financially.

Orders were coming in for the book from all over the United States. Every student that I had ordered one or more copies; I read for the women poets' group in Miami and received a heartwarming response, with certain affluent members writing checks for six, ten, or a dozen copies. Before the end of February I'd sold nearly four hundred copies of the book—and it was then that I wrote Br'er Williams a detailed letter, explaining my publication plans.

After waiting weeks for an answer, I picked up the phone and called Key West.

Tenn said, "Oh, Gil, I'm so sorry I haven't written you, but they were making the film of *Tattoo* here you know, and things are still sort of hectic. I'm downstairs, your letter's upstairs, and besides I couldn't figure out what you meant about the book—so tell me again, will you, baby?"

I explained the whole publication plan minutely; there was a small silence and then he said, "Ye-es, Gil, but I don't think a poet of your reputation should pay to have his book published, do you?"

I bit my tongue, counted five and told him, "I'm not paying, sweetie, I'm simply getting advance paid wholesale orders, and I'll make eight hundred bucks at the retail price, on the first edition."

"Oh-h?" said Tenn. "Well, I guess that's all right then. What is it you want me to do, baby?"

I said slowly, "I want you, as I carefully explained in my letter, to buy one hundred copies, which I'll have shipped to you. They'll cost you a hundred and eighty dollars, wholesale."

"Oh, is *that* all," T.W. said. "Well, God knows it's the least I can do for poetry. I'll put the check in the mail today—but please don't send me all those copies, baby. Just maybe a few I can give to special friends."

Several days, maybe a week, passed; then in early March I received the following note:

Dear Gil:

I left this check with Frank when I flew to Havana, but forgot to give him your address. I can't find it myself, so I'm sending this to the school.

Sorry about the delay. See you soon,

Love,
Tennessee

In the late summer of that year I took a vacation trip to Orlando, St. Augustine, and Savannah, laying the groundwork for the book which Tenn had insisted must be called *Go Looking*. He must have been deeply involved with his work for I did not see him again until late autumn.

Hurricane Carol took the roof off my publisher's warehouse in September, so the book's release date was set back, but October 26 found me autographing books at Burdine's, Miami's leading store, for a steady, day-long stream of students and friends.

I went to Ivey's in Orlando in November and had just returned from a weekend there, when I received a wire from Tenn saying he was on his way to the Towers Hotel and wished me to call him there.

He must have been delayed in arriving for I saw him first at Marion Vaccaro's at a supper party. He had on a white linen suit that set off his deep-tanned skin and he seemed contented and well.

We were a little stiff and formal for a few minutes, as old friends, meeting after a long time frequently are, and when I asked what he'd been writing, he answered briefly, "A comedy—I think."

"Comedy?" I said. "What's it called?"

He fixed a cigarette in its holder as he answered, "*Cat on a Hot Tin Roof*."

Someone joined us at this point, so I was unable to ask any more questions about the play, nor did we discuss it further during his visit. There are times, with Williams, when something tells me to keep off the subject of his work, and this was one of those times.

I lunched with him beside that tiresome pool at the Robert Clay and he looked at *Go Looking*, of which I'd brought him three copies. He thought the foreword was all right and we both said we liked the make-up of the book as a whole.

After that a little blank silence fell, and I said slowly, "You know, I've decided to start saving up for a trip to Europe, soon as I've paid back that money I owe you."

He scowled at me, alerted. "What money? You don't owe me any money."

I said, "Why, sure I do. You sent me a hundred eighty dollars to cover the wholesale cost of a hundred books."

He looked totally surprised as he answered, "Oh, really did I do

that? Well, hell, I should have, and don't you ever say another
word about paying that money back or I'll be insulted."

This is the conversation which I remember best from his brief
visit. The check he'd written had meant so little to him, he'd quite
forgotten it. He did not know that if he hadn't sent it, I might
have been unable to bring out Go Looking, on time, the previous
autumn.

Tennessee flew out to Hollywood. I made some club and TV
appearances, and read a few reviews of the poems that trickled in.
However, most of the editors of big-time newspapers and magazines who'd reviewed my earlier books seemed bent upon ignoring
this selection of my best work plus some forty-odd new poems
which had appeared in quality magazines. For a number of years
I'd noted that many books by good poets, listed under Books
Received by the Times and Tribune, were not reviewed. However,
I hadn't been prepared for Go Looking's being neglected, and my
Christmas was darkened by the suspicion that the editors had
mistakenly put the book in a vanity-press category.

In February, 1955, I lectured and read from the volume at the
University of Tampa. There were cocktail parties, teas, and radio
interviews; then I went on to Savannah where I read once again,
after twenty-odd years, for the Poetry Society of Georgia.

I heard nothing from Tenn in California, but there is an un-
dated letter to his grandfather—written, I think, in January—
which tells something of what he'd been doing.

He was casting Cat with Kazan and watching over the last
weeks of The Rose Tattoo. Anna Magnani and Burt Lancaster had
had their first fight on the set the day before and he'd have liked
to remain as referee, should one be needed for the picture's last
weeks of shooting, but he had to fly east to pass judgment on
Barbara Bel Geddes as Maggie in Cat. The play was being produced by the Playwrights company and he was reassured by this as
well as having Kazan as his director.

Frank Merlo and the dog would fly to Key West—and the letter
to Mr. Dakin closed with this:

If I didn't have to put this play on now I would be in St. Louis with you. I think about you every day. You must get out of bed as often as you can. I know it takes patience and effort, but we are depending on you to be ready and able to return to Key West when we go back in the early Spring. That's the nicest time of year there, you remember.

> Much love from
>
> Tom

When Mr. Dakin suffered a stroke later on in the winter and was taken to a St. Louis hospital, T.W. flew down to see him, and I cannot forget what he told me about this visit.

"You know how it is in hospitals. When I got in the room, I saw at once he'd soiled his bed—this poor old thing who was always so fastidious—so I sent for the nurse and orderly. As soon as he knew I was there the old man sat straight up like a little picked sparrow. He held out his thin arms to me and crowed, "Oh, this is a day, this a *wonderful* day," and I cried. The attendants came soon and made a big fuss because I was there, but I knew they'd been neglecting him, and I swear it was almost more than I could bear."

Cat on a Hot Tin Roof went into rehearsal with Barbara Bel Geddes as Maggie, Ben Gazzara as Brick Pollitt, Burl Ives as the awesome, coarse-spoken tyrannical Big Daddy, and Mildred Dunnock as Big Mama. Elia Kazan insisted upon a different third act for the play to give it a more positive ending as well as to bring Big Daddy back for a final scene, and Williams wrote the new last act with a private trepidation.

On St. Valentine's Day he received news that his grandfather had died two months short of becoming ninety-eight. Tenn and Mr. Dakin had planned for his centennial a party far more gala than Big Daddy's birthday shindig in *Cat*—and now, this event would never be celebrated.

Paul Bigelow flew down to St. Louis with Tenn, who had with him a blanket of English violets, outlined with a St. Andrew's cross of white carnations.

Mrs. Williams had planned a chapel service with no music, but

Paul told her he'd often heard Mr. Dakin say he'd like to have a special arrangement of "Crossing the Bar" played at his funeral, so this wish was carried out.

The two men flew back to New York; Mr. Dakin's daughter took his body out by train to Waynesville, Ohio, where he would be buried beside his wife. And perhaps it is Edwina who should have the final say here about the old man, in the telegram she sent to his former parish at Clarksdale, Mississippi:

Father fell asleep this morning. We do not grieve for him for he was ready and anxious to enter into that rest that remaineth for the people of God.

6

ONCE, AUDREY WOOD TOLD ME, "YOU KNOW, IT'S FUNNY SOME-times, about Williams. He really didn't know what he had in *Cat* until I told him, but *I* knew as soon as I'd read it."

Be that as it may, Miss Wood's clairvoyance—or, perhaps canny judgment—was not to spare her a thoroughly baffling evening with her unpredictable client.

Cat on a Hot Tin Roof opened at the Morosco on March 24, 1955, at 8:40. At approximately eleven P.M. the side doors of the theater swung outward, and just as Audrey and Bill Liebling stepped over the threshold into the alley, the playwright, pacing there, charged upon them head down, screaming, "Rats! Rats! Leaving a sinking ship!"

He stood and berated Audrey and Bill while they tried vainly to

tell him the applause and calls had been terrific and that they'd
simply taken the side exit to avoid being caught in the crowded
aisles.

There are several versions of what happened after this. Audrey
said to me one day over the phone, "I'll tell you some time about
this evening, my love, but the act takes a full twenty minutes and
I'm not up to it today."

She never got around to telling me the full tale and when I
asked her about it during a hectic, constantly interrupted interview
in her office, she said, "Oh, that's all coming out in *Esquire*, dear.
All you have to do is get the December issue."

I did, and here's what I found, to augment the foregoing description of the alley scene given me by Tennessee. Presumably,
the following account was relayed to David Newman, author of
the *Esquire* article, by Miss Wood.

There was to be a large party for cast, relatives and friends given
by Helen Hayes in honor of the costume designer, Lucinda Ballard. Audrey, of course, was invited, as was the author of the
evening. However, director Elia Kazan decided to have a little get-
together at his place for a select few before heading on to the big
do. In this case, Williams was invited, but Audrey for some
reason was not—although she and Kazan are good friends. Unfortunately, no one bothered to inform Williams of this fact.

He deduced that her absence at Kazan's soiree was evidence of
her disenchantment with the play, her displeasure at the opening
and her lack of interest in himself. Meanwhile, at the Ballard
affair, Audrey Wood and her agent-husband William Liebling
were enjoying themselves. "Then," she recalls, "people began
drifting over from Kazan's with stories. They told me Williams
was outraged because I had deserted him, didn't love him anymore, and had lost interest in him. As more people began to
come, the stories got more and more disturbing." By the time
Williams arrived at the big party, she was close to tears. There
followed one of those trenchant evenings wherein the very atmosphere is bathed in abashed mortification. Williams, upon arriving,
assumed a morose attitude and refused to acknowledge his agent's
presence. He stayed on the other side of the room, much like a
boy at his first dancing class, and wouldn't look at her.

Lucinda Ballard, the concerned friend of both, tried to act as arbitrator. Shuttling back and forth between client and client's representative she tried to mollify both. "You mustn't hurt Audrey," she scolded Williams, but he would have none of it, convinced he had been abandoned.

Finally, Audrey remembers, "I turned to my husband and said, 'Let us leave. This is ridiculous. This monster is breaking my heart.'" They exited to the checkroom and there, also departing, was Mr. Tennessee Williams. At this point, William Liebling, party of the third part, friend to one, husband to the other, decided to try his hand at patching up. He insisted they all get in a cab and ride down to Times Square, pick up the papers, and read the reviews together. He commandeered a taxi and hustled the two grim ones in, diplomatically sitting between them. ("I wouldn't let even the hem of my dress touch Williams.") When they got the papers they found the only place open nearby was Toffenetti's, a sort of family dinery in Times Square. Williams sat on one side of the table hoarding a mountainous collection of congratulatory wires which he wouldn't let her see. At three a.m. the headwaiter approached their table and Williams, still silent, looked up, sure, according to Audrey, that he was going to receive some compliment on his rave reviews. Instead the waiter said, "Aren't you Audrey Wood? Excuse me, but I have a friend who has written a play."

"Williams was livid," she recalls. "Livid. He sat there in stony silence. I got home and couldn't sleep. The next morning I called him and said, 'I want to see you. Lunch.' But when he arrived for lunch, he was as charming as always. Didn't mention a word about last night. Just forgot all about it, as if it never happened. This kind of thing," she said, with a sigh that shook her small frame, "can get to be wearing."*

What had happened, of course, is this: refusing to listen to Audrey's protestations of faith and good news in the alley, Tenn went on to the party at Miss Hayes', convinced that his agent had, indeed, abandoned a sinking ship. It was simply another instance of his being unable at certain moments to hear any good thing

---

* From "The Agent as Catalyst," by David Newman. *Esquire* Magazine, December 1962, p. 261.

because of vividly imagined, unreasoning, monstrous suspicions filling all the space in his head.

Just after the play's opening a certain coolness developed between him, Donald Windham, and Fred Melton as a result of a misunderstanding.

Tennessee told me afterward, "When I met those two in the bar at the first intermission, they didn't say one word. They just looked at me with scorn and contempt."

When I repeated this accusation to Donald, he let out a howl of laughing outrage and cried, "Now, there, you see. The truth is he made Fred and me promise, when he gave us our tickets, that we wouldn't open our mouths to him at the theater about the play."

Donald has since admitted that he was not, in truth, bowled over by *Cat*, so it may be that Tenn was partially right in this instance, as to the reaction he detected in the face of Windham, if not Melton. Nevertheless, whatever the actuality of this contretemps, I feel sure, looking back, that Tenn was undergoing at this time one of the most difficult half-years of his life. As he'd written his grandfather, the fall of 1954 and the winter of 1955 had been one of his busiest periods in recent years. The failure of *Camino Real* had left him morbidly wary and pessimistic; Mr. Dakin had died during the play's rehearsals, and finally, he'd not been happy with several things about *Cat*.

Certainly it was no time for me to visit him in Key West. However, when I called him in April to ask if I might come, he seemed pleased, so I drove down with a man who was doing some fine work in my classes—only to experience the most baffling pair of days I ever spent with anyone, anywhere.

When Jack and I arrived Friday evening, Tenn gave us cocktails. Almost immediately two children from the neighborhood came in bringing a large angora cat which Williams fondled, talking tenderly, tiredly to the children while ignoring my friend and me.

Later, he was stubbornly silent as we sat at a restaurant bar awaiting a table, and when Jack remarked upon our sitting there, saying nothing, he said stiffly, "I think it's restful, not talking."

At the table he warmed up sufficiently to refer to the waitress as a bitch he'd had an unpleasant time with the evening before while dining with Françoise Sagan. Paying the check, he left an extravagant tip and when I said, "Now, really, that's too damn much," he laughed and said, "Yes, but that's for calling her a bitch—in case she heard me."

That evening Françoise Sagan came to his house with her sister, a young Frenchman, and another girl, and except for my wickedly stating that I thought Katherine Anne Porter a greater writer than Colette—thereby provoking a volley of rattling Gallic protests—all seemed to go well.

It was not so, alas, with events in the Duncan Street house next day. Just after my host had come in from his morning stint in the backyard studio, we sat around drinking rum in glum silence. Whatever subject I tried to introduce seemed to be the wrong one, and when I said, timorously, that he must be very proud of having copped both the Pulitzer Prize and the Drama Critics Circle Award for *Cat*, the playwright snorted, "The hell with the prizes. I wrote *Cat* for the money."

I sat frozen by this remark, knowing full well how he'd slaved, how much about honesty and truth he'd tried (and succeeded) in saying in it. Yet, here he was, making a statement which both he and I knew to be as bold an example of mendacity as any his play contained.

I was, in fact, so furious with Williams for his whole attitude toward me on this visit (an attitude which I didn't, and still don't, understand) that I heaved a half-drunken sigh of relief when he uncurled himself on the sofa, saying he was going upstairs for a nap.

He'd been asleep nearly an hour when an emissary guest of Budd Schulberg's arrived, asking if we could all come over to Budd's for cocktails, so I went up to speak to Tenn. He was decidedly peevish at being awakened and said that he didn't feel like going to the Schulbergs'.

I said, "Okay," and went downstairs to tell the waiting gentleman Tenn wasn't feeling well.

The gentleman said, "Oh, that's too bad. But can't you and your friend come, anyway?"

I said, "Just a moment," and went back up to ask T.W. about this.

He looked at me with puffed, resentful eyes—and not knowing at all what I'd done to merit this snide treatment, I decided to dispense with any further efforts at tact.

I told him, "It may be a rude thing to do as your guest, Tenn Williams, but this guy downstairs seems to want Jack and me to come over and I'd love to meet Budd Schulberg, so I'm damned well going."

Williams gave me a long, evaluating look, after which he said, "We-ll, all right, then. Go tell him we'll all come."

Later, as we made ready to leave the house, he seemed in better spirits but he was annoyed with me for insisting he put on a fresh sport shirt, and flatly refused to change his rumpled, rather soiled slacks.

He was at home in Key West, he said, and the hell with how he looked to anyone at the party. Mr. and Mrs. Schulberg and guests could take him as he was.

At the party he was quite amiable and everyone had a fine time, I think. I did, anyhow. I liked Budd right away, and was delighted to be able to talk to him about Scott Fitzgerald, whom I'd always admired, and whom he'd known so well.

On the way back to Duncan Street, my friend Jack took some snapshots of Tenn and me which turned out well. You'd think to look at the two of us hams smiling upon each other, we'd had a serene weekend, but God knows I was feeling far from affectionate toward T.W. as that camera clicked away.

Back at his white gate he stood for a stiff moment to see us off, waved, turned, and skipped gleefully toward the veranda. Jack, looking back with me, said softly, "He's already forgotten we're alive," and I agreed. What's more, I was quite willing for the time being, to forget the existence of Tenn—since, as I've said, I couldn't, for once, imagine what I'd done to bring on his moody sulks throughout this visit.

In the past there'd been times when he'd have been more than justified in giving me the cold treatment, but this was no such time. However, I now believe there were two reasons for his behavior. I have a feeling he took an instant, unreasoning dislike to my inoffensive friend, and also that something (God knows what) had happened to upset him before our arrival.

If it seems churlish of me to have given this account of an uncomfortable visit, so be it. I have included it because it's true that Williams sometimes does behave toward his friends in a reasonless, resentful manner without explanation, and because such rudeness on the part of a usually tolerant, patient man is an instance of sufficient rareness to be commented upon.

Anyhow, it has always been consoling to me to know that Tenn almost never holds grudges without good reason, and that often, following an absurdly cantankerous performance, he is the embodiment of innocence and sweetness—as for instance he was, lunching happily with Audrey Wood on the day following that earth-shaking fracas after the opening of *Cat*.

As for our next meeting, his attitude was, fortunately, most friendly.

The autumn of 1955 found me working in the book department at Burdine's because of having lost a class through the nasty machinations of a jealous little straw-boss at my school, who resented my making more money than he did. I was now selling five days a week in the store, and teaching four evening classes.

It was a brutal schedule, but I was feeling fine and not minding it. I'd heard nothing from Tenn since my Key West visit, so I was surprised when our mutual friend, Eddie Birk, called me at Burdine's and told me, "I've got someone here wants to speak to you, Gilly."

I waited, then heard that lilting familiar voice, "Gil, man—what you doin' down there? I bet you're really makin' the loot now, aren't you?"

"Damned little," I said. "How're you, T.W.?"

"I'm fine, and want to see you," the voice said. "How 'bout coming out here right after work. I'll pay the cab fare, baby."

"Never mind that," I said. "I can pay for my taxi. See you in 'bout an hour, daddy-o."

I taxied out to Coconut Grove and as we careened into Eddie's gravel driveway old T.W. came bounding out, bucks in hand, determined to pay my driver.

We hugged each other like long-lost brothers and went into the house, where Eddie, blond and smiling behind his bar, was whipping up lethal concoctions.

Then all at once we were drinking, cracking nuts, talking about everything and everyone and Tenn told me, "Guess what, baby, I just saw Tallulah in New York. She's coming down soon to do *Streetcar* at the Grove Theatre."

At nine o'clock we sat down to a candlelight dinner on Eddie's terrace, with thick steaks and good Chianti—and nobody once said a mumblin' word about my inexplicable two-day visit to Key West, in April.

Miss Bankhead and Tennessee came to town simultaneously in early January. Tenn knew how anxious I was to see her, and on the first night after his arrival he told me, "I'm going to rehearsal tomorrow morning, so you come to the hotel and we'll drive out together."

I found him next morning sitting in the Robert Clay bar, reading a newspaper and having a Coke without alcohol.

"Lord," he said, "I didn't get much sleep last night—and this morning, trying to work, I forgot I'd taken my pep-up pill and took another one. I'm so groggy I just don't half know what I'm doing, baby."

We got into the Thunderbird and set off on a hazardous ride. I don't drive, and as far as I'm concerned Tenn doesn't either sometimes. This morning, in a hypertensive state, he drove unsteadily and slowly out toward the old Engle estate where Miss Bankhead was staying, through a positive foray of baleful looks from other motorists. We swerved into the sandy driveway to the old stucco Engle house and Tenn ended up braking the car in a large laurel bush, just under the drawing-room windows.

He clambered out and told me, "You'd better wait out here a few minutes. I know she'll want to see you, but I don't know what shape the rehearsal's in, so I don't dare take you in with me."

I sat down in a lawn chair facing the long front porch and presently Tallulah came out with Tenn. He started guiding her toward me and as I walked up the veranda steps, he said, "Er-Tallulah, this is Gilbert Maxwell," whereupon Miss Bankhead squinted in my direction and said, "Oh, good Lord, Tennessee, *I* know Gilbert."

We embraced briefly and in answer to my inquiry as to the state of her health, Miss B. said she'd be all right if it weren't for this daytime rehearsing, on account of she'd been a night owl all her life.

She squeezed my shoulder and said, "Gilbert, darling, I can't let you see this rehearsal, but there's the swimming pool. It's all yours—shorts and towels in the bathhouse—but if you don't want to swim, you don't have to, of course. Tennessee, take Gilbert 'round to the side door and give him anything he wants—give him some Scotch, give him some coffee, give him *anything.*"

She dispatched us both with a wave of her small hand and we dutifully went around the house, into the big kitchen where I met Tallulah's colored cook and butler.

There was a bar in the middle of the kitchen and the cook said, "How 're you, Mr. Maxwell? I'm Rose Reilly, the mad Irishman. Seems as if we ought to've met before, but I guess we never did."

Tenn made me a Scotch and soda and went back to the rehearsal in the front part of the house. Meanwhile, in the breakfast alcove, I'd spotted Sandy Campbell, a friend of Don Windham's, who was doing the newsboy in *Streetcar,* so I went out to chat with him. We could hear the rehearsal going on up in the front rooms, and every now and then Tallulah wandered back our way to wink at us cheerfully; also, once, to perform a funny ballet step involving one leg and a door jamb.

After a while, when Sandy had to go on, I drifted out into the grounds where I found a pretty, young Negro actress, who asked where I'd got the highball. I told her, and sneaked her one. Her name was Vinette Carroll and we sat down together at the bar. After a while Van Heflin's sister, who was playing Stella, came out. Rose Reilly introduced us and I said, "Miss Heflin, do you think Miss B's likely to blame me for this child's having a Scotch?"

"She sure will," Miss Heflin said, "and Vinette better get it down fast."

Miss Heflin disappeared, and Rose Reilly and I began to discuss Miss Bankhead.

"Well," Rose said, "I was with her for years and years in New York till finally I couldn't take her schedule anymore, so I left. But she wanted me back, so when she found out I had myself a nice little city government job she called up nobody less than Mayor Wagner. She told him I was a good friend of hers—a poor thing, being terribly underpaid by the city—and that she needed me, so darned if I didn't end up right back with her again."

We talked on a while about Tallu and I said, "Rose, do you know what I've always said about Miss B.?"

"No," Rose said, beating a cake. "I know what I've always said, but you tell me, first."

I told her then: "I've always said there's just too much of her— too much physical, mental, and spiritual energy, bound up in one little package."

Rose nodded. "That's pretty good—but what I always say is, everybody thinks the atomic age started in the forties, but I know it started back in 1903 the day she was born, down there in Jasper, Alabama."

Vinette finished her drink and said stoutly, "Well, all I've got to say is, she's the sweetest thing I ever met."

Fortunately, she'd just slid the empty glass under the bar when Tallulah danced in and came around to the icebox, opposite where I sat. She smiled at me and nodded, popping a vitamin pill in her mouth, washing it down with tomato juice.

"You know, you look good," she said.

"You look good, too," I said. "Wonderful, in fact."

There were several actors in the kitchen now, as well as Rose and the butler, and all her remarks after that were made for the benefit of the group.

She asked, "How long's it been since we last saw each other, Gilbert?"

I said, "A long time. Nine years, darling."

"Too long," she said, shaking her head. She pirouetted across the kitchen, turned and announced: "This man writes the most divine poetry, darlings." Then, great, dark eyes glowing, she asked,

"Let's see, Gilbert, the last time I saw you, you were the editor of NBC's magazine, weren't you?"

"Associate editor," I said—and she nodded, winked, and whirled out, having told the kitchen at large about her friend.

It is this sort of thing that makes one love Tallulah, and I mention it here because it is typical of her manners that she should have wanted her company to know what she thought of me and my work. As she'd told Tenn, we'd known each other for years—ever since 1934, when, having discovered my first book of poems through her friend Stephan Cole, she ordered a dozen copies to give to friends. She'd had me up for a memorable evening at the Gotham. I had been with her on several occasions backstage down the years, and though I could never lay claim to being a close friend of hers, I'd had many exhilarating hours with her. Now she was here. I was going to see something of her again, this time with Tenn; and I couldn't have been more pleased.

That evening, dressed rather casually, Tenn and I went downtown to a penthouse restaurant for dinner and when the *maître d'*, after too long a wait, seated us at a table smack in the path of the door, still keeping us waiting for service, I got mad.

I said, "This is ridiculous, Tennessee, and if you're not going to do something, I will." Before he could protest I waved the lordly headwaiter over and told him, "This is Mr. Tennessee Williams. He and I are on our way to spend the evening with Miss Tallulah Bankhead, and since we're already late we'd like some service."

The old boy bowed and scraped, turned fast, and snapped his fingers. A waiter and busboy came flying and all went merrily, with countless small attentions, ere the meal was over.

"Now, you see," I said, "what a little name-dropping can do in Miami," and Tenn sighed, "Yes, but what a hell of a way to get attention."

"Never mind," I said. "It worked."

We arrived at Miss Bankhead's around nine to find her holding an after-dinner kaffee klatsch with the cast and she cried out at once to Tenn, "Oh, surely you didn't drive out here, did you? Tennessee Williams, don't you ever get behind the wheel of that car again."

This was the first I knew of her having seen us nose into the laurel bush the previous morning, so I hastened to assure her we'd come by taxi.

Miss Bankhead then backed into a corner, sang a verse of "Bye, Bye, Blackbird," and after that, having been applauded, sat down to talk with Tenn about the character of Blanche.

The cast members gradually drifted away, leaving the three of us together, and Tenn asked me to read a poem.

Tallulah, who was wearing gold slacks and a soft cream-colored blouse, sat down before me on the floor, arms on my knees, and lowered her head to listen while I read "Go Looking."

She said that she loved it; we went on to talk about some mutual old friends, about poetry, and the theater, and I told her, "You're going to have a surprise, I think, when this play opens at the Grove. Having done the Big Show, you've got a vast new audience of teen-agers now, you know."

Miss B. said that she hoped all would go well. The actors came back suddenly, all at once, and everyone started playing parlor games.

As rehearsals became more and more strenuous, I saw a lot of Tenn and Herbert Machiz, the play's director, but nothing at all of Tallulah. Then, a few nights before the opening I called Tenn after my class as he'd asked me to do, at the Engle estate, and Tallu answered the phone rather sleepily.

I said, "Oh, Lord. Tenn asked me to call him there. I'm afraid I waked you out of a sound sleep, darling, I'm so sorry."

She sighed plaintively, "No, you didn't sweetheart. I'm just lying here drowsing, waiting for this sleeping pill to take over. I'm all alone, though. Tenn and all the others have gone to the air field to meet Frank Merlo."

The famous voice sounded forlorn, and I hung up the receiver feeling a little sad.

In the late afternoon, one day before the play's opening, Tenn and I sat and watched a last run-through of Streetcar. Tallulah came on with her suitcase, looking fragile and lovely. Her first lines, plaintively spoken, sent a chill down my spine and as the scene progressed I saw that Tenn was as moved as I was.

He said quietly, "This is going to be a beautiful performance. I'm not the least bit worried, so let's go have our dinner."

On the opening night of *Streetcar* I took a copy of my book *Go Looking* with me to the theater for Tallulah. I was a little hesitant about trying to slip it around to the dressing room, but I ran into the theater's publicity man, who said, "Oh, go ahead, take it back, she'll be so pleased."

When I got to the dressing room, Rose Reilly was there and she said, looking scared, "Lord, Mr. Maxwell, you know Miss Bankhead well as I do; you better get out of here quick."

I said, "You're right," and turned to go, but just as I stepped into the corridor a small tornado in mink whirled up, roaring, "What are you *doing* back here? You know better than this."

I said, "Yes, I do. I'm sorry," and fled, wondering how I could have had little enough sense to have invaded a star's dressing room before an opening performance.

Tenn had his own party that night for dinner. I'd dined with Winifred McConville, with whom I'd come to the theater—both of us rather the worse for cocktails and after-dinner imbibing. Furthermore, I am positive that most of the Coconut Grove theater audience was in a like, if not worse, condition, and it was this sort of mass drunkenness that poor Miss Bankhead—as valiant a lady as ever set foot on a stage—was forced to cope with that evening.

She entered to great applause and the opening scene went brilliantly. Then, suddenly, as she pointed to the liquor and cried, "I spy! I spy!"—a hundred people in that lushed-up house began to laugh. They kept on laughing at moments throughout the play; there was no stopping them, and I sat grinding my teeth, marveling that any star could carry on in the face of such ribald bad manners.

After the play I arrived backstage in time to find Tenn posing with Tallulah for the *Time* photographers. She saw me in the doorway and cried, "Gilbert, darling, look behind you. That's my sister Eugenia and I want you to meet her."

I turned, introducing myself to Eugenia. We said the usual trite things to each other, and then I saw Vinette Carroll standing rather apart. I went to her and said, "I want you to go with me to the big party Gilda Dahlberg's giving," and she said, rather hesitantly, that she would be glad to.

Somehow I got separated from Winifred McConville backstage and as Vinette and I waited for her in the theater lobby, Tallulah came out, wearing her mink. She sauntered over to where we stood and, looking up at me like a small girl, asked softly, "Are you coming to the party?"

"I sure am," I said. "I'll see you."

As Miss B. left us, Vinette seemed strangely hesitant. She said, "Lord, Mr. Maxwell, this is Miami. I don't know about going out there."

We were moving toward the sidewalk, and now, exactly as if on cue, Miss Bankhead beckoned to the girl from a car. Vinette went over for a momentary conference and came back to tell me, "Miss B. says she could see by my face what I was thinking. She says this party's for her, that I'm a member of her cast, and she won't go one single step unless I do, so I guess I can go, after all."

The party was simply incredible. Mrs. Dahlberg had borrowed the Ray Wheatley estate, and the activities centered around an enormous indoor pool with bars seemingly everywhere. Gore Vidal arrived; I excused myself to Vinette, and he and I chatted a few minutes in the library. Then I went out and found Tallulah lying on a chaise longue by the pool. I sat near her as a number of people came to pay court, and suddenly the society editor of the Miami News came to me and said wistfully, "I'd so love to talk to her."

"Then don't be silly," I said. "Sit down here."

I urged her forward, telling Miss B., "Tallulah, this is my good friend Joan Nielson, from the News. She's always been so wonderful to me about publicity for my classes."

Tallulah leaned forward, extending a tiny hand, saying, "So glad to meet you, Joan darling, this man's a divine poet . . ." Then in the same breath she whirled on me, rumbling, "You are the most tactless fool. I'm going to tell everybody here what you did to me tonight."

She rattled on about my backstage visit, saying how everybody knew it was bad luck to visit backstage before an opening, and I looked humbly penitent until she ended up telling the assembled group we'd been friends twenty-two years.

After that, I wandered out to the bar where the newspaper people were whooping it up, and the last thing I remember is standing with my arms around Katherine Dunham and the television interviewer Jackie Pearce, loaded right to the gills.

Somehow I got myself a taxi and made it home but once I got there, I fell down on the bed and let go with a good crying jag. There'd been too much booze and excitement, and besides I was heartsick about the way that audience had received Miss Bankhead.

I hadn't seen Tenn all night, having been unable to find him anywhere at the party. Actually, he, Winnie McConville, and some others had gone out in the early hours for scrambled eggs, at which time Mr. Williams made a remark which was to start a small feud between himself and his star.

My phone rang next day and the voice of a Miami *Times* reporter, who was also the local news gleaner for *Time* magazine, asked me if I'd heard Mr. Williams' exact remark about Miss Bankhead the night before.

I had—from Winnie to whom he'd made it—but I said, "Joe, I want you to listen to me most carefully. I don't know what Tenn said, since I wasn't with him all night, but I can tell you this: whatever it was, it's not important, because he was loaded, like everyone else last night. What's more, Miss Bankhead has had her trials with this play; she's exhausted, much too thin, and not well at all, so I beg you, don't try to make anything out of this meaningless incident."

The man agreed, and that might have been the end of this ridiculous nonsense, except for an unfortunate circumstance. Two days later another ex-reporter from the *News* was sitting in my living room with Winnie and me, discussing the show, when Winnie, to my horror, blurted out Tenn's exact remark. The guy who was present lost no time in relaying this tasty tidbit to the reporter who'd called me up, and as a result, *Time* promptly came out with an item quoting Tenn.

Miss Bankhead was justifiably angry, and there followed a glacial attitude on her part toward Tennessee. Understandably upset about the whole incident, Tenn wrote her a letter of apology, to which he received no reply, and he felt very bad about everything.

It was after the opening of *Streetcar* in New York at City Center that he wrote the following letter to the *New York Times*, and since it speaks for itself, I quote the entire piece—feeling it unnecessary to stress the fact that this gesture was the act of a gentleman to right any wrong he may have done to a lady while he was not himself.

To the Drama Editor:

To the considerable and lively controversy about Tallulah Bankhead as Blanche DuBois, in the recent City Center revival of my play, "A Streetcar Named Desire," I would like "just for the record," as they say, to add my personal acknowledgment, praise and thanksgiving for what I think is probably the most heroic accomplishment in acting since Laurette Taylor returned, in the Chicago winter of 1944–45, to stand all her admirers and her doubters on their ears in "The Glass Menagerie."

I have loved all the Blanches I've seen, and I think the question of which was the best is irrelevant to the recent revival. Several weeks ago, on the morning after the opening in Coconut Grove, Miami, Fla., the director and I called on Miss Bankhead in her boudoir where this small, mighty woman was crouched in bed, looking like the ghost of Tallulah and as quiet as a mouse. I sat there gravely and talked to her with the most unsparing honesty that I've ever used in my life, not cruelly, on purpose, but with an utter candor. It seemed the only thing that could save the situation.

If you know and love Tallulah as I do, you will not find it reprehensible that she asked me meekly if she had played Blanche better than anyone else had played her. I hope you will forgive me for having answered, "No, your performance was the worst I have seen." The remarkable thing is that she looked at me and nodded in sad acquiescence to this opinion.

Contrary to rumor, I have never stated publicly, to my sober recollection, that she had ruined my play. What I said was phrased in barroom lingo. I was talking to myself, not to all who would listen, though certainly into my cups. But that morning, after the opening, Tallulah and I talked quietly and gently together in a totally truthful vein.

She kept listening and nodding, which may have been an unprecedented behavior in her career. The director and I gave her notes. I went back that night, and every note she was given was taken and brilliantly followed in performance. I left town, then, because I knew that I had hurt her deeply (though for her good) and that she would feel more comfortable without me watching her work.

I doubt that any actress has ever worked harder, for Miss Bankhead is a great "pro," as true as they make them. I think she knew, all at once, that her legend, the audience which her legend had drawn about her, presented an obstacle which her deepest instinct as an artist demanded that she conquer, and for those next three weeks she set about this conquest with a dedication that was one of those things that make faith in the human potential, the human spirit, seem far from sentimental: that give it justification. Think for a moment of the manifold disadvantages which I won't name that beset her in this awful effort! She had only two weeks' rehearsal.

When the play opened at the City Center, this small, mighty woman had met and conquered the challenge. Of course, there were few people there who had my peculiar advantage of knowing what she'd been through, and only a few of her critics appeared to sense it. To me she brought to mind the return of some great matador to the bull ring in Madrid, for the first time after having been almost fatally gored, and facing his most dangerous bull with his finest valor, a bullfighter such as Belmonte or Manolete, conquering himself with his spectators and his bull, all at once and together, with brilliant capework and no standing back from the "terrain of the bull." I'm not ashamed to say that I shed tears almost all the way through and that when the play was finished I rushed up to her and fell to my knees at her feet.

The human drama, the play of a woman's great valor and an artist's truth, her own, far superseded, and even eclipsed, to my eye, the performance of my own play. Such an experience in the life of a playwright demands some tribute from him, and this late, awkward confession is my effort to give it.

Tennessee Williams.*

_____

* March 4, 1956.

Tallulah did not immediately forgive Tennessee, but it was inevitable that she should. When he returned to Miami, after a trip North to see the Center opening, he told me, "Well—I knelt at her feet up there on opening night."

"And what was her reaction to this gesture?" I asked, grinning.

Tennessee guffawed. "She received it with queenly dignity, as her just due."

As for what I thought of Miss Bankhead's Miami performance in *Streetcar*, I have this to say: I watched her closing scene several times—always with tightened throat and a blur between me and the stage. She was a moving, strangely tragic Blanche, and no mistake.

7

I NEVER FAIL TO REMEMBER THE SPRING AND SUMMER OF 1956 IN Miami as one of the happiest periods I ever spent with Tenn.

George Keathley, owner and director of Studio M, a tiny theater on Bird Road, had been after Tenn for some time to write a play which he could produce. Tenn, as I have said before, had worked occasionally the past year on a long one-act called *Sweet Bird of Youth*, and he decided to try the piece out at Studio M, under George's direction.

George, a friend of mine who also taught at the Lindsey Hopkins Vocational School, was and still is a good-looking young man with dark hair, extraordinarily light blue, bright eyes and a blunt nose which adds to the rather gypsyish charm of his irregular face.

He seldom failed to send me tickets for his opening nights and when he'd come out at the second intermission to ask eagerly (as if my opinion really mattered) what I thought of the show, I was always glad to say I thought he'd done a good job. Although I felt, in those days, that George sometimes failed to shape a play into an integrated whole, I always marveled at his ability to take a group of rank amateurs and make them look, one and all, like professionals. George was strong on characterization. He worked with the burning intensity of an artist as well as a vigorous young man, and he had the sort of magnetic charm which made most of his performers anxious to do their best for him.

From the start of the *Sweet Bird* project there was the problem of finding a professional to play the leading role of Ariadne Del Lago, the aging, decadent, disillusioned movie star, and George came up with an actress of distinction in Vienna and Germany, with whom he had once studied acting in New York. Her name was Margrit Wyler and I will say even before telling how I first met her, or speaking of her work in *Sweet Bird*, that I have never known a person whom I came more swiftly to admire than this warm, sincere woman who is also an artist.

I met her at a party that Marion Vaccaro gave for Hermione Gingold, who was visitng Hoke McDonald, an old friend of mine in Miami. Hoke had suggested I come out to his house in Coconut Grove the next day to have brunch with his guest while he was at his office, and I was trying hard, seated next to Miss Gingold on the porch of Marion's waterfront house, to get acquainted with her.

Miss Gingold, however, was in a strangely taciturn mood. She spoke rarely during the afternoon and I was so intrigued and puzzled by this behavior on the part of a comedienne of celebrated wit, that I gave only polite, perfunctory attention to another lady who sat on a small sofa near-by. She was a handsome woman with great eyes, beautiful skin, and fine bone structure who looked at me with a friendly interest she made no attempt to conceal as she talked to me casually; and though I had been introduced to her as Miss Wyler, I did not actually realize at the time that she was to star in Tenn's play.

Rehearsals started on *Sweet Bird,* and, bored by now with my teaching at Lindsey Hopkins (some of my students took the first-year course in creative writing seven consecutive years), I welcomed Tenn's invitation to attend the initial readings of the play.

On the first evening Miss Wyler sat under a worklight reading her part in a slow, relaxed manner, and when she reached the entrance of the Negro bellhop, Fly, into the St. Cloud hotel room, Tenn and George suggested I read with her. I agreed, and having no idea of Fly's character, proceeded to give it an old Southern darky interpretation, to the ill-concealed astonishment of Miss Wyler, the delight of Keathley, and a completely hysterical reaction from Tennessee. Because of this the evening got off on a note of camaraderie, and as we all said good night, I had a feeling Margrit Wyler and I would become real friends.

The rehearsals of *Sweet Bird* were a joy, I think, for everyone concerned. As they progressed, Tennessee began to write and rewrite, and before long it was evident that he was whipping together a three-act play. Far from the harrowing problems of Broadway, he could let himself go, which he did with a rollicking, infectious enthusiasm.

Much of his happiness was due to Margrit Wyler's work in the play, as I found out one afternoon in the first week of rehearsals. He rolled up in his Thunderbird, came across my lawn at a quick trot, entered my living room, said howdy-do to several people already present, and sat down on the sofa with a dreamy, somehow satisfied air.

Someone asked how the play was going and he answered, "I don't really know. This actress is so great I can't tell whether it's the play that's so good, or whether it's Margrit Wyler making it seem that way."

The conversation turned gradually to other topics and he sat withdrawn, unaware, I'm sure, of anything that was being said in the room.

Then, as though he and I were quite alone, he suddenly looked at me and asked, "Gil, I think God is the most evident thing in the universe, don't you?"

I said, "Yes, I guess I do, Tennessee."

He nodded. "Gil, do you pray?"

I said, "Yes," and while the other people present (I cannot, significantly, remember who they were) listened and watched in surprise, our two-way exchange continued.

Tenn said, "I do too, you know. But never at any regular time, except just before a play opens on Broadway. It's always a bad night for me, with lots of people around, so I go into the bathroom, the only place where I can be alone, and kneel and ask God to please let the actors get through the evening."

He said all this not caring whether the people in that room were sophisticates, cynics, or atheists; and as I look back, I think I know what had caused him to speak so earnestly. It is the terrible speech of the heckler in *Sweet Bird*, and I believe he'd just written it that morning. The speech occurs in a conversation between the heckler and the mistress of Boss Finley, the old political reactionary, just before Boss's hypocritical address in which he will claim that the voice of God called him to a holy mission.

MISS LUCY: Wait till they turn down the chandeliers in the ballroom. . . . Why don't you switch to a question that won't hurt his daughter?

HECKLER: I don't want to hurt his daughter. But he's going to hold her up as the fair white virgin exposed to black lust in the South, and that's his build-up, his lead into his Voice of God speech.

MISS LUCY: He honestly believes it.

HECKLER: I don't believe it. I believe that the silence of God, the absolute speechlessness of Him is a long, long and awful thing that the whole world is lost because of. I think it's yet to be broken to any man, living or any yet lived on earth—no exceptions, and least of all Boss Finley.

Because of Tennessee's early years in rectories, he has an ingrained religious streak and it is my guess that, like a small boy, having scared himself by the dark speech quoted above, he had come to me that spring afternoon for some reassurance of God's existence.

I feel, too, that he was looking ahead, with the play growing slowly, steadily into a drama of powerful lusts and loves and hates—thinking of the Broadway show and of the prayer he would say for Margrit Wyler on opening night.

This whole incident—everything Tenn said that afternoon—impressed me, and if what I've said here sounds sentimental, I could not care less. There is this simple, even childlike, facet of Tennessee Williams' complex nature of many selves, and I am unfailingly charmed by its occasional disarming manifestation. It is a facet of self which I have not witnessed to any degree of late in my sometimes sad, harassed friend, and that is why I remember the Miami *Sweet Bird* period with such nostalgia.

As the rehearsals went on I was fascinated by the taking out and putting in of scenes, the work of Allen Mixon as the gigolo, and most of all, by the things that Margrit Wyler was doing with her role, as well as her fascinating self. She was lonely in Miami, and I began to go out with her after the show, with one or more friends, to some late restaurant. Then, she telephoned one day to ask me to come out to the theater to pass judgment on a negligee she planned to wear, and I said, "Margrit, I think I must tell you I've seldom met anyone I've been so drawn to on short acquaintance as I have to you," and she answered in her beautifully modulated voice with its patina of accent, "But, Geelbert, this is a mu-tual thing. I cannot explain it, but I tell you I already feel closer to you than I ever have even to George whom I love dearly and have known twelve years."

It is impossible to produce on paper the earnest warmth of her voice as she said these words. However, anyone who saw and heard her in Miami as Ariadne Del Lago will know what I mean, for she brought to that pitiful, lost character a dignity and pathos, a strength and sincerity which came of two things only: her fine talent and the indisputable greatness of her inner self.

There are so many flash images of this magic spring that still have power to move me. I see myself going to the window of my apartment as the Thunderbird braked to a stop on the side lawn, and then I see Tenn running like a kid, calling, "All right, Gil, baby, break out the ham and the grits. Rehearsal at eight, you know."

I see him on a day when, shopping for groceries, we'd also stopped to pick up my laundry, running with the big bundle of shirts under one arm toward the house; and later, mop in hand, swabbing up the floor of my kitchen when the rain had blown in, singing with me an old hillbilly song, and laughing about some of the crazy characters who made up our circle that year.

There were lunches at Captain Tom's wharf restaurant, over the Miami river. There were evening dinners at my place or at Tenn's suite in the Towers—and always there were the long evening hours in which I watched Tennessee, George, Margrit, Allen Mixon, and my old friend Jimmy Reese, brought down from New York to play Boss Finley, shaping *Sweet Bird* into a memorable drama out at the little theater.

I am sentimental about this time, too, because of the party Tenn and I gave for Miss Billie Burke who'd come to star at the Coconut Grove Playhouse in *The Solid Gold Cadillac* and to stay with Marion Vaccaro, who, years ago, as a girl just out of college, had been governess to Miss Burke's daughter, Patricia Ziegfeld.

Tenn and I dropped into a men's clothing shop one afternoon in Coral Gables where as a gag he bought for himself and me sport shirts exactly alike in cloth and pattern, though his was green and mine was pink. On the way home, I said wistfully, "I just love Miss Burke. I'd like to give her a little party next Sunday," and Tenn said, "Well, for heaven's sake, give it then, and let me pay for it—but let us have it at your place."

He insisted on giving me several large bills—and for once I spared no horses as to liquid and solid refreshments. There were three kinds of booze and a spread in which everything from red and black caviar to cucumber sandwiches appeared on the coffee table.

Sunday afternoon I rang up Tenn to ask, "Should we wear our new sport shirts for the party?" and he answered promptly, "Yes, with matching sunbonnets."

The cars began to roll up around five; Tenn rounded the corner with a couple of young actresses, Maria Brittaneva and Cloris Leachman, beside him on the Thunderbird's front seat. Just after that Marion Vaccaro drove up in her lavender Cadillac with her brother George and Miss Burke—and the Cuban family upstairs leaned so far out their front window they nearly pitched headlong onto the lawn before the house.

Miss Burke, who does not drink, had her tea and a special sandwich made with Pepperidge Farm bread which Marion's cook had made for her. The rest of us drank martinis and after my third (I have no idea why) I asked Miss Burke bluntly how she felt about dying. Tennessee cried out, "Why Gil, you can't ask Miss Burke a thing like that," but Miss Burke said gently, "Not at all, Mr. Williams. This man has asked a pertinent question and I shall give him a straight answer." She turned to me and said, "Actually, I face death with less and less trepidation each year that I live."

I said, "You think, then, there's something afterward?" and she answered, "Of course. I know there is. But besides, you see, I'm growing steadily older, and there's really not much left for me to live for. My daughter is married, with a child of her own, so I'm not needed there and I have no idea, either, how long I can go on acting now." She added, "You see, Flo Ziegfeld and I were really lovers, you know. I suppose I should have married again but I never could, because Flo had spoiled me for any other man."

She said other memorable things that day, too—gravely, in a voice and manner quite unlike that of the comedienne who has fluttered birdlike across the screens of the world speaking in the tiny, saucily sweet treble that has become her trademark. She is a remarkable person in many ways, and I find myself thinking now of a thing Tenn said about her one night at the supper table at the Miami Beach Surf Club.

Miss Burke had just told me, her blue eyes shining, "Oh, you don't know how thrilled I am just to be sitting here with Mr. Williams," when Tenn leaned and said into my other ear, "Why, she's the most beautiful woman at this table."

She was that—and the most beautiful woman at my party, too, outshining the younger actresses and all the town ladies who sat around her.

That afternoon, as I helped her into Marion's Cadillac she told me, "Now, if you ever get out to Hollywood, you must come to see me," and I did not dream that one day I would see her again, out on the West Coast.

She went home in a few days and before long I had two fine letters from her in one of which she wrote, "What wonderful and dreadful drama is Mr. Williams writing now? Oh, how I should like to play one of his characters—but then, I am grateful for having been in the theater at all, even as one of its clowns."

The days in Miami passed, and night after night, I watched *Sweet Bird* growing, changing, constantly being rewritten. Several scenes were cut, and there were two which Broadway would never see that seemed to me superb.

In one, the boy, at that time called Phil Beam, comes to the evil Boss Finley's mansion to see Heavenly, the old man's daughter, whom Phil has unwittingly infected with gonorrhea. Finley's old-maid sister, Nonnie, tells him to go at once, before Boss learns he's there, but Phil, clutching the great bouquet of red roses he has brought for Heavenly, begins to reminisce with the old lady about a trip she and he and Heavenly once made to a school meet where he'd competed, in *The Valiant*, for a prize. As he reminds her of the return trip on the train to St. Cloud when the three of them happily sang a song, he and the old lady put their heads together and sing, "If you lacka me, like I lacka you," and Nonnie is reduced to tears. She begs Phil to go at once with his flowers, thinking she hears Boss in the house, and Phil, giving her a last hug before leaving, drops one rose on the porch.

Nonnie stoops quickly and slips it into her apron pocket just as Heavenly appears on the porch. The girl asks, "What was that you put in your pocket, Aunt Nonnie?" The old lady answers, "Nothing, darling, only a piece of trash," and Heavenly says sadly, "What an unkind way to speak of a rose."

There was this scene, yes, and one other, in which Boss Finley, seated with his daughter at the dining table on Easter Sunday, drawls, "Honey, move them God damned Easter lilies so's I can see your face." He also remarks, "Baby, you have just two expressions on your face. One's petulant, and the other's less pleasant." He goes on, nagging, and Heavenly says, "Oh, don't think you can fool me, Papa. I know you for what you are. Aunt Nonnie works like a Nigger, and there's just one air-conditioned room in this house—the one that you sleep in."

This was a fine scene of heartbreakingly bitter Southern family haranguing and there is no way to say what Jimmy Reese, with his droll voice and face overriding the sinister inner ugliness of Boss, managed to bring to the role. Sydney Blackmer would later give a terrifying impersonation of this old bigot and sadist at the Martin Beck in 1959, but I missed the touches of sly, snickering humor that Reese brought to the old boy and the wicked gleam in his eyes as he planned his deviltry.

Sweet Bird rehearsed for weeks at Studio M, with many changes of scenes, but through them all, Margrit Wyler remained, as Ariadne, what she had been since she first moved into the character: a tragic woman whose callousness, disillusionment, self-centered egotism, fear of failure and death seemed no more than surface manifestations. You felt, beneath all the apparent ugliness of despair, the lost Adriadne who had once been warm and simple—even perhaps unselfish. You felt her loneliness, her longing, her great need for love, and even in her most violent scenes with the gigolo she was using, who also was using her, an ironical, maternal emotion. It was there, and you felt that Ariadne, having been a fine woman once, could not help feeling inside herself a regretful concern for this "pitiful monster" who, looking into a mirror could not see, like her, "a monster with a difference—with the outcrying heart and soul of an artist," but only the flight of youth's sweet bird and "a face that tomorrow's sun will touch without mercy."

In reading over what I have had to say here of *Sweet Bird*, Tenn, sitting with me in an airport restaurant last spring, just after we'd seen his mother off for St. Louis, laid the manuscript down, lighted a cigarette and said, "Yes, you're right. *Sweet Bird* did lose something before we got it to New York"; and then he added quietly, "I'm afraid I work too long and too hard now on my plays."

And so I feel justified in saying that Broadway audiences did not see in this play a vehicle which, in its early stages, had a homely, touching warmth that seemed to me to be lacking in the final version.

As the play originally ended, Heavenly was kneeling in prayer at stage right, just after Boss Finley, his son, and Scudder, the doctor, had borne Phil Beam off to the graveyard to be castrated. There was a scream; then suddenly Ariadne appeared with a telephone at stage left, clicking the receiver, crying, "Operator, operator, someone called me. I know somebody called me," and even as she protested, Heavenly, with clasped hands prayed, "Oh, Lady, wrap me in your starry blue robe. Make my heart your perpetual Novena."

Margrit Wyler said to me one night at supper, "I'm not sure about that ending. It may be corn, but I will say this: every night when Heavenly makes that speech I get a shiver down my spine."

I said that I did, too—and I was sorry to see the ending finally changed.

The opening night of *Sweet Bird of Youth* came at last. At the first intermission I found Tenn walking the alley with a bottle on his hip, and thinking he was merely suffering the usual opening-night jitters, I said, "What the hell is this? You're in Miami, not Shubert Alley, man." He whirled on me and cried mournfully, "Oh, no, you don't understand. It's my mother. Can you imagine how I feel, knowing she's in there seeing this awful play, with all these sick, degenerate people in it?"

I made some perfunctory remark, keeping my thoughts to myself. But I was not surprised when Edwina, at a tea I gave for her later, turned to me and said wonderingly, "Gilbert, what's wrong with Tom, getting upset about my seeing this play? Doesn't he know I'm a sophisticated woman?"

We both laughed heartily over Tennessee's trepidations, but I understood his reaction. Common sense might tell him that Edwina, after reading some of his short stories, would be past shock, but he still could not help feeling that his gentle mother was far too much a lady to be exposed to these harsh creatures.

There were many parties throughout the *Sweet Bird* period, and I remember a huge one at Marion Vaccaro's when Tennessee was feeling but slight pain, if any. A male pianist-comedian, rounding out a solo engagement at the huge Coconut Grove Playhouse, came to our boy and said, perhaps in innocence, "Tenn, I haven't had a chance to see your play yet, but I do hope to, if it's still running when I finish at the Coconut Grove."

Tenn answered smoothly, "I expect it'll be there as long as you're at the Playhouse."

Not getting the drift, the gentleman went on, "I believe we played the same street in New York last year."

Tennessee asked sweetly, "Where were you? At the Bijou?"

Sweet Bird of Youth had all the earmarks of another success and he was in no mood for apprehensive remarks about it—innocent or intended.

All through that winter and spring I'd been reworking the novel, reading aloud lengthy passages from it to my long-suffering playwright friend. I had become apprehensive—since, rewriting certain sections *ad nauseam*, forever dissatisfied, I'd realized with alarm that one of the reasons for this lay in my having taught creative writing so long I'd begun to apply all the technical rules I'd given my students to my own work during a process of creation and re-creation when a writer should feel free of self-criticism. At the school, I was being tormented by a superior, as well as by the endless aggravation of students attached to me emotionally, and for these reasons I'd become obsessed with the idea of leaving Miami.

One day in March, driven beyond endurance by these problems, I'd walked into Tenn's hotel suite and told him as he lay comfortably propped up in bed, reading, "You've got to help me get away from this town and that damned school before I lose what's left of my mind."

Tenn dropped his magazine and stared. He said, "Why, Gil, I don't understand. I was just thinking the other day how, of all the people we've known together, you seem to've made the best adjustment."

"Adjustment?" I cried. "To what? To failure and frustration as a writer? To putting up with sex-starved middle-aged women like the one who comes to class wearing dark glasses in the evening and says she's cracking up because I won't sleep with her? All this—to say nothing of the unspeakable disappointment of trying to teach hundreds of unteachable amateurs how to write, for a lousy take-home salary that's dwindled to forty-eight dollars a week? This, I'm supposed to adjust to?"

Tenn looked briefly troubled. "Well," he said, "I'll admit the money's not much—but otherwise, I thought you were happy. . . ."

"How could you think that?" I yelled. "Unless you haven't been listening to all my complaints lately. Happy, your foot. I'm so goddamned miserable inside I'm in despair most of the time. I've got to have a change, do you hear me?"

He said that he did, and murmured something about seeing what he could do, while I made a mental note to remind him at intervals of just how strongly I felt about getting back to New York, and the subject was seemingly dropped. However, when Audrey Wood came down for the *Sweet Bird* opening, I was surprised as we sat one day by the pool, when Tenn said quietly, "Gil, tell Audrey the salary you're living on right now."

I told her, and nodding slowly, Miss Wood said, "It's a neat trick if you can do it."

Tenn said, "I've been listening to this novel of Gil's and I think you'd better read it, Audrey. In fact, I think you ought to take him on as a client."

He got up then and went for his swim, leaving his agent and me alone.

I told her, "You'd better not listen to Tenn, Audrey, I've been a failure as a writer so long now, I think there's a jinx on me."

"Well, I don't know about that," Audrey said. "I have lots of faith in Tennessee's judgment. After all, he brought me Carson McCullers and William Inge." She looked fondly out at her client, charging head down through the pool's blue water, and added, "I'd be willing to bet this man's done more for other writers than any established author in America."

She asked me to send her the novel which was two-thirds finished, and I said I'd mail it, so that it might reach her at MCA just after her return.

Several weeks later I received a letter from her saying she was turning the book over to Phyllis Jackson, MCA's fiction agent. She said also, "I have told Phyllis that I think there's a best-seller, a movie script, and a play in this manuscript."

Summer came on, with Tenn in and out of town, and in August I told him, hopefully, about the start of a project of mine with which he was later to become involved. My New York agent, Bertha Klausner, who'd read *The Sleeping Trees*, suggested I send it to Bette Davis, telling her that the book had the makings of a screenplay and that she might be interested in one of the women's roles. I did so, and, to my joyous surprise, promptly received an enthusiastic letter in which she said that she'd be happy to play any one of the leading women's parts, all three of which she considered magnificent.

Tenn, who thought the letter most gracious, told me that I should think about writing the screenplay as soon as I got my novel off my hands.

In the early fall he took me on a yachting trip. Hal Wallis, the Hollywood producer, was on board and so was the movie star Lizabeth Scott, who was under contract to Wallis.

We had a fine day and at one point Lizabeth asked, "Tennessee, back in the days when you were getting no recognition, what did you think would eventually happen to you?"

Tenn said slowly, "Oh, I don't know. I guess I just thought I'd go on writing plays nobody'd buy and trying to support myself at any old job I could find."

Lizabeth gave a little spontaneous gasp and leaped up to hug him, crying, "Oh, Tenn, I just love you for saying that."

Everyone laughed and I suggested she hug me, too, since I was still supporting myself at any old job *I* could find. Tenn mentioned the letter I'd had from Miss Davis; we talked about the possibilities of making a screenplay of *Trees*, and Hal Wallis asked, "Why haven't I seen this book? It sounds like something I could use."

I said that he could certainly see it, and agreed, since his hotel was far up on the Beach, to get a copy of the book out to the airport the next day.

Back in Miami after the boat trip, Tenn said, "There's no time to fool around now, Gil. I'll drive you to the airport tomorrow."

Next day, for some reason, we were quite late in starting, and I remember our perilously racing out in the Thunderbird to the airfield where we left *Trees* with a ticket agent.

In September I received a nice letter from Hal Wallis saying he'd liked the book immensely. He feared, however, since so much of the action occurred in the minds of the characters that there might be too many technical difficulties in adapting the plot for the screen.

Tennessee said flatly, "You must pay no attention to anyone's ideas as to what will or won't make a screenplay, baby, and if you don't hear from Miss Davis soon, I'll write her a letter myself."

This he did, in early October, and I am saddened by the thought that this letter, of all his letters that I own, has been lost, since I consider it an excellent example of his tact and generosity. He told Miss Davis that I was at present writing a second novel which he thought was my most important book to date, that I was greatly in need of a change from Miami and my teaching job, which the evolution of an acceptable screenplay with a star of her caliber might provide, and that he hoped her interest in *Trees* had not waned. Miss Davis answered in a short time, saying that her interest most certainly had not waned, and suggesting that I contact a director whom she liked.

Tennessee was charmed by the letter, and once again he said that I must keep thinking in terms of the screenplay of *Trees* myself. He said, "There's really nothing to writing a screenplay, and I'll help you all I can when you're ready to tackle it."

I'd long since decided to tackle it, once the novel was completed and Tennessee had got *Orpheus Descending* off his hands, but I knew the time wasn't yet right, especially for him, since his whole being at the moment was tied up with *Orpheus*. This play was of course the revised *Battle of Angels*. He'd been working on it seventeen years and as he talked about it to me I realized that the actuality of this play's becoming a success had become an obsession with him.

I have observed before that the humiliation of failure is a thing which Tenn finds intolerable, and as he worked on *Orpheus,* showing me no part of it, but occasionally quoting certain bright bits of dialogue, I became intensely eager to read the finished script.

The summer passed, with Tennessee, often in town, patiently listening to chapter after chapter of *The Long Pursuit's* revision. I'd moved to a small, cheerful house in the southeast section of town, and there Tenn, Marion Vaccaro, Winifred McConville, and I had Thanksgiving dinner, Marion having brought the turkey and chestnut dressing from her house on a big silver platter.

After dinner, somewhat drowsy from drinks and food, Tenn went to sleep while Marion and I were reading aloud from Millay. Marion departed shortly with the remains of her turkey, and Tenn, surprised by this action, expressed the opinion that she'd been displeased with him for having dozed off during our reading. I felt she'd perhaps been annoyed by some shortcoming of mine as a host; however, her unprecedented gesture of marching off with her salver of goodies was more or less futile, since two nights later at her house her mother invited me to help myself to the remaining turkey and dressing—which I did, with a lavish hand.

As the Christmas season approached, two young fellows whom I shall refer to in these pages as Richard One and Richard Two became a part of Tenn's and my circle in Miami.

Richard One, in a cocktail bar on Miami Beach one Sunday, came up and introduced himself to Tennessee. He was a muscular, Nordic-looking young man with slightly thinning, light-brown hair, a pleasant speaking voice, and a most agreeable manner. He was writing plays, he said, and had worked for a time in the offices of Eddie Dowling, who, I was later to learn, cherished considerable fondness for him. As I recall it, Tenn asked him to dinner with us, or perhaps to some party at my cottage or his hotel suite, and he soon became a member of the Robert Clay Poolside Sitters' Club in front of the Williams cabana.

I was augmenting my meager teaching income again this year by selling, this time in Jordan Marsh's book department. There, one day, a young man dropped in to see one of the salesgirls, and she introduced him to me, saying, "Dick, I want you to meet our poet."

This was Richard Two, a tall young man with a lean, aristocratic face and narrow sea-green eyes. I cottoned to him at once and impulsively asked him if he'd like to come to a barbecue the next Sunday which Winnie McConville was giving for Tennessee. Richard Two said that he would, but he has often told people, describing our meeting, "The funny thing is, I wasn't especially impressed by being asked to meet Mr. Williams. I'd spied Maxwell darting around that book department, yelling at the manager to come and help him find out what he'd done wrong at the goddamn cash register, and I thought, 'This guy I've got to know, somehow.' "

As for me, I was intrigued by what his salesgirl friend had to tell me about Richard Two after he'd gone. He'd recently been fired from a part-time job in this same department for spending too many afternoon hours in the coffee shop, gabbing with friends.

It hadn't mattered, though, his girl friend said, because this one always had several jobs going at once. Right now, he had just two, one with an employment agency, the other with a local funeral home where he lived.

Sunday came and Richard Two appeared on the small porch of my house, punctually at ten, with a good morning briskly spoken in the slightly nasal accent of his native New Hampshire. We had a leisurely highball, breakfasted, and took a bus up to Winifred McConville's home where she and a young couple next door were already at work on the barbecue and Brunswick stew. We all had several drinks, plus a test bowl of Brunswick stew and dozed off in the backyard, waking just in time to greet the evening's arrivals.

Marion Vaccaro was among these and I decided to talk with her about a small business proposition. Tenn had told me that if I could get someone to put up the money for me, I might buy a 1 per cent interest in *Orpheus*, so I took Marion aside to ask if she'd go in with me on such a deal. Marion said she'd think about it, and returned to the living room to corner Tennessee.

The party wore on with various games, dancing, and singing; our hostess retired, overcome, around ten o'clock, and we all moved over to the young couple's house. After a time the hostess, who is red-headed, Scotch and Irish, but mostly Irish, came roaring in to find out what the hell the couple had meant by taking over her party, and somehow everyone started yelling at everyone else— several good-naturedly, others with indignation. For some unaccountable reason Richard Two and Mrs. McConville began to call each other names; a young man about whose singing Richard Two had made a cutting remark sneaked out to the kitchen where he vengefully poured the last bottle of vodka down the sink before his departure—and, all in all, everyone started home after midnight convinced that he'd been present at quite an affair.

Winnie McConville was working in a Flagler Street department store, and when I suggested to Richard Two, downtown next day, that we drop in to see her, his mouth fell open. He said to Tenn, afterward, "I didn't see how any of us could be speaking after that awful mess the night before—and I was absolutely astounded when Winnie greeted Gil and me, all smiles and charm, precisely as though nothing unusual had happened."

He had yet to learn that what is said and done in one's cups late of an evening in Miami is not only often not mentioned, but happily not remembered by any party member in the sober light of a following day.

Most of the social life for our circle was centered now around the Robert Clay pool, in Tenn's suite at the Towers, at Marion's place, or at my little house, and again, I look fondly back on the month of December, 1956.

Tennessee, Richard One, Richard Two, Marion, and I spent a good many hours sitting around the pool, or dining out together. Mrs. Williams came on from St. Louis, and also Dr. Hugh Hyatt, Tenn's dental surgeon friend from Memphis, to stay through Christmas. Mrs. Williams insisted upon addressing me as Mr. Gilbert, and I told her that if she didn't lay off, I was going to start calling her Miss Edwina. In time she dropped the handle of my name, but she has always remained, since this visit, Miss Edwina to me.

Tenn was working frantically now on *Orpheus*, getting ready for

the New York opening. One day he and I went to see Joan Crawford in a picture called *Autumn Leaves*, with a young actor named
Cliff Robertson, and as the movie progressed with Robertson
turning in a fine, sensitive performance, Tenn said, "That's my
boy for *Orpheus*." He began negotiations for Robertson, who
ended up as Val Xavier, the lost young man in the play.

When Miss Edwina had been down in the late spring for *Sweet
Bird*, I'd had small chance to be with her, and I was glad to see
more of her on this visit. She, Tenn, and I lunched together,
talking about the ridiculous morality fracas over *Baby Doll* in
which Cardinal Spellman had got himself involved, and I was
impressed with the way Miss Edwina dealt with the press when
they asked her what she thought of the picture. She let the re-
porters know that it wasn't quite her dish of tea, but she also told
them firmly that her opinion of the film had nothing to do with its
alleged immorality. Her remarks were astutely pointed and when
the reporter quoted her, making her sound like an addlepated
Southern reactionary, she was justifiably annoyed.

"They make me sound like a fool," said Miss Edwina, "and
that's not fair, you know."

In the weeks before Christmas we had some nice gatherings and
the one that I remember best was a dinner party at my place when
Miss Edwina first told the story of Tenn's winning the essay
contest on the subject, "Can a Good Wife Be a Good Sport?"

One of my guests that night was a little elderly actress who'd
been in early films under the bewitching name of Dixie Cotton.
Having married a man named Browning she was now called
Brownie, and I remember her being impressed by something Mrs.
Williams did when we all went out for a drive. Miss Edwina said,
"You're not dressed very warmly, Mrs. Browning," and took off
her scarf to place it around the little actress's shoulders—a gesture
which Brownie has not forgotten.

One night when Tenn and I were dining at a restaurant near
Jordan Marsh, I told him, "You don't know how lucky you are,
still to have Miss Edwina. I'd give anything on God's earth if
Maude could come back, even for half an hour."

He looked up sharply, asking, "Do you really feel like that?"

"God, yes," I said. "And you'll feel the same way, too, when your mother's gone."

He came down to the store next day to ask me to help him shop for gifts for Miss Edwina and Rose, and he brought several beautiful things for both of them.

For some reason at which I can only conjecture, Tenn is not much concerned with the holiday season.

As I sat reading on December 25 at the Towers while he banged away at the typewriter, I was surprised when Doc Hyatt came in, looking upset.

He said, "Tennessee, do you know your mother's packing to leave for St. Louis?"

Tenn looked up and blinked. He said, "Packing? Why?"

"Because," said Doc Hyatt, "this is two P.M. on Christmas Day; she's right here in the hotel and she hasn't heard from you since yesterday."

"Oh, Lord," said Tennessee, "I'd forgotten it's Christmas Day. I'll go take her to lunch."

He reached for the phone and rang Miss Edwina while Doc and I looked at each other, incredulous.

At the time the situation was one I could hardly believe, but I have since decided something about Tenn and Christmas. He cannot bear it, I think, remembering the old holidays when he and Grand and his grandfather and Rose were all together, so he just forgets about it. I can't bear it either, having lost my mother just after the season, but I can't forget Christmas Day—and so I suppose he is luckier than I and many other people who find the year-end holidays nostalgically sad, if not actually unendurable.

That Christmas of 1956 was a great one for me in one way, though, and I was feeling unusually hopeful. Earlier in the month, when I'd once again asked Tenn if he couldn't do something to help me get out of Miami, he'd answered, "I mean to do something for you—indirectly."

Later he'd told me, "I spoke to Audrey in New York this morning and she said, 'I think I can get this boy some money.'"

In Christmas week a letter came from Audrey, telling me that a national organization which sometimes helps writers had made me a grant on which to finish my novel, and that I'd be getting a one-hundred-fifty-dollar check monthly for the next ten months.

It was typical of Tenn that I should not learn until later that the money had come from a fund he'd set up in the name of his sister. Audrey had asked for the money, yes, but it had been Tenn who'd said, "Please tell them that I'd like them to make this award to Gilbert Maxwell."

Miss Edwina went back to St. Louis and Tenn made ready to leave for Key West.

On the way to the airport he insisted upon stuffing three ten-dollar bills in my pocket, saying, "I forgot to buy you a present, so take this and have yourself a New Year's party."

I'd given him a copy of Millay's Collected Poems, and he'd left it with me, to keep for him until he came back in a week or so. It is presently stored, with two hundred other books of mine, in Miami.

On the last day of my stint at Jordan Marsh, I asked for an afternoon off.

Richard Two and I shopped for the party, and we had it New Year's Day. I'd asked everyone I liked; the small house was jammed; and if my neighbor next door hadn't offered her grounds as a parking lot, there'd have been no place for the cars.

The party began at three in the afternoon. Late guests arrived around evening with Christmas bottles, and the welkin was still a-ring at three A.M. All the neighbors, except those who'd been asked to the whingding, arose in arms against Maxwell, and as a result my square landlord ordered me to move.

Richard Two went with me to look for a place, and after much searching we ended up with an apartment just half a block away. Tenn returned in time to help me move, which we did, loading the Thunderbird fore and aft, and Richard Two still remembers Tenn's anxious plea, "Don't scratch the paint, baby, please don't scratch my paint."

I was working like something demented now on my novel. Richard Two, because of cavorting with me and Tenn, plus the general convivial life of the holidays, had lost his berth at the funeral home, so I suggested he move into my place and help with the book, taking dictation, typing and retyping the revised manuscript.

So Richard was with me in those days, working on an hourly basis, while Tenn, at the Towers, was putting the last touches on *Orpheus Descending*. Marion Vaccaro had decided to put some money into the play for herself, for me, and her mother, and we were all looking forward tensely to the Broadway opening.

One day Tenn called and asked, "Would you like me to read my play to you and Dick?"

I said we'd love it, and that evening, after my class, he came over with his script.

He sat in a big chair under a bridge lamp and read the whole play through. He reads beautifully, being a born actor, and I sat there thinking as the characters leaped from his pages, "This is the best; this really is his best."

At one point, worn out from a day of writing and my evening class, I dozed off for half a second. Tenn didn't miss that bit and several days later when the reading of the play came up in discussion, he told Marion, "Well, I'm not too sure about it. Gil went to sleep in the second act."

I was chagrined, and stumbled and stammered, explaining.

The reading had been an absorbing experience—and it was a bleak moment for me when Richard Two suddenly rushed into the house next day, sputtering, "What fools we were last night. Why didn't we have a tape recorder back of Williams' chair?"

Dick Two and I have always been regretful about our lack of foresight in this case, and both of us still speak sadly of not having got on tape that unselfconscious, moving rendition of *Orpheus* by its creator.

The winter and spring of 1957 was a busy, harassing period for everyone. Tenn was in New York with *Orpheus* and I was having a devilish time with the last few chapters of my novel, as well as with one head of my school, whom I now recognized as an inexplicable enemy.

On the first night of the new spring term he assigned me a room off a connecting bridge between two buildings where students tramped constantly past. Reading aloud a great deal, lecturing, directing student discussions, I needed complete concentration, so I closed my door and lowered the shades of my windows.

Next evening, incensed by this innocent action, the principal attacked me in the registration office, stamped his feet and screamed at me like a bantam cock before swarms of arriving students and teachers.

I said only, "You must not speak to me like that," and went to my classroom, shaken.

However, one of my loyal students, who'd heard the commotion, charged into the office yelling, "Now, I am a taxpayer, by God, and I am sick of watching the persecution of an excellent teacher whom I admire also as a man, and whose salary my money is helping to pay." She struck the registration desk with her fist and bellowed, "Where is that worm? I dare him to come out and face me."

At her approach the gentleman had hidden, squatting down behind his desk, and the next day I made a federal case out of his performance before one of the school's heads. Some semblance of peace was temporarily restored, but I knew beyond doubt that time had run out for me with the Dade County school system. This man whom I had to work under no longer wanted me around, and I was more than ready to go.

In addition to all this I'd begun to have a real problem at home with Richard Two. He who had seemed so industrious, handling three jobs at once, now had no employment except the few hours of typing which I could give him. Through laziness and neglect he'd lost his job with the phone company and had lately been borrowing from me. The worst was yet to come, but the air in my place was thick with resentment, and there was shortly to be a showdown between this drone and me.

As to Tenn and *Orpheus*—he had met and liked a snake-fancier student of mine named Mary who'd paralyzed my short-story class by turning up one night with a seven-foot boa constrictor called Juanita draped about her shoulders. Mary had promised Tenn some fine snake skins for the hero's jacket in *Orpheus*, but when the time came to deliver the goods she'd apparently disappeared into the Okefinokee Swamp where she sometimes resided.

Tenn was in New York working on the *Orpheus* production. I'd written both him and Audrey about some matter, and got no reply, so I casually remarked in a letter to Phyllis Jackson, my MCA fiction agent, that if I could lay hands on either him or Miss Wood, I'd gladly boil them in oil. I then had a letter from Audrey, saying, "No, dear, this lady's not for burning, and I beg you to forgive what seems to be negligence on mine and Tennessee's part. We are up to our ears in this play."

Shortly after this the phone rang one day and it was Tenn, wild with annoyance because Mary could not be found and his costume designer, Lucinda Ballard, was without a set of snake skins. I said lamely that I hadn't been able to locate Mary, and Tenn wailed, "Oh, God, doesn't that woman realize what she's done? Why, this is big business, Gil. Where in hell can I get snake skins at this late date?"

He hung up, harassed, but get a snake-skin jacket he did, and *Orpheus Descending* opened at the Martin Beck on March 21, 1957, under the direction of Harold Clurman, with Maureen Stapleton and Cliff Robertson in the leads.

The play received both good and bad notices. Tenn told me via long distance that there seemed a good chance of its running a while, but the next thing I knew, Marion Vaccaro called to tell me, "I've had the first over-call, my dear, so naturally, if we make any money, you must pay your share of this."

I said, "Of course"—and that's the last time either Marion or I have spoken of *Orpheus*, which ran for a few weeks only.

Tenn came back to Miami after his opening, not seeming to me to be in bad spirits at all. Perhaps, though, I was rather insensitive to the woes of others in April and May of that year, for I now had on my hands an insoluble problem.

Richard Two had ceased to make the slightest pretense at seeking a job. I'd come home from a rugged evening of teaching to find him spread out on his bed with a book, or looking idly out of the living room window. He had a brooding, melancholy air, and was short-tempered with his unwilling host upon whom he was wholly dependent. He was in debt to me for his share of the rent and food, and even his beer and cigarette money. I had grown tired enough of this, but when I discovered that several friends of mine whom he disliked were staying away from my house because of his ugly silences or downright rudeness when they'd called, I went into vigorous action. I urged Richard Two to go out and find something, *anything* to support himself, and when he made no effort in this direction, I moved him, bag and baggage, twice, out on the front porch. In my absence he climbed back the first time through the porch windows; the second time he sat among his bags and looked pathetic until I broke down and offered to lend him twenty-five dollars more if he'd really go after a job.

He seemed elated, and made great promises, none of which were kept—for Richard, to my slowly dawning astonishment, was on a single-minded campaign. Both he and Richard One had been driving Tenn around in the Thunderbird all winter, but now, Richard Two—brooding and calculating—decided really to promote himself with Mr. Williams.

Determined upon serving a famous man, he yearned to become driver, valet, amanuensis, and *most particularly* traveling companion to Tenn, who, he was sure, would be striking out soon either for the Virgin Islands or Europe.

Now I am a man who admires subtlety and this bold, brash project of Richard's was truly frightening to watch. Furthermore, since Mr. Williams already had two available traveling companions in the persons of Marion Vaccaro and Frank Merlo, I told Richard Two that he hadn't a prayer. He failed to agree with me, and I kept on watching, while he went about his project with the most naively blatant display of opportunism I ever expect to witness.

About this time, too, something happened which was destined to help cook this young man's goose to a turn. Seeing the state of mind I was in, the friction between me and my free-loading guest, Tenn said, "You two are never going to be able to make it under this roof unless something's done about Dick's indebtedness. Now, Gil, I want you to tell me the exact sum of his debt to you and I'll write you a check for the amount, which Dick will pay back to me."

On the day he left for Key West he gave me a check for one

hundred twenty-five dollars and we all had a farewell drink at the airport—but if Tenn and I thought my problems with Dick were at an end, we were both mistaken. This boy continued to borrow from me as well as to run up a large bill on my phone—and before the month of May was out, so was Richard—of my apartment, that is.

Meanwhile (I cannot remember whether it was at Christmas or in the spring), an event had occurred which surprised me. At dinner one evening with Tenn, his mother, Doc Hyatt, and Marion Vaccaro, Doc said, "Gil, if you're so eager to go to Europe, why don't you go on a package tour, like I did? The round trip, all expenses, would cost you just about seven hundred dollars."

Tenn dropped his fork, demanding, "What's this? Gil's not going to Europe. He'd do nothing but waste his time over there for the next two or three months and never finish his novel. No sir, he must not go."

There was a silence in which everyone looked mildly astonished. Then Marion asked quietly, "Gilbert, how much would it mean to you to go to Europe?"

I said, "It's the one thing I've always wanted to do more than anything. I've been dreaming about it for years."

Marion's hazel eyes met mine as she said, even more quietly, "Then, my dear, you must go," and the subject was dropped.

I wondered that night why Tenn was so vehement about my not going abroad on the funds he'd got me, but of course I had no way of knowing what went on in his mind.

When he and Richard Two saw me off on the train for New York in June, I still had no real suspicion regarding my old friend's motives in this case. However, I have since made up my mind as to what they were: though he had not told me his plans, Tenn had decided to spend the summer in New York with an analyst, and he wanted me there also.

I could be wrong in this belief, but I think not, and if I am right I still have no complaints. I am pleased to think that Tenn may have wanted and needed my company during a trying ordeal. What's more, I had no inkling as my train rattled north over the Florida flatlands, of what was about to befall me. I was in for a fabulous, varied, harrowing, hilarious summer with T.W., both Richards, and loads of other friends, old and new.

Jack Barefield met me at the station in New York and I stayed the first night at his Macdougal Alley apartment, haunted for me by its former tenant, my old friend Lulu Vollmer, who'd written her play, *Sunup*, while living there. Next day I moved into the Hotel Earle and began calling up friends, one of whom was the poet Gertrude Claytor, a Virginia lady for whom I have great respect and regard.

Tenn had said to me before I left Miami, "I know you've been emotionally upset lately, both by the school and by your home situation, but the one thing you must do at once is to finish that novel. If you don't it's going to be bad for you psychologically—in fact, you'll hate yourself."

I agreed, and even though I was so excited about New York after years of absence that I felt like kissing the paving stones, I did immediately set about winding up *The Long Pursuit*. Mrs. Claytor offered me her typist as well as a room in her apartment to work in, and there the typist and I polished up the last two chapters of the book. I took it at once to Phyllis Jackson at MCA and hoped for the best.

On my first weekend I took a train to Connecticut to visit Nancy, who was now married and had a new baby. We'd talked by long distance phone over the years, but the human voice does not noticeably alter with the passage of time, and I knew as we walked toward each other at the railway station that we were both somewhat shaken by the changes nine years had wrought. I said, almost at once, "Your hair's not the same, Nan, it's darker," and she retorted, "Well, you don't look quite as you used to either, Gilly."

We had a fine time after this exchange, laughing and reminiscing for two days, but I was saddened by memories of the summer of 1947 when my Nan was the most beautiful girl in the Village and I, with no gray at temple or brow, could still be taken for a man of twenty-eight.

The bird of time was on the wing and I rode back to New York on Sunday, thinking as I gazed out at the green countryside how much less durable is man than an elm or a lilac bush.

Just before I'd left Miami, Tenn and I had spoken one day of these matters, noting that the Reaper had been scything off our friends in an alarming way during the past decade, but I was ill-prepared for one shock I sustained about a week after my visit to Nancy.

I'd repeatedly called an old friend of my college days, and, receiving no answer, had told myself, "Well, after all, it's summer. Norma's somewhere in the country."

Tenn had come East and I was on my way to dine with him at Herbert Machiz' place one afternoon when another lady out of my past hailed me from the sidewalk café of the Fifth Avenue Hotel. I stopped to have a fast drink with her, and when I asked about Norma she told me this gay and lovely woman had recently died of a brain tumor—so recently, in fact, the telephone company hadn't got around to disconnecting her phone.

I took a bus up to Machiz in a dazed state—and got thoroughly plastered before the evening was over. I realize now that I must have been greatly disturbed, for I remember picking a fight with my host about Miss Bankhead's experience in Miami, and Tennessee's telling me I was unfair to raise hell with Herbert as a director about things that had happened to Miss B. through no direct fault of his.

For that matter, I was soon to discover, a few evenings later at Gertrude Claytor's, that Tenn, who'd already started analysis, was in no state of inner serenity either.

Gertrude had said, "I'm going to give a small dinner party for you," and I'd said, "Wonderful. Shall I ask Tennessee?" She said that she'd be delighted and Tenn had accepted the invitation.

There were two older men at the party, a younger woman and man, who were engaged, and Laura Benet, the poet.

The evening started off nicely, I thought, but I did notice that the two older gents, who were professorial and literary, seemed strangely silent. Gertrude had a fine cook and the meal was Virginian, with hot biscuits, fried chicken, and everything else dear to the Southerner's palate.

Conversation and excellent wine flowed freely between Gertrude, Tenn, Laura Benet, and me throughout the meal, and afterward we all settled down in the drawing room. The two elderly men were still silent and I thought I now knew why, but I also guessed as the evening wore on that I'd catch it in the long run from Tenn. Finally the younger woman said, "Mr. Williams, I want to quarrel with you about the ending of *Summer and Smoke*. I wish you'd tell me why you leave Alma Winemiller like that, picking up a traveling salesman."

There was a split second's silence before T.W. sighed, "Well, honey, if you don't understand why I did that, I'm afraid it's a little late for me to try to explain it to you."

We left a few minutes after that and Gertrude's front door had scarcely closed before Tenn whirled on me, demanding, "Why did you subject me to this? Those people hated me. Why, those two old guys either ignored me or just sat there and stared at me with purest venom."

"You are nuts," I said. "I knew you were going to come up with something like this, and it's just not true. Those men were awed and shy at meeting a man as famous as you. After all, you should understand that. You're shy. . . ."

"No such thing," said T.W. "Those people despise me."

We were out in the street by now and I countered lamely, "Well, anyhow, Gertrude gave us a lovely dinner."

"Mrs. Claytor's all right. I like her," Tenn said flatly. "But by God, I can pay for my own dinner. Come on, I'll buy you a nightcap."

This was the start, then, of our summer of excitement and misadventures.

Mrs. Claytor gave me tickets to *My Fair Lady* and I saw it with a new companion; Richard One arrived in town, and he and Tenn and I were often out together. We were bouncing along 57th Street West one day when I suddenly yelled, "Frank!" and we all stopped in joyous astonishment. The tall blond man in horn-rimmed glasses was Frank Krause, a former roommate of mine whom I'd introduced to Tenn in 1942. Neither of us had seen him for years and now there was great rejoicing as he joined us on our way to a French restaurant.

Tenn took the three of us that evening to visit his friend Marcus Romero, the Brazilian consul, who had a West Side hotel apartment. Marcus spoke English with an oddly mixed notion of syntax and idiom, but he was so amiable, so hospitable, so much a man of good will, I found it easy to understand him.

Tenn said that he liked Marcus' apartment; Marcus remarked casually that there was a vacant one the same size next door, and Tenn said he'd like to see it.

The manager came up with the key; we all walked through the place, and Tenn, in eight minutes flat, wrote a check for a month's rent.

"Now, this," he said firmly, "will be known as my West Side pad, and we shall have freedom and fun here the rest of this summer."

Frank Krause was not happy with his living conditions at the moment, so Tenn told him, "This solves your problem, man. Just move in here tomorrow."

I'd moved up to the West Side Y, where Richard One soon came also to stay, and a few days later Tenn phoned me there to ask if I'd like to accompany him to Chinatown.

I said I'd be glad to, but that I was meeting Gertrude Claytor for lunch.

"That's fine," Tenn said. "I like Mrs. Claytor. Ask her to have lunch with you and me at the Algonquin and we'll all go to Chinatown."

We did, returning laden down with paper lanterns, blue and gold wind chimes, a set of bead portieres.

When we'd gotten everything hung in the West Side pad, we all sat down to evaluate the result and Tenn said happily, "We'll put a sign over the door that says, 'This apartment is *supposed* to be tacky.'"

There were parties somewhere almost every evening now, but we were all busy in the daytime. The analyst had tried to persuade Tenn to stop working, and he'd more or less promised to do so, but he was actually getting up early each morning, working as usual, before keeping his couch appointment. I was out seeing editors, talking about my novel, and when it came back from a house where Phyllis Jackson had sent it, she coldly remarked that if I had all these editorial contacts, she didn't see why I needed her. I said, so be it, and took my manuscript away with me from her office.

I was also trying to get a job with a publishing house, but the best I could find was some free-lance manuscript reading with George Braziller and Julian Messner.

Frank Krause was job hunting too, and Richard One was writing a play, but nothing anybody was doing seemed to interfere with his evening activities. If Tenn was busy elsewhere, Richard One and I were invariably out together whooping it up, and I recall one gala night when we closed a bar on Lexington.

There was a small orchestra and when one o'clock came the manager locked the doors, leaving only himself, the musicians, Richard and me in the place. The girl vocalist began to improvise with the orchestra men and for the first time I sat enthralled in the midst of a real gone, after-hours jive session.

It had been fun, but when I told Tenn about it next day, adding, "Richard was broke last night so I treated him," Tenn asked, "How much was the bill?"

"Well . . . eighteen dollars," I said.

"That's a lot of money," said Tenn.

We were waiting for Richard One to join us at dinner in a restaurant near the West Side pad. He came, so did the menu, and Tenn asked, "What're you having, Gil?" I told him. He ordered for himself, then turned and told Richard, "Tonight you're on your own, boy, and what's more I want you to give Gil nine dollars as your half of you all's spree last night."

Richard cheerfully agreed and we all had a laugh—but I began to see something clearly that evening. Tenn was feeling responsible for me this summer. He was worrying for fear I'd fritter my time away in carousing, so I resolved to give him a daily account of my rounds with the publishers.

He kept saying, from time to time, "Of course you'll go back to Miami. You must go back and resume your teaching," and there was nothing I could do to convince him that I could not go back, that the school principal did not want me back, that he wished, indeed, to replace me with one of his own friends, and finally, that I'd be damned if I would go back under any conditions.

I began to see, though, that I'd need something in black and white, so I wrote the principal asking about the fall session. He replied, saying that since I'd not yet arranged for my teaching certificate for fall, he'd assumed I wasn't returning and had hired a replacement.

I read the letter to Papa Tenn at the West Side pad. He said, "Well, that's from the horse's mouth, all right," and I sighed in relief, believing I'd now convinced him that Miami was henceforth for the gulls and snowbirds as far as I was concerned.

We used to meet often in the lounge of the Mayflower Hotel after a swim at the Y, and it was there that I said to Tenn one afternoon, "Well, my money's not going to last much longer and it's a shame, because I honestly think if I could hang on here through the fall, I might make some sort of connection with a publishing firm."

"Then you must have a little more loot," said Tenn. "I'll see what I can do," and a day later he wrote a letter to the Organization asking its head to extend my money grant for another three months.

In July an accident befell me at a party in Brooklyn Heights. There was a raised threshold to the door that led to my host's garden and I'd been sitting in his front room watching people trip over it, thinking, "What fools they are, can't they see that raised threshold?"

Half an hour later I measured my length in the garden, striking my forehead on the sharp spike of a low ornamental fence. I thought I'd sustained a slight cut, but when I turned up at Roosevelt Hospital next morning the interne coolly informed me that he could see my skull.

Since ten hours had passed, he was afraid to stitch the cut, so he butterflied it, informing me, "You're going to have a scar, and while it won't be too bad, it's also not going to win you any beauty awards, m'friend."

My host called to say he'd put in a claim for me with the company which had insured his place, and Tenn said philosophically, "Oh well, scars are always interesting."

There were parties, parties, parties all this summer; but when Richard Two arrived, there was one gala which proved to be unforgettable.

Now, Richard Two's humor is based upon the employment of cruelty. The idea is always to strike with cutting wit(?) at a man's most vulnerable deficiency. If he is aging, too stout, balding, or has some physical affliction, this is grist to young Richard's mill. I, however, was not only loaded but in a foul temper the night he decided to needle me before a room full of people at the West Side pad, and on this night I outdid myself. The result was violence and vitriol on my part, with various guests, including Richard Two, flying in all directions.

It was a reprehensible, dreadful performance, and I have this to say: once I got over the remorse of a two-day hangover, I never for a moment regretted attacking this guy who has spent his maladjusted life since his teens in attacking other people, using despicable verbal weapons which should be contraband in any civilized group.

I was ashamed of myself for embarrassing Tenn at his party, but since I'd seen and heard him, a few nights before, order out a couple of critical guests who'd disparaged his work, I could not bring myself to don sackcloth after my own outburst.

Unstable as I was, however, it was a bad time for me to have acted up, for Tenn was more disturbed than I thought at the moment, and the next day he lit into me in no uncertain terms.

Sick and miserable, I asked him on the phone that morning if he thought there was a chance of my getting the money he'd asked for from the fund, and he retorted, "I don't know. That's not a charitable organization, Gil."

We arranged to go to lunch, and there, over whiskey sours, while he wavered between righteous anger and helpless laughter over a couple of pot shots I'd taken at a pair of last night's offensive guests, he informed me, "I have called Winifred McConville this morning and told her to get you back to Miami where you belong."

I laid down my fork and said evenly, "You know damned well there's no job waiting for me down there—and, even if there were, I wouldn't go. I'm going to stay right here and find some kind of employment."

"You are *not*," said Williams. "If you do, you'll end up in Bellevue."

I said, "Now, you listen to me, man, while I tell you something over this lavish lunch you're paying for: you've been kind in getting me that fifteen hundred dollars and kinder still to've asked for more—but you are not God, and not you nor anyone else is going to tell me what I *must* do. You ought to know that by now."

There was a silence; then, in mutual self-defense we spoke of casual things. We said good-by stiffly outside the restaurant and Tenn hailed a taxi while I turned west toward the Y, jaw set, more than ever determined to get my jobless, loused-up life into shape.

Tenn took off by plane next day for the Virgin Islands, far from well, with Frank Krause, who's a male nurse by profession, as a fortunate traveling companion.

In a few days the lady who had charge of funds at the Organization called and asked me to come to see her. We had a friendly talk and she told me, "Yes, I think we can get a grant extension for you." Next, the insurance man came to the Y and settled with me, while the bandage was still on my forehead, for less than the scar I emerged with was worth—and then I went out and got me a job.

Meanwhile, at the Long Island estate of a friend named Gordon, I learned he'd just returned from the Virgin Islands. There, he said, he'd heard from Tenn that I was drinking myself to death, would soon land in the charity ward at Bellevue, and that he, T.W., had washed his hands of me.

"So this," said Gordon, flatly, "is the kind of friend you have in Tennessee Williams."

I answered slowly, "I don't doubt he said those things and they don't matter. He shouldn't be talking like that, but he actually

believes it all right now. As for you, however, I will ask not only
why you've felt it necessary to relay all this crap to me, but what, as
a friend, you have ever done for me? Williams has given me
money, admired my work, and helped me as much as he could to
get on with it. He's introduced me to fascinating, famous people,
had me at his rehearsals, taken me to plays in orchestra seats,
wined and dined me in New York's best restaurants—whereas,
when I have come to see you on weekends, I've often brought my
own booze, not to mention occasional sacks of victuals. I feel
therefore that you are a bit out of line this evening."

About two weeks later the phone rang in my room at the Y and
Tenn's voice said, "Gil, I'm in Havana. I've been worried about
you, man. How you gettin' along?"

"Fine," I said. "I have a job in a bookstore, I got two hundred
and fifty dollars for the cut on my forehead, and Miss S. is coming
through with the loot from the fund, which you asked for."

"Oh yeh?" quoth Tennessee. "Well, sir, your fortunes sure have
changed, haven't they?"

He said he'd be home soon and was anxious to see me. I said I
was anxious to see him, too, and I was. As soon as he got back I
repeated all the news I'd heard from the Islands, and he turned
both crimson and white, avowing his absolute innocence.

We got together for dinner one evening at Barefield's. Gordon
rang up, and after a chat with Jack, asked to speak to me. As I
talked with him briefly, Tenn yelled from the living room, "Tell
Gordon I'd like to speak to him."

He sailed into the bedroom, took the phone from me, and told
Gordon off for three minutes, but the best he could come up with
was that Gordon had quoted him out of context, while he was in
his cups.

When he got back to the living room he found Jack and me
rolling wildly around on the sofa. I'd never really thought the
whole business anything but hilarious, and now I found it unbearably so.

The summer was over. Williams and I were still friends and the
West Side pad was no more. He had let it go only a week after a
certain woman columnist had chattered, in possible envy,

What famous playwright is going regularly to an analyst and, at the same time, throwing Nero-like orgies in his West Side apartment?

The day I read this I let out a mixed whoop of indignation and helpless mirth. If the lady'd dropped in, unasked, on one of those "orgies," she'd have found they consisted of poetry readings and parlor games, topped off with a lavish banquet of cold cuts, potato salad, and cole slaw from the corner delicatessen.

True, she might have got some kicks from one evening when a young Jewish fellow came straight over from hearing Billy Graham at Madison Square Garden and sat down to explain to our rectory-reared playwright the plan of salvation through Jesus Christ. Tenn sat, solemnly attentive, now and then nodding his head, asking earnest questions while I sat listening in absolute disbelief, asking myself, "In the name of sweet heaven, what is the meaning of this?" However, on second thought, I'm glad the columnist didn't drop in since I feel perfectly sure her presence would have cast a scornful chill on the warm atmosphere of Williams' West Side pad, which was early Won Ton in decor and *supposed* to be tacky.

8

AT THE BOOKSTORE, I WAS HIRED AT FORTY-FIVE DOLLARS A WEEK by a slim, sandy-looking young man who, rain or shine, walked over each morning from his apartment to this ancient, honored book emporium carrying a tightly furled umbrella. He was supposed to be floor manager, but he was actually no more than a sort of monitor for the motley collection of clerks who worked under him. The store manager was an efficient machine of a woman to whom I took an instant, uncontrollable dislike that was shortly to prove disastrous.

The floorwalker, Sandy Shanks (I'll call him that), discovering my last book of poems was still in print, ordered a half-dozen copies for the Fine Arts department.

I introduced myself around the departmental floor, and when I shook hands with a young man in Philosophy, I had the instinctual impression of having met a creative personality.

The boy's name was Frederick. He had deep-set, shining brown eyes, a squarish, high-colored face, and curly dark hair which he wore low on his forehead in the manner of the young Mark Antony.

When Frederick found out that I was a poet, I saw a gleam in his eye which I thought I recognized, and when he'd read some of the poems in *Go Looking*, commenting upon them in a way no layman could, I said, "You might as well confess. You write poems, too."

Young Frederick admitted that he did, and I asked him to bring some of his things to the store.

In bed one night at the Y I took his sheaf of papers and began to read, first attentively, then with a kind of excitement I hadn't felt since Howard Griffin, my protégé of 1945, had first shown me some of his things.

Frederick said he hadn't been sending his poems out, and I urged him to do so, telling him to look up the poetry markets in *Writer's Digest*. We began to lunch together; he swam with me at the Y, and always when we had a free moment in the store, we talked about poetry and poets.

I had thought of myself as being obsessed by poetry in my salad days but I was to learn, as time passed, that I was a restrained bard indeed compared to this twenty-two-year-old fanatic.

Frederick thought poetry, read poetry, talked poetry every hour of his waking day and often had nightmares in which he leaped up, or strode about, uttering such rhythmic, fantastic fragments as, "Look, oh, look, the room is filled with giraffes," or "Seven white doves have just flown in through the ceiling."

I was warned of these exhibitions by his suite-mate at the Sutton Hotel, but I did not receive the full impact of the night performances until later on when he and I rented a place together.

Tenn came into the bookstore one day, graciously autographed all his books which the saleswoman had in Fine Arts, met Sandy Shanks the floorwalker, young Frederick, and the very nice, dark woman head of Juveniles where I'd landed because of once having been a children's book manuscript reader for the Viking Press.

Then one day, the monstrous manageress had someone fired in the fiction wing of the shop and I made an appointment with Sandy Shanks for Frank Krause, who was promptly hired.

One day the manageress stalked up to me as I was doing a department display and snapped out, apparently under the impression she was speaking to an unskilled laborer, "Don't you ever again let me see that stockroom in the shape you left it yesterday, understand?"

I looked at this broad as though she'd taken leave of her senses, walked over to Sandy Shanks, repeated her remark, and asked, "What is this place—something straight out of Dickens? I don't care how you phrase it, I want you to tell that female she's never to speak to me again as long as I'm here."

The poor guy flushed brick red, muttering something about my not being required to take such rudeness, and from that day on neither the manageress nor I acknowledged each other's existence. The handwriting was on the wall—but I, as usual, going sunnily about my business, failed to heed the hints my department head kept throwing out about September's being a good time for a man who might want to better himself, to be out filing an application at some good department store.

Tenn dropped in one day and when he sat down in Juveniles to talk with me a few minutes, several clerks came over to chat with him.

Next day Sandy Shanks told me, "I hired you to sell books in this shop, not to hold court over there with Tennessee Williams," and I, mistaking his poker-faced dryness for a sample of his native New England humor, laughed merrily.

In no time at all then, two things happened. Frederick and I decided at lunch one day to make a stab at finding an apartment, and the following payday Sandy Shanks called me aside to tell me, "I know this will come as a shock to you, but I'm going to let you go."

I was flabbergasted, but I said, wide-eyed, "You must be kidding. Where could a man go from here? This is the bottom of the ladder."

He had the grace to smile but he repeated, "I'm sorry—that's how it's got to be."

I said, "Why? You've always seemed to like me."

"Who I like's got nothing to do with it," said our bespectacled martinet. "I have to get along with those people upstairs. You see, everyone here thinks you're just in the store on a lark."

"Sandy," I said, "this dull, dry, eight-hour daily grind under your goddamned fluorescent lights that make both customers and clerks look like dead things is not my conception of a lark."

"I know, but that's not all." Sandy Shanks leaned toward me to speak confidentially. "I've seen how you and the manager have been looking at each other, and frankly I'm afraid if you stayed here, you and that woman would get in a fist fight right on this floor before Christmas."

I looked at him, nodding slowly.

I said, "Now, you are talkin'. I think that, too, so maybe I'd better go."

Sandy Shanks grinned at me for the first time as he clapped my shoulder. "In that case I think you should take a little extra time on your lunch hour today to apply at one of the big stores."

I said I would, and two hours later returned from a trip down Fifth Avenue, signed up for the silver department of a store which the carriage trade fondly refers to as New York's last stand of graciousness.

That afternoon I called Tenn and told him, "You won't believe this—but your beamish boy's been fired from this Scrooge establishment."

Tenn said, "Well, I wish I could say I'm sorry, but I can't. The goddamn place is a sweatshop, baby. See you at the Mayflower lounge in an hour."

So that was the end of me and the manageress of the book-store—until a day six years later when a call came through from her to my publishing firm asking a monetary favor. I said silkily, "Let me, as editor in chief here, handle this one," and I did, reminding her of who I was, where and when I'd known her, silently reminding myself, "The mills of the gods grind slowly, but they grind exceeding fine."

I gave Tenn a bright moment describing the above transaction, and sent him into a fit of giggles as I finished, "I am—as you have reason to know—an eye for an eye, tooth for a tooth man, in the strictest Biblical sense."

But Tenn is too, alas; and while neither of us holds malice overlong, every now and then as the bowl o'erflows and the evening wears away, one of us astounds a group of friends by suddenly sitting up, bawling, "Don't you dare talk about my behavior. Why, my God, when I *think* of what you did to me in Miami last winter . . ."

This sort of thing is likely to end up in a free-for-all circus, with Tenn and me in stitches—but there are several events of which we seldom speak, and one has to do with *Suddenly Last Summer*.

One crisp autumn night when Richard One and I were downing a few at an East Side hangout, we rang up Tenn, who said, "Sure, come right over. I'd love to see you both."

He seemed unusually cheerful as he made us drinks and sat us down before a chirruping fire in his living room. Then, almost shyly, he asked, "Would you all like to hear my new play?"

I was surprised, knowing the analyst had insisted upon his taking a vacation from work, and anyway I couldn't see how he'd had time to write a play in the past hectic summer, but I said, "You bet I would," and Richard One said, "Oh, yes, please."

Tenn got his manuscript and began to read with great clarity and dramatic fervor, but somehow, tanked up as I was, I seemed to be hearing too clearly—and I didn't *like* what I was hearing.

I caught Richard One's eye which also looked doubtful, and all of a sudden (I swear I could not help myself) I stood up, snorting, "This is no *Streetcar*, and I'm going home."

I headed somewhat unevenly for the door and Tenn sprang after me, grabbing my arm, yelling, "Gil, for God's sake, come back here and tell me what you mean by this. Please . . . let me finish reading the play." I shrugged and returned to my chair to sit unreceptively silent while he read the entire script, and when he'd read the doctor's conclusive speech I was still unhappy. I hadn't been able to make myself like the play. Its theme of universal devourment repelled me, and I was sickened by its cannibalistic scene, as well as by the powerful story of the sea turtles, which sums God up as a cruel, indifferent deity.

I could not say that I'd liked it, and Richard One was guarded in his remarks, so Tenn went into a panic. He threw the script to the floor and cried, "I knew it! I knew it! This time Audrey's really betrayed me. The damn play's no good, yet she's willing to let me make a fool of myself, putting it on Off Broadway."

There was more of this which I heard in a kind of half stupor. I was sad and sorry, but this was the first play of Williams' since *The Lady of Larkspur Lotion* I'd found deeply offensive, and I refused to lie about the way the piece had both impressed and depressed me.

We three seemed to part amiably enough, however, some time after midnight.

Next evening as Richard One and I sat in a French restaurant talking over the fracas, my companion gave me a gleam-eyed look and said slowly, "Nevertheless, if this number turns out to be a hit, you can bet your sweet ass we're going to eat humble pie."

I said, "Lord, that's right. I'll go call him this minute."

I spoke cheerily into the phone, expecting T.W. to be able to laugh about the previous night's shenanigans, but this time I was in for a lethal shock.

He said, in a voice that sounded truly hurt, "We-ll, I don't know, Gil. You sent me to the analyst twice today. . . . I never thought a time would come when you'd get up and walk out on a play of mine while I was reading it to you."

I felt a slight nausea in the pit of my stomach; then I took the bit in my teeth and said firmly, "Tenn Williams, you knew better than to read me *anything*, with five martinis in me."

"Ye-es," Tenn said, "but you knew what you were hearing, and what you were saying, too."

"All right, I did, yes," I said. "I did not like this play and I could not lie about it."

"Well, maybe not," Tenn said. "But I don't think I have ever . . ."

"Now, stop right there," I said. "You certainly have: once in Key West, about that first version of my novel; and once two months ago in Miami when I started reading you two opening pages of a novel and you sat straight up in my living room and yelled out before both Richards, 'No, no, no. Put that down. I can tell that's old work, and I won't listen to it.' "

There was a still, thoughtful silence. I said quietly, "Tenn, tomorrow's my day off from the store. What about lunch?"

Tenn hesitated, then he said, "All right, why not? The Sun Luck West at twelve-thirty?"

I left the phone feeling better, but if I thought this was the end of me and *Suddenly Last Summer*, I was misled. I was to be haunted by the play in one way or another for the next few years, as I shall later reveal, and there is still some resentment within my playwright friend toward an old side-kick, who once in a lifetime dared to say, "This is something of yours I have failed to appreciate."

I wrote a rough draft of this whole episode and when Tenn read the following paragraph, he delighted me by falling into my unintentionally laid trap. Please follow the italics and asterisk.

Criticism of Tenn's behavior as a person is a prerogative which, as an old friend, I insist upon. Criticism of his work is another thing. I made the mistake of doing that just once, and the result was catastrophic, so I shall not do it again. *Criticism of himself Williams can take and be humble; any derogatory comment on anything he has written is neither to be borne nor tolerated.* He has said in *Suddenly Last Summer* "The work of a poet is the life of a poet—and vice versa—the life of a poet is the work of a poet, I mean you can't separate them . . ."* I have always thought this a highflown, rather ambiguous, inept statement to make about poets in general, but perhaps it is true of Tenn that his work *is* his life and his life is his work.

So there we have it. The reader will note that what I said in italics is beautifully corroborated in my friend's footnote.

* Mrs. Venable made that remark, a part of her adoration of Sebastian—it wasn't the author speaking for himself. A poet's work is his escape from his life—at least in my case.   T.W.

One thing has come to me lately, though, and because of this thing—even more than the danger of causing estrangement between us—I shall be careful never again to tell Tenn that I dislike a play of his, for here is a note I made another day:

Sometimes when I have heard him say *my work*, it was in the deferential way another man might say, *my mother, my sister;* and again, in the tender way of one who says, *my lover, my child, my old, true, constant friend.*

When a man's work means this to him, a friend walks softly, carrying no big stick.

At some time in the fall of 1957 Cornelius Coffin Williams died alone after an asthmatic attack, in a hotel room in Knoxville.

On the day Tenn received news of his father's death, he had been scheduled to appear with Mike Wallace on a TV program. He begged to be excused, but he was not allowed to be and no one but himself knew the state of his emotions as he sat, fortified by Scotch, his face wreathed in cigarette smoke, deliberately parrying Wallace's cunningly pointed questions about his work and his life.

I have since been able to surmise the state of his mind and heart that night from several things he has told me about Cornelius.

He has said, "You'd have been crazy about my father, Gil. He had a wonderful sense of humor and you two would have got along fine. Cornelius had a terribly sad, lonely life and I can't help feeling now, how much he was misunderstood."

T.W. has read me an impressive biographical sketch about C.C. called "The Man in the Overstuffed Chair." When it is published, the reader who wishes to do so may satisfy himself as to the distressing conditions prevalent in the Williams' home in St. Louis when Tenn's grandparents were living with Edwina and C.C. in the forties. It is not my business to give here such an intimate, devastating picture of a household as this sensitive piece contains. I do remember, however, two things which Tenn has told me about his father that seem pertinent to these memoirs.

He said, "C.C. was a man who found it hard ever to say anything sentimental but he felt deeply—I know that now. I can never forget one time when he went with me to see my sister in the state asylum. He bore up pretty well till we'd left her. Then, in the hall, he dropped his face in his hands and tried to control himself, but he couldn't. He laid his arm against the wall, leaned his face against it and cried like a helpless child. And there's another thing, too, I wish you'd say in your book. Mother has said in hers that my brother came home after the funeral in Knoxville and told her, 'Neither Tom nor I shed a tear.' That is not true. I cried."

It is evident that his father's passing affected Tenn far more than he could know in 1957. He has since come to feel not only sympathy and compassion for C.C. but a nostalgic regret that he and this lonely man were never able to communicate except in a kind of yearning, mutely embarrassed discomfort in each other's presence—both the older man and the younger being "condemned to solitary confinement" within the prisons of their "own lonely skins."*

I always see Tenn and me, in the fall of 1957, at the Mayflower Hotel lounge where we sat and looked out through plate-glass windows at the trees of Central Park blazing red and gold across the street. We nearly always met in this place after my day at Altman's, Tenn's day of writing and analysis, and it was here I first said to him, "Bertha Klausner has suggested that I ought to write your biography."

My friend sat thoughtful a moment, turning his glass on the table before he answered, "Well, perhaps you could. But let's wait till after *Sweet Bird of Youth* has opened."

It was in the lounge, too, one day, that we had an exchange which was farcical. In discussing a major novelist who had just published an incredibly poor book, I said, "Lord, why does a great writer go on and on when he's so obviously said all he has to say"—and saw on my playwright's countenance an instant, half-

---

* From *Orpheus Descending*.

amused look, as of one who says wryly, "*Touché*, Mephistopheles."
But I am not one to let a bit like that go unchallenged. I said at
once. "Now I *have* got you where the hair's short. That was a
perfectly innocent remark, but even if it had been a crack, for once
you can't put me on the defensive without admitting you think
you're great."

It was one of the more delicious moments we've shared, and
both of us enjoyed it.

The lounge was the place, too, where, with Frank Krause, I met
Josephine Healy, an old friend of Tenn's. Jo had known him and
Don Windham since the forties when she was with the Theatre
Guild, and on this day, as always, she and Tenn were discussing a
prospective visit to Rose, in whom Jo had always taken an interest.
Jo had left the Guild to become secretary to Winthrop Rockefeller, later to Gypsy Rose Lee. She was now with Celeste Holm
and when she learned I'd liked this actress's work in films, she
asked Frank and me up to the Holm duplex on Central Park
West. We had drinks there and a pleasant hour with Miss Holm,
who has, I think, the most incredibly blue eyes in Christendom.

I was to see more of Jo through the years, no more of Miss
Holm, since she and Miss Healy were destined to part company in
the not distant future.

In the middle of autumn *The Long Pursuit* came back from the
last publisher to which I ever had heart to send it. Audrey Wood
had told me the book gave evidence of being a best-seller, and that
she saw in it both a play and a motion picture. Phyllis Jackson had
wept over certain passages. A few days after the last chapters were
finished I'd read them aloud to Tennessee and he'd cried, un-
ashamed.

The book had gone, through three different agents, to at least
ten major publishing houses whose editors' reactions had ranged
(God alone knows why) from indifference to downright belliger-
ence and indignation. One had suggested that it might be made
suitable for his firm if I were willing to make some changes, none
of which he seemed willing, or able, to specify. The final publisher
had kept the manuscript two months. When I called to ask about
it, he'd said, "The first half of your book is magnificent, so we'd

like a little more time for a final editor's reading." I waited and
one day he called me at the bookstore to tell me, "This book came
as near as any ever has to being accepted here, but we have chosen
a first novel by H. instead."

He named the daughter of a well-known American writer. The
novel landed startlingly soon after publication on the 29¢ counters
of the Marboro bookstores and Liggett's drugstore.

I said to Tenn, "This does it. I'm now going to relegate *The
Long Pursuit* to a closet shelf." Tenn said, "No, don't. I think the
trouble is, you're offering an honest, profound work to a shallow-
minded world. But on the other hand, maybe it's just the first
chapter that needs rewriting."

I said, "I've already rewritten the first chapter sixty times, and
besides, it's more than the first chapter. There's something radically wrong, but there doesn't seem to be one editor or agent in
New York who's able to tell me what it is, and I'm not detached
enough about my own work to find out for myself."

Recently Tennessee said to me, after reading the passage in
which I stated that he hadn't wanted me to go to Europe in the
summer of his analysis because he wanted me in town, "You were
wrong about that, Gil. I was glad you were here, yes, but I'm
neither so dependent nor so selfish as to have insisted you stay for
any such reason. I was honestly afraid you wouldn't finish that fine
novel. It *is* a fine novel. I still believe in it, and you'll sell it, after
this book is published."

Here, indeed, is a typical reaction of Tenn's. He could never say
die on *Battle of Angels* for seventeen years and it finally became
both a Broadway play and a motion picture. I put in six years on
Pursuit, and I'm beginning to think he may be right about its
outcome, too.

Publishers and editors are notoriously blind judges as well as
inadequate critics of manuscripts. Thus, Tenn has again encour-
aged me not to give up on a project, even as he has often un-
knowingly sent me, shamed by his own fiercely persistent efforts,
to my typewirter, when, depressed by careless refusal letters from
editors of publishing firms or magazines, I could see no reason for
going on working.

Perhaps this is the most important influence he has had on a number of writers. Bill Inge has said, "Some writers help others just by being. Tennessee has certainly helped me by being." And God knows, such an encouraging influence, both conscious and unconscious, is needed in a country where a general indifference to artists and to quality work of all kinds is not merely regrettable and shameful, but obscene.

It is my belief that the average editor, being a frustrated creep who never had the guts to try to make it as a writer, hates all living authors. He seems also to forget that his function as an editor, if he would aspire to being more than a comma-changer, is to tell a writer what is wrong with his manuscript and what he must do to make it publishable.

Once in a century a man arises in this country who can fulfill these functions; however, the last one that I can remember died some years ago. His name was Maxwell Perkins.

One day at the lounge I told Tenn, "I may have done a crazy thing, but I've found a hotel penthouse for Frederick and me. It's not cheap, but we'd be paying no more than we're paying separately—and of course there's always the saving of being able to cook and eat in."

We walked up together to the West Side hotel, took the elevator to the top floor, and climbed a short flight of stairs. I unlocked the penthouse door and flung it open. The lights were out but the curtains of the picture window were pulled back. We stood for a moment gazing out at the lights of Jersey and the boats gliding slowly along the Hudson, then I switched the lamps on in the charmingly furnished room-and-a-half with its kitchenette window through which you could see Radio City, and said, "Voilà. Mah home, suh."

Tenn looked all around, nodding. "Yes," he said, "I can see how you had to have this."

Frederick, who'd seen the place and approved it, left in a few days to spend the holidays with his family in Ohio.

At the Sutton Hotel, after watching his abortive attempts at packing, I took over and somehow got all his stuff in his bags. I went with him to Grand Central and saw him off with autographed copies of *The Sleeping Trees* and *Go Looking* tucked under his arm.

Altman's silver department was fun, and I made friends on the fourth floor whom I would enjoy for years to come. The Avenue windows this year, filled with little animated animals and human figures, were truly enchanting. There was snow, a country store, a lake with sleighs, an old-fashioned kitchen, and a child's voice that lilted merrily out over the sidewalk crowds of old and young children, "We're going to have a barnyard Christmas, on the farm this year."

Every poet is more than half a child, so when young Frederick returned just after New Year's, I took him from the train to the store where he stood enthralled and wide-eyed till I urged him on up the cold, sun-struck street.

Tenn was one of our first guests at the penthouse. I was busy cooking Sunday dinner, so I told Frederick, "Time now for you to peel the peaches, kid."

He got the peaches from the ice box and absently accepted the knife I gave him. Then, while I wrestled with pots at the stove he wandered from the kitchen to the picture window, peach in one hand, paring knife in the other, rambling on, "Yes, Tennessee— but that *other* poem of Eliot's . . . You know, the one that starts . . ."

Every now and then I bellowed, "Freddie, peel the peaches," gleefully enjoying the look of wonderment on Tenn's face, till finally in the midst of a poem Fred was quoting, old T.W. leaped up and cried, "Oh, good God A'mighty, gimme that knife. *I'll* peel the peaches."

That afternoon as I walked him toward Central Park, T.W. made some remark about Frederick's being truly out of this world, and I said, "Yes, I know. I can't believe he's for real most of the time myself, but the boy writes good poetry, so I've resigned myself to going on for a while, as Paul used to do with you, telling him all day long, 'Hang up your shirt, bundle your laundry, brush your teeth, go to the bathroom, Freddie.' "

I stayed at Altman's for the white sale after Christmas; then I lived on unemployment insurance, while Frederick went on working at the bookstore.

On my birthday in February Dick Orme arrived from New Orleans and both he and Tenn came over.

Tenn brought me a bottle of Scotch with a card that said, "Sympathy, dear." Dick had just won eight hundred dollars on a horse race, and when he left us for another engagement, fifteen minutes had hardly passed before the desk clerk phoned to say there was a package for me, which turned out to be a second bottle of booze from old Dick.

One day just before the opening of his dual show *Garden District*, when I was at Tenn's place, he said, "Come over with me to the York. I want you to see Robert Soule's set."

There was the evil garden of *Suddenly Last Summer*, terrifyingly real, and I admired it.

Tenn said, "You're going to be impressed with the play, I think, Gil"—and that was that. No matter how or for what reason it happened, I was given no opening-night tickets to *Garden District* nor asked to the cast party, as was Richard One.

Some weeks later Tenn called to ask if Frederick and I'd like to see the show. He said there'd be tickets at the box office, so the poet and I, unable to afford a taxi, plowed our way from the East Side subway through six inches of new-fallen snow to the York Theatre.

As the man in the box office handed me the tickets he said, "That's $9.45, Mr. Maxwell."

I felt rather than saw Frederick turn pale as I answered, "I think there's some mistake. These tickets are complimentary."

The guy looked uncertain as he insisted, "I have no such instructions from Mr. Williams, sir."

I took a deep breath and told him, "Then I think you'd better phone Mr. Williams."

The theater manager was summoned; there was a whispered conference and a call that was briskly terminated one minute after the box-office man had said hello. His face was crimson as he handed me the tickets, murmuring profuse apologies.

When we got to Tenn's apartment after the show, he had cooled off somewhat, but he was still mildly indignant.

He said, knowing damn well what was in my mind, "How embarrassing, Gil. You know I never meant you to pay for those tickets."

I guessed he might be able to see from my face that I was amused, but I wickedly let him think what he pleased.

There'd been one awful instant at the theater when I'd thought, "Maybe he did this to get even"; then in the next second, I'd known he was incapable of any such small-time vengeance, and had become firm with the greedy box-office man.

Frederick had been mad about both the play and the production. I'd liked its pace and timing, the direction, the setting, the fine performances. I was charmed by the one-act, *Something Unspoken*, with Eleanor Phelps and Hortense Alden, impressed by Anne Meacham as Catherine Holly in *Suddenly Last Summer*—and Frederick's enthusiasm was almost, not quite, contagious: I could admire *Suddenly* as a brilliant tour de force in playwriting, but I could never honestly say that I liked it.

As the winter passed, there were lean times at the penthouse in which the youthful bard and I could barely manage the rent and grocery bills.

Tenn went down to Florida, from where he occasionally phoned. Richard Two was still in debt to me, but I was unable, either by pleas or threats, to collect the small amount he owed me that could have meant so much at the moment. By April I was scared—and then, as so often happens, the extraordinary occurred. I'd been unable to get any free-lance work from publishers after making the rounds all the past summer and fall, but one day in April I was at a house, just having seen an editor, when I ran into another one out in the hall. He grabbed me and cried, "Mr. Maxwell, I'm so glad to see you. The only phone number you left here last summer was Tennessee Williams' answering service and those operators couldn't tell me where you are now. Come right into my office."

The man had an assignment for me to rewrite a Russian stage and film actress's autobiography. When I left his office I had a verbal agreement that I would be paid a thousand dollars for making a publishable book out of the bulky, amateurish manuscript I was toting home.

I started to work immediately and Frederick began typing up the replotted, totally rewritten chapters of the book, receiving payment from me by the page. It was a good arrangement for a project which would occupy us both till the following September.

In the penthouse all winter and throughout the colder days of spring, the wind had blown through the loose skylight above the bathroom, freezing the anatomy of whoever might be in the shower or using the john. This, one could endure, since after a few minutes one might return to the wall-to-wall carpeting, the ever-attractive river view from the living room's picture window. What one could not bear was the failure in early summer of the ancient hotel's hot-water pipes—and so with reluctance Frederick and I said farewell to our secluded eyric high over Broadway.

The place was haunted for me anyhow, by painful memories of firsts of the month when our limited incomes barely stretched to meet the rent and phone bills, and by one ghastly day when Richard One, who'd been drinking too much for several weeks, came to me with helpless tears streaking his small-boy face.

"Oh, God," he cried, "help me. For God's sake *help* me. Promise you won't let them take me away. . . . Oh, please, Gil, promise me."

Neither Frederick nor I had seen a man with delirium tremens before, but now that we were faced with the problem we suddenly knew what to do. We immersed Richard One in a tub of luke-warm water and forcibly held him there singing in some kind of patois resembling French—a language he can't speak, sober—until he was able to re-enter the dubious winter world of the unemployed writer, frustrated, embittered, egomaniacal, and temporarily despairing.

Before we left the hotel Tenn asked me one day as the lobby door was opened for us by a small man whose hands trembled slightly, "Who the hell is that?"

I said, "That, my friend, is the beggar you see sitting outside Macy's with a box of pencils, shaking like ye olde aspen leaf, with a card 'round his neck that reads, 'I HAVE PARKINSON'S DISEASE.' He has a room here, and when he's not 'working' he's vacationing in Philadelphia. The only other distinction this hotel has is that old Mrs. Drew once had a suite here in which Miss Ethel Barrymore as a young, uncertain actress briefly resided."

I left the hotel with some nostaglia, but little pain. Frederick was bored by the idea of finding a new habitat, so I did most of the looking, coming up at last with what had once been a big front drawing room—now with kitchen attached—in a reconverted brownstone that had once housed Herbert Hoover.

We warmed the place with several gatherings at which George Keathley, Tennessee, and my beloved Margrit Wyler, just back from acting in Germany, were present. There were many parties, and always in the evenings, open house. Richard Two had moved to New York from Miami, where on one of his visits, Tennessee, with Marion Vaccaro and George Black, had made up a sizable gift check to help this mortician's assistant return to the North.

Dick Two fully expected to find immediate employment, so on his first evening in town he entertained Richard One, Frederick, and me at dinner at the Fleur de Lis restaurant. The bill came to thirty dollars, but the prodigal was briskly undaunted. Tomorrow he would pos-*itively* be starting a most remunerative job.

The job did not come through, and one week later Richard Two was borrowing from one and all to meet the demands of his land-lady, the cafeteria, and the corner beer joint.

From the first the front drawing room of the old house in West 71st was an evening hang-out for every friend and acquaintance of mine who had nowhere else to go. The two regular paying guests were Richards One and Two, who somehow always managed to scrape up enough loot to pitch in on a fifth of rum and contribute a dollar each toward the dinner I'd shopped for and cooked. Frederick and these two always tipsily did up the dishes, and presently half a set of quite decent stainless-steel tableware given me by a friend ended up in the downstairs garbage cans.

The whole summer was a montage of work and after-nightfall gatherings, with Tenn, returning from out of town, leaping from a taxi to yell under our windows, "Gil, you home?" or ringing the bell and charging, *surprise, surprise,* up the stairs with a bottle of Scotch.

It was during this summer, too, that I first got the full distrust treatment from him, for I remember his sitting in the one big chair, looking mournfully down the long living room to the kitchen where I was mixing a salad, sadly intoning, "They say you hate me but I don't think so, because God knows I don't think you could ever say meaner things to my back than you say to my face."

"That's for sure," I said firmly. "I haven't yet joined the back-biting small coterie of hypocrites, envious failures, and bootlicking sycophants who surround you, daddy-o."

I had no idea then that the absurd belief of my hatred for him was actually to grow in his mind until it became a conviction.

For a long time I'd been working on the screenplay of *The Sleeping Trees*, occasionally asking T.W. a technical question or two, but he hadn't yet seen the typescript.

In the early fall I delivered the manuscript of the actress's autobiography. I was living now on the last of the thousand I'd been paid for this job of replotting, cutting, revising, completely rewriting, sentence by sentence, paragraph by painful paragraph, a book originally put together by a beauteous lady who could speak and write in Russian and French, but not English. She'd been allowed the choice in her contract of either giving me credit in her book's front pages for my work, or remaining discreetly mum.

She chose the latter alternative.

Tenn took one look at the manuscript and snorted, "The job was worth three thousand," and I agreed, reminding myself nonetheless, that without the one thousand I'd never have lived from the first of the year 1958 till the early fall.

Williams was not talking much about his own work this autumn, but I knew that he was revising *Sweet Bird of Youth* for a spring production.

I went back to Altman's, with Frederick, to sell in the book department.

At T.W.'s one evening in early December, my host asked casually, "Gil, could you use a nice silk robe?"

I said that I could and would, whereupon he disappeared into the bedroom, returning with a dressing gown of embossed brown silk. He put it on and the sleeves completely covered his hands, while the skirt swirled about his feet in voluminous folds like a high-styled bridal gown.

Frederick and I let out a couple of helpless yoks and Tenn said, poker-faced, "Bill Liebling gave me this, but you know it must have been bought for Bill Inge."

The robe was long worn out before Paul Bigelow cleared up that mystery. I told him the tale last year and he said at once, "Of course it was for Bill Inge. Liebling just bought two identical garments for Bill and Tenn, and got the boxes mixed."

My one regret is that I could not have seen Inge, who is over six feet, in the robe that was meant for Tenn who is five foot seven.

Soon after this, Tenn went down to Miami. He was trying out a comedy called *Period of Adjustment*, which he rehearsed and directed at the Coconut Grove Theatre from December 18 until its opening, December 29. He returned after the first of the year to begin rehearsals on *Sweet Bird of Youth*.

That year I was not asked to stay on at Altman's for the white sale, so, with no free-lance work coming in from publishers, I was in a precarious state. I called Tenn, who said, "How near broke are you, Gil, baby?"

I said, "I'm down to thirty bucks."

He said, "Oh, Lord, it's urgent, then. Meet me at the Seven Arts Club at eleven."

I met him, bearing a finished draft of *All on a Summer's Day*— the screenplay of *The Sleeping Trees*. We went at once into the theater where we found Geraldine Page and Paul Newman onstage, smoking, apparently mumbling to themselves. Elia Kazan was sitting relaxed in a front row seat and when Tenn clapped him on the shoulder and asked, "Gadge, you remember ole Gilbert, don't you?" Kazan shook hands and said, "Sure."

We sat in the row behind him for a few minutes while Page, lying on a sofa and covered with her fur coat, continued to murmur lines to Newman, who murmured back. The two of them occasionally seemed to be looking out directly into Tenn's face and mine, so I was not surprised when Kazan turned to say sotto voce, "Tenn, I'd be glad to have Gilbert come along in a few days to a run-through, but I don't think it's good for him to be here just now. I think it's making them nervous."

I rose at once, saying I understood, and Tenn asked me to wait for him in the lobby.

Out there I found Sydney Blackmer, who was playing Boss Finley, and Virgilia Chew, who was doing Aunt Nonny. I introduced myself, and Sydney and I got into a conversation about his former wife, Lenore Ulric, who had often been a party guest of Bill Hughes' when he and I lived in the Harvard Annex.

"She was the warmest, sweetest, most generous woman I ever knew," Blackmer said. "You always had to restrain her from giving away everything she had—even her clothes—to anyone who was in need."

We talked for about an hour. Miss Page appeared, waved at us, and disappeared. Then Paul Newman came out, asking, "Where's Gerry?"

"In the privy," said Sydney Blackmer.

"Yon privy?" Paul asked, pointing, and Blackmer said, "Yes."

I'd always wanted to meet Newman so I walked over and told him who I was. He shook hands, saying, like a small-town Southern boy, "Howdy, Gilbert," and we started to talk about the motion picture of *Cat on a Hot Tin Roof*, which he'd made the past year with Elizabeth Taylor. We were discussing the impossibility of believing that he, as Brick Pollitt, could have been supposed to sleep in the same room with Liz Taylor as Maggie, not touching her, when a pair of puppyish schoolgirls bounded into the lobby with their nauseating requests for autographs.

Paul turned with a kind of amiable resignation to serve them, and I went back to rejoin Sydney and Virgilia.

When Tenn came out a moment later the two of us went forth into the bitter cold day to seek some warming refreshment. We found a bar, and as he climbed up on the stool, rosy-faced, cheerful, Tenn took the screenplay from me, saying, "We'll drink to this, baby. It ought to be good and I'll bet it is, so you turn it right over to Audrey and she'll get going."

Before we left the bar he'd slipped a check for a hundred dollars into my hand. We moved over to the luncheon table to join the young man from *Esquire* who was interviewing him, and I felt less anxiety than I had for days about the forbidding weather outside, not to mention the frugal state of my icebox.

A few days after this he called to ask Frederick and me to a runthrough of *Sweet Bird* at the New Amsterdam roof, adding, "Last night I heard Diana Barrymore give a magnificent reading of *Suddenly Last Summer* at Herbert Machiz'. I liked her tremendously. She'll be at the rehearsal tonight and I'll introduce you. This is someone you must know."

Miss Barrymore came to the rehearsal that night with a friend of Herbert Machiz and Tenn took Frederick and me over to meet her. We talked for a minute or two, then I asked Diana if she remembered a friend of mine who'd been on the road with her in *Saint Joan*.

"Oh, yes," she said. "I loved him. Have you heard from him lately?"

I said I hadn't and she leaned confidentially over the back of her seat to tell me, "He's in the *clink*, my dear—for the second time. I'll tell you about it later."

Kazan called the rehearsal to order, dispatching a man to move through the house and dispose of everyone who was not there by invitation. I could see Margrit Wyler, who was "standing by" for Miss Page, sitting down near the front; Miss Page and Newman were taking their places onstage; but I was intent on studying Diana Barrymore, who had moved across the aisle to sit alone, hunched in her seat, and, from the moment the action started, to smoke incessantly when she was not chewing a fingernail.

At the first intermission she went down to speak to someone onstage and as she stood on tiptoe in the harsh glare of the work light I saw that the bones of her neck and spine, revealed by her low-cut black dress, were much too evident. I had now a superficial impression of a sort of urchin-girl-woman, too thin, high strung, supersensitive, and somehow touching.

When she came back up the aisle to join Frederick and me, and spied Tenn's jacket on a chair with its pint protruding from the pocket, she grasped my arm, saying with a low chuckle, "That was me up till two years ago."

We chatted a little and I told her I'd like her to see a screen play I'd just finished, so she promptly scrawled her phone number on a scrap of paper.

Two days later I called, and when I told her my name she echoed on a questioning note, "*Gilbert Maxwell?*"

I reminded her of our meeting and she was immediately gracious. She would like to see both the novel and the screenplay, so why didn't I come for cocktails on Thursday, with Freddie?

We showed up on time at her place on East 61st and I know now that neither Frederick nor I shall ever forget our first impression of Diana and her little pad.

She met us at the door, beautifully made up, wearing a silk blouse, slacks, and ballet slippers, and led us through a foyer where the walls were covered with framed pictures of John Barrymore, on past her gold-and-white combination bar and kitchen, into her small living room. The pastel silk drapes that covered one wall were billowing a little from a fan, soft music was coming from a hidden hi-fi, and the air was sweet with some expensive scent, freshly sprayed from an atomizer.

She took our coats and, as I relinquished mine, pointed at a dry-cleaner's tag attached to my suit sleeve, crying, "What on earth is this, my dear?" then, above my apologies, "Well, at least we know you're *clean.*"

She was receiving in style today, as she nearly always was, and in no time at all two guests arrived—her publicity manager, Phil Bloom, and a young man with the astrological sign of Pisces, whom she called "My Fish." The dark young man, just emerged from the bathroom, had been introduced as Bill Morrow. He was now helping her mix the drinks, and he, I was soon to learn, was to her, Too, Too, or Little Too, since she'd recently decided he was simply too far out.

Diana drank coffee while we downed her Scotch and her vodka. Everyone got a glow on; then Phil Bloom and I, having discussed Sidney Lanier as an antecedent of Tennessee's, began to toss some of the poet's great lines back and forth.

Diana turned from talking to the Fish and asked, "Sidney Lanier? Who's *he*?"

Bloom and I jumped on her with both feet and she said with her husky, almost guttural laugh, "Well, I'm so-rry, but I only read Ellery Queen and Tennessee Williams. I'm an authority on Williams, through."

The whole informal afternoon was delightful and rollicking, and I marveled at this ex-alcoholic, with her well-stocked bar, ready to mix anyone any sort of drink he wanted, sitting there sipping her coffee, bright-faced, gay, seemingly more elated than anyone else.

She was at once a lady and a hoyden—hospitable, quick-moving, rompish—but I felt most of all, beneath her obvious enjoyment of the moment—her evident earthy love of life—a person of great warmth, reaching out desperately for affection with a child's half-fearful, almost-frantic desire to please.

I was intrigued by this woman, but there was more to my whole reaction than that. It was something I could not wholly comprehend, much less find words for, and when I left her apartment that evening I knew that I'd somehow get to know her, not merely better, but well.

I called next day to thank her for the party and we conversed on a number of subjects. She was a fine cook, she said, and when I told her that I cooked too, we agreed that we must each fix a dinner for the other. We talked a great deal about Tennessee, and I suddenly knew that he'd become an obsession with her, both as a man and a playwright. She was eager to play *Sweet Bird of Youth*, either on the road or in London, and that was why she'd been chain-smoking, gnawing her nails, as she watched Geraldine Page rehearse.

She began to call me every day at six o'clock, and sometimes Frederick was ready to slaughter me, since, in that one-room apartment, he was frequently forced to hear only one side of our raucous, hilarious conversations.

One day she phoned to say she had tickets for an ANTA assembly production of Tennessee's one-act play on D. H. Lawrence—*I Rise in Flame, Cried the Phoenix*. She would like me to escort her to this morning show and to be her luncheon guest at Sardi's.

I arrived at the theater early, and so did Audrey Wood, who paused in the lobby to speak with me briefly about the screenplay, which she'd read and returned to me with suggested changes. She then asked, aware of my uncertain financial state, how I'd like to go out to California to the Huntington Hartford Foundation for writers and artists, where, housed and fed without cost, I might finish my third novel that was now half done. I assured her I'd be glad to be in any place right now where I could work, safely housed and fed, and she said, "All right, my love, I'll see what I can do."

Tennessee, who'd flown down from the *Sweet Bird* engagement in Boston, bounced in, fresh-faced, about this time, calling out, "Audrey," and then, in apparent astonishment, "Gil, what you doin' here, man?"

I said that I was waiting for Diana, and he and Audrey went on into the theater.

As I moved toward the glass front doors of the lobby a cab pulled up, and Diana in her new blue mink coat stepped out of it. When we took our seats behind a gentleman who turned to greet her effusively, Miss Barrymore was graciousness itself, but as I helped her off with the new coat she whispered, "This is one of those good friends who disappeared when I was a down-and-out drunk. I wouldn't take *anything* for his seeing me here this minute with you, wearing my mink."

I had always thought *Phoenix* away and beyond the best of Tenn's one-act plays and this production, with Alfred Ryder as Lawrence, Viveca Lindfors as his wife Frieda, and Rosemary

Harris as their friend Brett, was extremely well acted under Tom Brennan's direction.

Diana and I went off in high spirits to Sardi's where a waiter showed us to a side table. Diana picked up her menu and told me, "Lord, how wonderful it is to be able to sit down again in a good restaurant, select what you want to eat, and be able to pay for it. Order yourself another martini, dear, and anything you want on this menu, because thanks to my book, I can now afford it. Besides, this comes under the head of professional entertainment."

I'd just started on the second martini when I spied Nancy Cushman at a nearby table. I waved and she came over to speak to Diana, reminding her of the time they'd played *The Philadelphia Story* together. When I took Nancy back to her seat, she said softly, "Diana looks wonderful, Gil, and you don't know how glad I am to see her like this."

The lunch hour stretched into two. I had my food, plus a third martini, and before we rose from the table Diana and I had learned a great deal about each other.

She asked me about my family and listened while I told her more than I'd told anyone in years. It was somehow incredibly easy to talk to her, and spirited by the martinis, I literally let go.

I told her how my mother had left my father when I was eighteen months old, taking me home to Washington, Georgia, where I grew up with her, my grandparents, an old, blind, addled great-aunt and my feeble-minded uncle. I told her how my father had tried to kidnap me when I was three, and how, after that, my mother lived in blanch-faced terror of him.

I said, "When I started to school I was told never to speak to a stranger because he might be my daddy, so I used to hurry through the streets, looking neither right nor left, but straight ahead. I was afraid of everything, in my childhood. I was a natural-born extrovert-introvert, forced into scared introversion, and as a result, a misfit and a sissy. I was never happy till I grew up and went to work for my father in Atlanta, where I found out he was just as selfish and self-centered as my mother had said he was. That did something to me, I don't know what, but anyway I came home and did all the things at school I'd always longed to do. I went out for football, dated girls, and sailed through my last year of high school, suddenly popular, completely assured of my own attractions for the first time in my whole life. I turned into an out-and-out extrovert—loving it, and almost stopped being scared. Anyhow, I became as little afraid as any human being with such a background ever can be."

Diana had listened to my long harangue with interest, now and again nodding, "Oh, yes, I understand that," and as I finished she said, "Now I know why I felt drawn to you when we met. How could I help being, when so much that happened to you, happened in different ways, to me, too. Only—you never became alcoholic."

I asked, "Is it true, as you said in your book, there was just nobody when you were down and out?"

She said, "Well, yes, almost. There was always my one friend, Bob Applewhite, who never left me; then later, when things were really terrible, Violla Rubber, my present manager, came along to do something for me."

She spoke then of her mother, Blanche Oelrichs, the poetess who called herself Michael Strange, of John Barrymore, Ethel, and Lionel, and I learned she was fond of her aunt.

She said, "I admire Aunt Ethel because she's always been a good mother. She hasn't done anything on the screen for a long time, and I haven't heard from her recently, but I hope she's all right, Aunt Ethel. I do hope she is."

We left the restaurant arm in arm and took a taxi uptown, sitting close together, still talking of many things, but more lightly, laughing, enjoying each other's company. I left her at her door and took the taxi on up to West 71st Street.

When I got there I had an impulse to call her. I did, and we went on talking over the phone, about Tennessee and ourselves.

There was a glow all through me as I hung up the receiver, and it was not all due to martinis. I had begun to feel toward this girl a closeness which, after this luncheon, I clearly understood.

Like Tennessee, we had grown up surrounded by love and hate, each of us, in different ways, with no father. There was a bond between us—a thing Tenn must have sensed when he had told me with quiet conviction that I must know Diana.

The three of us were to become close to each other now—to form a trio dubbed by Diana, The Living Playwright, The Living Actress, The Living Poet.

I never knew why she thought of us and herself in this way; I only know that the terms were affectionate, that they were destined to stick, and that they meant something special to her.

9

When "Sweet Bird" returned to town in early March, Tenn informed me at lunch at Jim Downey's that Geraldine Page was giving a great performance as Ariadne Del Lago.

Frank Merlo phoned on March 8 to tell me that Tenn's opening-night list of guests was unusually large. He said, "I'm having to put you and Frederick in the first row mezzanine. I hope you won't mind that you're not in the orchestra."

I said that we'd rather be in the mezzanine and he sighed in weary relief as he hung up.

I sighed in relief on the play's opening day when a check for a co-signed loan from the Bankers Trust arrived in the morning mail. Frederick was back in a bookstore, but I'd had no free-lance work since January, so the loan was vitally important.

Neither Frederick nor I had ever been to a Williams opening on Broadway and we were immensely excited, approaching the theater, as we glimpsed Tenn and Frank crossing the street, and yelled to them.

As a champion and devotee of Margrit Wyler's I was determined to be unimpressed by Miss Page even if she made her entrance bare-backed on a white horse with her hair in flames, but it was plain from the start that she was playing with volcanic power. *Sweet Bird* had been considerably stylized by Elia Kazan, but Sydney Blackmer brought a sinister reality to the bigoted tyrant, Boss Finley, and Paul Newman was ingenious, charming, and pathetic as Chance Wayne, the young prodigal who, defying his fate for love of Boss's daughter, refused to be scared out of town by the old man and his loutish son.

When Miss Page as Ariadne Del Lago received the news via long distance from a Hollywood columnist of her unsuspected triumph in her latest film, she stalked to the front of the stage, faced the audience, and cried, "My picture has broken all box-office records."

The house went instantly wild—and I was one of those hundreds who stood up, beating my hands together, shouting bravos.

At the end of the play, Newman, having refused the actress's pleas to skip town with her even though the younger Finley and a doctor were waiting to castrate him, stepped through the curtains and said, straight to the audience:

I don't ask for your pity, but just for your understanding—not even that—no. Just for recognition of me in you, and the enemy, time, in us all.

He stepped back through the curtains and closed them—and once again a storm shook the Martin Beck. I gave up trying to count the curtain calls and Frederick and I left the theater keyed high with the realization that Tenn and Elia Kazan had stupendously scored once more. It was a great night for everyone, for Cheryl Crawford as *Sweet Bird's* producer, for Audrey Wood, for Jo Mielziner, the scene designer, and all the cast.

Next day the gentlemen of the fourth estate raised their collective voices in a paean comparable to their chorused acclaim of *Cat on a Hot Tin Roof*—forgiving America's leading playwright for *Orpheus Descending*, forgetting their less-than-felicitous-reception of that ill-fated drama.

Tenn left town for Key West after the opening, so he was not present for Diana Barrymore's New Haven tryout of *Suddenly Last Summer*. She asked Frederick and me for the second night, and we three made a tour of the Yale campus in the afternoon, guided by my old friend Dean Loomis Havemeyer, whom I hadn't seen for a decade.

Jack Barefield arrived around six and Diana assembled a dinner party which included an Italian sculptress and an actress, Alice Nunn, who, working once as a waitress near a shabby hotel where Diana was on her uppers, had sent up trays of food to sustain a fellow actress.

In the restaurant Diana sat beside me and whispered, "Order the best now, love. This is my party and I've got money to pay for it."

The play was directed by Herbert Machiz, with Cathleen Nesbitt turning in a fine performance as Mrs. Venable, but my attention was fixed from the start on Diana as the mentally disturbed Catherine Holly.

As she made her first entrance in white, looking twenty-five and no older, the audience broke into applause for this girl who had come back to them from a world of the living dead. She proceeded to astound them then with a dynamic, mad, scared, and terrifying inner emotion as she built her performance. The Barrymore talent was there in this thing she projected, as well as in the powerful, husky voice, but I was most impressed by her mobile hands that were not the big hands of her father, but rather the small poet's hands which her mother, Michael Strange, had bequeathed her.

The theater was not filled on this cold night in New Haven, but those who were there told her with loud applause, as she took her bows, of their own personal pride in her triumph over a family weakness which once had all but destroyed her.

Backstage, Barefield introduced me to Miss Violla Rubber, Miss

Barrymore's manager. There was a full moment's pause before the lady accepted my proffered hand, and I got the distinct impression that I, as a new friend of Diana's, was being weighed and found wanting. I had no time to brood upon this impression, however, for Diana appeared on cue, her own hand gaily outstretched, crying, "Come with me, Gil. You have to meet Miss Nesbitt."

Cathleen Nesbitt was charming and I liked the camaraderie and mutual respect that seemed to exist between the older actress and the younger.

Later as we all parted outside in the cold, Diana gave me a great hug, kissed me, and told me, "I'm going to miss you on the road, love, but I'll be calling you around six, so please be home." I had no idea that she meant this, but as the weeks passed the calls came, from Detroit, and from Chicago where Tenn saw the play and praised her performance. In Chicago, stricken with laryngitis, she held a press conference and that night, before the curtain, appeared voiceless but plainly sober to face her audience.

Chicago's critics, headed by Claudia Cassidy, rewarded her with unstinting praise for her first performance, assuring her run in Chicago.

But she was always lonely in Chicago, and once, calling, she asked me, "What's happening there right now, Gil?"

I said, "Oh, the usual thing. Dinner's on the stove. Frederick's out in the kitchen mixing rum and fruit juice, and both Richards should be here soon."

She said in sadness, "Oh, God, how I envy you all. I wish I could be there, or else that someone I love was here with me."

The tour was successful; she was earning good money and reading the sort of notices she'd always hoped for, but it was not small circle of loved and loving friends around her.

After her return in the spring she told me one day, "It's disgraceful that a man of your talents shouldn't be with a publishing house. I think I can do something."

She called the World Publishing Company in Cleveland and talked to her friend William Buckley. Then she phoned back to say I'd get a call from William Targ, editor in chief of the New

York office, whereupon I thanked her and said, surprised, that I'd met Bill Targ in Miami.

Bill called me up and when we talked in his office he said, "Gil, for heaven's sake, you didn't have to come to me through Miss Barrymore. Why didn't you let me know you were back in town?"

I said that I'd thought he was out in Cleveland, and he assured me I'd be getting some work from World.

I went there in late May for three weeks to replace an editor who was sick. Bill Targ, and Jerome Fried, the managing editor, liked some things that I did, so from that time on Fried occasionally called me for an assignment.

Meanwhile, Frederick had been sent by an agency to another publishing house where I had connections. I called a woman editor there whom I'd known for years. She spoke to the editor who was hiring an assistant and the man called me at World to say that he was trying to decide between Frederick and another young fellow. I assured him briskly of Fred's capabilities and he said, "Then he's my boy, I think."

And so once more—Diana having helped me, I having been able to say a good word for Frederick—the household in West 71st became temporarily solvent.

While I was still at World, Tenn returned to town and asked me to a Saturday matinee of *The Nervous Set*. When we went out for a wee drop at intermission I walked up to the bar, head high, announcing, "Now, I'm going to buy you a drink, my friend."

T.W., mounting the bar stool, almost fell off. He said, "Oh God, the millennium's here. Bartender, this way, quick."

In speaking of the relationship between Diana and Tennessee, I must make it clear that her absorption in the playwright and his plays was the all-important, ruling force of her life in 1959. She had stopped drinking in order to play *Streetcar* well; she had scored the past year on the road in *Cat*; she had just returned from a triumph in *Suddenly Last Summer*; and now she was out to move heaven and earth to play *Sweet Bird* in London. But this was not all by any means, since she had for the man, as well as the playwright, an idolatrous love that proved to be little short of traumatic.

The truth of all this was brought forcibly home to me when she said one day on the phone, "I've been unfair to you, Gil, and now that I've come to love you just for yourself, I'm so ashamed of what I've done, I must get it off my conscience. Did you know— did you actually realize I was using you for weeks after we met, merely to get closer to Williams?"

I said, "Sure, I knew that."

She gasped. "You *did*—and you didn't mind?"

"Of course not," I told her. "What difference could it make, now that I know you sincerely care about me? After all, if it hadn't been for Tenn, I'd have never met you. And, if you hadn't been so mad about him, you'd never have seen enough of me to get to know me well—so if we're going to be technical, you could say I was using Tenn to get to you. Everyone uses everyone else—you know that."

She agreed that this was true, but she was by no means eased of conscience about her own wiles. She had contempt for people who used other people to get ahead, and I have heard her rage against a young actor whom she suspected of sleeping around in order to get to Hollywood. She herself had never done such a thing and she was outraged to think that anyone she was fond of could be so morally callous.

There were times too when she raved against the whole Royal Family, but she had enormous respect for their name in the theater. And she was also more attached to the Barrymores than she cared to admit, as I found out on June 13 when Ethel Barrymore died in Hollywood.

I called to offer my sympathy, to ask if she'd be flying out to the funeral, and to say that I'd thought perhaps she'd want to forego the party Tenn and I were giving at my place that night.

She said, "Well—I don't know, Gil. Some of my friends think I ought to fly out, but I'm undecided. I hate the thought of facing those photographers and cameramen after all my unhappiness out there—and as for the party, I think I'd like to come, if you think it would look all right."

I said, "Of course, no one will misunderstand," and she told me, "You see, the main thing Aunt Ethel's death means to me is the end of a dynasty—and I can't feel too bad about her. She was old and sick, so I like to think, if there is a heaven, she's up there right this minute with Daddy and Lionel, having a marvelous reunion. Yes, love, I'll come to the party. I'd much rather be with all of you there than here at home by myself."

Her speech was significant—but not nearly so telling as the events which ensued that night and in the small hours near morning.

I'd planned a little gathering, mainly so that Claire Luce, the actress (not the playwright-ambassadress), might have an evening with a certain old-time director friend of hers. That's what I'd planned—but I began to realize as Frederick and I dashed about, redding-up the apartment, that our guest list had gradually grown to a dozen and a half. There were the two Richards, a painter who played an old instrument and sang folk songs, a young man from Georgia who fancied himself (and was, to some extent) a raconteur, Miss Luce, Tennessee, Frederick, and me to start with.

Then Diana arrived, hurrying upstairs with two bottles of Scotch. She wore a white, sleeveless dress and a short haircut, and a deep tan, head to toe, after her recent stay in the Virgin Islands.

She'd scarcely sat down before the bell rang again. Frederick answered the door; two women stepped in, one dressed in black, both wearing Hallowe'en masks, and Tennessee yelled, "It's Anna. Oh, I'm so glad."

It was indeed Anna—last name, Magnani—with her secretary-interpreter Mrs. Donald Cook, Tenn having completely surprised me.

The party began to swing and I wandered dazed by stardust from group to group as the Georgia raconteur held forth, followed by the painter-singer who gave us "Bar'br'y Allen" and "Green Sleeves." Miss Luce sat and sketched Miss Magnani; there was a toast to Ethel Barrymore; and then everything began to get fuzzy to me, though I do remember sitting on the floor with my head in Anna's lap while she stroked my hair and plaintively crooned, "Come with me to Italy, Oh, come with me to Italy."

It seems I was very sad; and Anna, seeing me so, was filled with compassion.

Diana, being cold sober, went home ahead of anyone. After a while the phone rang and I faintly heard Frederick, far off, saying, "Oh, Gilbert *can't* come, Diana. He'd never make it."

She had grown frightened alone, and wanted me with her, but I was sound asleep, slumped in a chair. Tenn and Richard Two went over instead, to find her almost hysterical.

When I woke next morning, I saw Richard One curled up on the long green sofa. The phone began to ring, a couple of the guests returned for Bloody Marys—and when I phoned Diana after brunch she said it would be all right if the two Richards and I came over.

We were all rather high, and I was not too shocked when she showed me what appeared to be a black bruise that covered her whole right thigh, knee to hip. She said that it was no bruise, it was a burn. She'd taken a couple of pills to make her sleep, had awakened hungry, got up and gone to the kitchen to fix herself some eggs. She'd come to, lying on the floor, half in the upturned frying pan, half in the spilled hot butter she'd placed in the pan before she fainted.

Someone rang up on the phone and she screamed at him, "You're never to call me again, do you understand? All that part of my life's behind me now, you bastard."

She was shaking and tense, and I asked before I could stop myself, "Have you been drinking, Diana?"

Instantly then she turned into a kind of virago as she screamed to the two Richards, "How *dare* he suggest such a thing and pretend to be my friend? Get him out. *Now!*"

Before we knew it, she'd flung open the front door and literally shoved us out. I was flabbergasted, and remorseful all the way home in a taxi. I called her as soon as I got in, and we both wept, apologizing.

She told me then all in a rush that she'd been in such a state the night before, she hadn't realized when Tenn suggested she take a pill that she'd taken one earlier. She had no memory of anything until she woke, sprawled in the grease, and the most frightening

thing was that when she had dragged herself back to h
she'd seen a plate of scrambled eggs on the bedside table.

She wept, ashamed of having ordered me out of her pad, saying she could understand how I must have thought from her actions that she was tight, but that she could not bear my suggesting she'd touched alcohol—much less my *believing* she might have.

When her doctor looked at her, he told her manager the burn was so bad she might possibly lose her leg. He began to use an iodine spray, however, and Diana was soon up and about, crossing the street, bandaged, to dine with Tenn at the Colony, and later, rehearsing *Streetcar* for a week's engagement in Pennsylvania.

Neither she nor anyone else ever knew why she became hysterical after going home from my party, but I have always felt her reaction was rooted in one of two things: she was either more shaken than she knew by Ethel's death, or more disturbed than she'd realized by the choice she had to make between flying out to the funeral and remaining at home.

Diana was a person of extremes within whose tortured mind and spirit such forces as fierce resentment, sick remorse, compassion, hate, and love were often rampant.

George Keathley was to direct her in *Streetcar* and the readings were held at her apartment. She lay on her bed with a canopy over her because she could not at first bear even a sheet to touch the iodine-sprayed burn, and read with the actors. She liked the looks of Richard Two, so, thinking that he might be right for the small part of the newsboy whom Blanche Dubois desires, she had him read, in the bedroom, for Keathley and Violla Rubber.

Unhappily, however, neither Miss Rubber nor George was sufficiently impressed with Dick's approach to the role, so nothing came of that venture.

She was up, bandaged, for the first rehearsals, and though I shuddered for her in the violent scenes where Stanley Kowalski throws Blanche about, she told me that the young man playing the bumptious Pole had managed to fake it so well he hadn't hurt her.

The state of her mind and nervous system was another thing, and I did not like the high-strung sound of her voice when she called me from the small Pennsylvania town where she would appear. I knew that she was constantly on the phone to New York for she told me one day, having called Bob Applewhite earlier, "I told Apple, 'This is a party line,' and Apple said, 'Not anymore it isn't.'"

She was desperately worried, nerve-wracked, terrified of being alone—because she was scared, first of all, that she might not be able to give the performance of her life for Tennessee Williams, and second, that something would happen to prevent his coming up for her opening.

He was busy, working on both *Period of Adjustment* and *Night of the Iguana*, but I was reasonably sure that nothing would keep him from going to see her, and nothing did.

He, Frederick, and I were driven up by Violla Rubber's male secretary and when we got there Vi was waiting to greet us at a small motel near the theater.

She took me aside at once to tell me, "It's because of you he's here. I know that and I'm grateful."

I said, "That's not true, Vi. He'd have come without me," but she insisted, "No, he's been asked before when he didn't show up. You brought him, and I want you to know the drinks and the dinner are on me tonight. You must see he doesn't pay for anything."

I shrugged and agreed. It was untrue that Tenn wouldn't have come without me, but there was no use trying to convince Vi or Diana of that fact. I'd long since learned, the impetuous, extravagant-minded people of the theater believe or disbelieve what they wish to, regardless of logic or reason, and this was just one more minor example of a sometimes vexing phenomenon.

Our party had seats down front in the orchestra. The house was hushed awaiting Diana's entrance, and when she appeared I heard a chorus of stifled gasps all around me, "Oh, Lord, look at her. She's so *thin*."

This was an understatement and it seemed to me I could see her white-faced tension even under her recent tan and the makeup, but none of that mattered. On this night she gave one of the most astounding performances of Blanche Dubois I'd ever seen. She did not attempt a heavy Southern accent, her voice at times seemed near to breaking with exhaustion, yet Blanche emerged three-dimensional, pathetic, brave—in the final scenes, unmistakably mad—and Diana took bow after bow, to bravos.

Vi Rubber was waiting at the dressing-room door when Tenn, Frederick, and I got there, and she said to me, "You go in first, Gil."

I stepped in, closing the door, trying to hide the shock I felt at the sight of Diana. She stood there drenched in sweat, shaking, crying, cursing the electricians for a light that hadn't gone on, and when I took her in my arms I felt her heart pounding too hard, too fast. She was truly not much more than skin and bones and as she clung to me, weeping hysterically, I tried to tell her how wonderful she had been, how much everyone had loved her. I stepped back and opened the door and Tennessee came in.

He put his arms tight around her and told her, "My darling, you were tremendous. You have a great voice and you are a Barrymore."

She seemed to relax then, but she could not quite stop crying.

We went out to a restaurant for supper, and after a great deal of persuasion from us all, Diana ordered a steak.

When George Keathley came in, he sat down beside me, and I told him, "That was marvelous direction, George. I saw all your little special touches—there were some things I've never seen in Streetcar before," and he thanked me. Then he looked at Diana and said, "Thank God, she's eating. I don't know when she's had an actual meal. Lord, Gilbert, you can't imagine what I've been through, night after night spooning into this girl's mouth the little food I could get her to swallow."

We both looked at her cutting the steak, talking nineteen to the dozen, her face shining bright, and I said, "I know. But whatever she and you have been through has been worth it. He has seen her in Streetcar—and he has told her the things she's been literally dying to hear."

She went on to play engagements in other towns, and when Vi

and I met her at the airport on her return, she ran toward us across the field, wearing slacks and ballet slippers, high-spirited, radiant, apparently in love with life. She was still quite thin, but she told me she'd eaten a big lunch on the plane and was feeling unusually well.

Just after her return she called to say one day that Tennessee was taking her up to see his sister. He had promised to take me sometime, and when I reminded him of this he asked me to go along with them.

The limousine called for Diana and me at her place and I remember, as we drove over to pick up Tenn, how lovely she looked, wearing a severe black dress and no make-up except lipstick. On the way upstate to Stony Lodge we talked of many things, including my screenplay in which Bette Davis was still interested. Audrey Wood had been unsuccessful in selling it, but two independent would-be producers, a man and a woman, had been working on its sale, with Audrey and MCA still in control, and there now seemed a possibility of its being bought before Christmas.

Diana and Tenn both gave me some strong advice as to the investment of the money which hadn't yet appeared, and after exhausting this subject, we spoke of Richard Two. He'd been out of work for some time. Diana, upset about not being able to take him on the road, had asked me if I thought it would be all right for her to give him a little consolation present of a hundred dollars. I'd advised her to give him fifty, since he was notoriously open-handed with excess cash in his pocket, and today we were laughing about the fact that her check, which I'd cashed at my bank, had bounced—she being, as she often was, temporarily overdrawn.

We were not laughing, however, about the fact that I hadn't spoken to Richard Two for several weeks because of an unnecessarily cruel thing he'd said to me in a room full of friends and when Tenn, ever forgiving, said, "Oh, Gil, you know he's miserable not being up there with your group in the evenings; call him up, man, and let him come home again," Diana sat erect to say flatly, "Absolutely not, Tennessee. I know all about this and Gil mustn't see him."

She was always like that. She would say, "If you are my friend, I love you, and if somebody has hurt you, he has hurt me, too, so I won't see that person myself."

We drove on, talking of lighter matters until we came to the great gates of Stony Lodge. The road to the main buildings wound through wooded paths past a swimming pool and tennis courts, and when we came to the cottage where Rose lived, Tenn said, "Gil, let me go in with Diana. We'll be out soon."

I waited with the chauffeur, noting the quiet charm of the place and three attractive young women playing cards on the terrace. After a while Tenn and Diana came out with Rose and I had a swift impression of a small woman wearing a varicolored bright cloak with a hood, thrown back. As I came up to shake hands with her I saw that she had a heart-shaped, perfect face, unbelievably clear, silver-gray eyes, and brown hair touched with gray which she wore rather short, smoothed back from her forehead over her small ears.

She greeted me warmly and when we were in the limousine with me on the front seat, I turned to ask Rose what she felt like having for lunch. She said, "Some rice," and smiled at me as she lighted a cigarette.

We drove to a terraced restaurant at Tappan Hill where we sat at a table beside some great windows that gave on a view of woods and hills. Diana and Rose had Coca-Colas while Tenn and I drank martinis, and we talked happily together. Rose said that she didn't remember having seen John Barrymore on the screen, but when I asked if she'd seen any plays of Tenn's she said tersely, "Yes, one. *The Rose Tattoo*. Very poor."

Tenn choked on his drink as he set it down, remarking, "Very astute critic," and the meal progressed.

After lunch Diana and Rose retired to the ladies' room, Tenn and I to the gents' and I said to him as we entered, "She's lovely, but I know what you mean now. I don't see how you've borne it."

He said, "Well, after thirty years, you learn to bear it. You have to."

He had to make a phone call to Carson McCullers, whom we planned to call on at Nyack, so Diana and Rose and I took a walk in the garden.

I asked, "What is this flower, Rose?" and she said, "I don't know. Delphinium, I think—and of course, that red thing is salvia."

I asked her then what life had been like in the rectories with her grandparents and she said, "Well, I always enjoyed it, but you see, Tom was with my grandparents so much more than I ever was."

I checked with Tenn on this later, and he said that her memory was correct.

When we reached Carson's old white Victorian house the maid let us in and we found her mistress waiting for us in a big chair by the fireplace. She was wearing a white dress and the sudden smile that illumined her face as we entered was at once impish, welcoming, and joyous. It was evident, even as we seated ourselves— Tenn on the sofa with me, Rose on a couch next to the wall, Diana in a big chair facing the room—that Carson was extremely happy to see Tennessee.

She said, "I'm drinking lemonade for the moment, but you all must have a highball."

The maid brought drinks for Tenn and me, Cokes for Rose and Diana, and we settled down to talk.

Tenn told Carson that the house looked lovely and when she said, "Yes, but I must have these floors scraped and repainted," he insisted the floors didn't need it.

He and Carson began to talk about a prospective stage version of Carson's *Ballad of the Sad Café*, for which she hoped to get Anna Magnani, and Tenn suggested she autograph a copy of the book for Anna.

The maid brought the book. There was a small silence as Carson sat with poised pen; then she looked at Tenn and asked, "How do you spell ballad?"

Tennessee, so help me God, replied slowly, "B-a-l-l-e-d." I looked at Rose, who gave me a wink through her cigarette smoke, then at

Diana, who was sitting quite still with her mouth slightly open, and the room rocked with laughter.

I remember telling Carson a little later that my favorite short story of hers was "The Jockey." I said that I thought it an exquisite, subtle piece of work, and asked, "How on earth did you get the idea for that story?"

Carson looked at me poker-faced for a moment before she answered all in one flat breath, "Well, I was in Saratoga," and that was that. When we told her that I seemed to be on the verge of selling my screenplay, she said at once, "Come and kiss me," which I did.

After a moment she asked, "Gilbert, honey, do you like tomatoes?" I said that I loved them and could never get any good ones in New York, so she told me, "Then go out back in the garden and pick what's there. I'd love you to have them."

I turned to ask Diana if she'd like to help me, whereupon she leaped from her chair with alacrity, shouting a fervent "Yes."

Outside I realized that she had been sitting there on the edge of her seat, cold sober, not only shy of Miss McCullers, whose work she'd had to confess she hadn't read, but also aware of tensions which I hadn't felt, for she said now, dashing from bush to bush, picking, "Oh, God, I wish there were a few more ripe tomatoes so we wouldn't have to go right back."

She said this with a laugh, and I took the remark at its face value, but she'd meant it seriously—for more disturbing reasons than I recognized, as I was soon to learn.

Tenn and I were on our third drink when Rose suddenly stood up and announced, "Well, Tom, it's time for me to get back for supper," so we took our leave, over Carson's hospitable urgings to stay for dinner with her.

On the way back to the lodge Rose and Tenn talked of several things; then, she said softly, "Tom, remember me to Colonel Lindbergh when you see him again."

I caught my breath, but Diana said quickly, "Oh, that's right, of course. Lindbergh used to live around here."

Rose said her quiet good-by to us at the entrance to the terrace surrounding her cottage, and Tenn took her arm to walk with her to the door. He had not reached it before Diana broke down completely. She wept with her face in her hands, her whole body shaking, and I could not, to save my life, think of anything to say to her. She was still crying when Tenn got back to the car and we rode in silence, neither he nor I able to utter a word until her sobs ended and she sat back, fumbling for a cigarette.

We did not speak of Rose all the long way back to New York. Tenn asked us up for a drink at his place and when we reached the living room he said, sinking onto the sofa, "Diana, darling, would you make us a cocktail? Something special, with a little absinthe I have in there."

Diana went into the kitchen and as she busied herself, Tenn rose and walked toward the hi-fi. He said absently, "Let's hear *Butterfly*," and by the time Diana returned with the cocktails, "Un Bel Dì" was blasting out over the peaceful neighborhood at the height of the hi-fi's volume.

Tenn listened a moment. Then he said, "No, that's not the 'Un Bel Dì' I wanted," and got up and changed the record. He did not turn down the volume and we sat there with the sound blaring loud enough to fill Carnegie Hall.

Finally, after Diana had made us a second drink he rose to turn it lower, but when I said quietly, "Tenn, I must go now, I have an appointment with Jack Barefield," he whirled upon me, crying "You're not going anywhere. Call and break that date with Jack. You cannot leave me."

There was no arguing with the tone of that voice so I went to the telephone. When I came back and sat down in a chair opposite him and Diana on the sofa, there was a second's silence. And then he unloosed a torrent of articulate anguish which I cannot and will not try to recapture. I remember fragments of his speech, such as, "She was the best of us all, do you understand? More beautiful, more intelligent, sweeter and warmer than anyone. Not one of us was fit to stoop and tie her shoes. . . . The torments this girl has endured are not to be mentioned; yet she stands there before you, triumphant, with her head up and her shoulders back and looks you in the face and silently tells you, this brave little

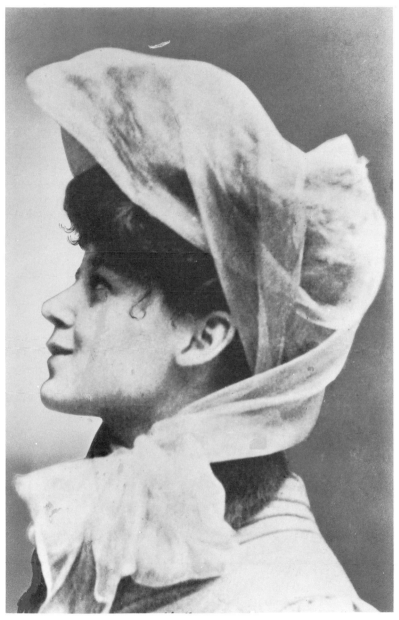

Miss Edwina at about the time she met Cornelius: from the triple frame on Tennessee's dresser

Tom at the age of two with his father

Rose and Tom, Columbus, Mississippi

Grandfather and Tom at 53 Arundel Place, 1944

Tennessee, Fred Melton, Donald Windham, and friend

Tennessee and Donald Windham, 1944, at the time of *You Touched Me*

Tennessee in 1945, just after *The Glass Menagerie* opened (Tayloe Gwathmey)

Tennessee and Frank in Key West

First anniversary celebration for *A Streetcar Named Desire* (Friedman Engeler)

Vivien Leigh, Tennessee, and Elia Kazan

Diana Barrymore

Tennessee and Gilbert Maxwell,
1945 (Tayloe Gwathmey)

Tennessee and Gilbert Maxwell, 1945 (Tayloe Gwathmey)

John Huston and Tennessee in Mexico during the filming of *The Night of the Iguana*, 1963

creature, 'Look at me. Somehow, I came through, I am here.
. . .' "

It seems to me almost a sacrilege even to try to reconstruct this
speech which affected me more deeply than anything he has put
on paper; and I know of no way to describe what I felt then and
feel now, except to say that I had never heard such agonies of love,
despair, and regret as came from the soul of this man while "Un
Bel Dì" soared above us, there in the Sunday dusk. I sat numbed
as his voice died out—and again Diana turned her head, weeping
with her face pressed into the back of the sofa.

After a while Tennessee grew reasonably calm and stood up and
said, "Now, I'll call Anna. We'll go over there."

Magnani said that we were to come right over, so we took a taxi
to the Hampshire House. Tenn and Diana were both calmed
down by this time, and when Anna, arms outstretched to greet us,
ushered us into her living room where Mrs. Cook also waited, I
breathed more easily. Anna was everywhere, bouncing about the
room, dispatching Mrs. Cook for drinks—bending over to clasp
her hands between her knees, rising to point at me and crying with
her black eyes dancing, "Oh, you, *bello, bello.*"

Tennessee shouted, "She's saying, 'You're beautiful,' Gil," and
Anna still dancing cried again, "Oh, I love to look at you today.
You look like a leetle cat, *just* like a leetle cat."

I shook with laughter as I told her, "It's just a little sun tan,
Anna, plus some sleep, and the fact that I'm sober."

Tennessee translated quickly and Anna said that I must never,
never be drunk again. Then she jumped up on the sofa on her
knees, took Diana's thin arms in her hands and told her, "Oh,
Diana, my darling, *no.* You cannot do this, you know. For the
stage—for romance—you mus' not be like this."

Diana said, "Oh, I know, Anna. You mean I'm not sexy this
way," and the party began to swing.

Anna was making *The Fugitive Kind* with Brando and she
besought Tennessee to come up next day to watch them work,
telling him, "I need you. I go home and make no good picture, I
don' care, but for you I must make art. You come tomorrow,
Tennessee. Do not desert me." Her hair was in curlers and she

ripped them out, letting them fall, telling him, "Now I am woman again, now I kees you"—and she did.

It was lovely being with Anna, and as we went on to an Italian restaurant for dinner the warmth of the woman stayed with us. It was late when we left the restaurant, coming out into the deserted stillness of Fifth Avenue. I said good night there to Tenn and Diana, but as I walked toward the subway in Radio City, I felt all at once flatly exhausted. The day had been hilarious, delightful, unbearably shattering and poignant by turns—and I wanted to go home and sleep.

I had met Rose Williams at last—and now I knew more about Tennessee than I'd known before—far more than I understood fully or could ever put into words.

Next day, Diana called me. She said, "You were extraordinary yesterday. You had a lot to drink and never showed it. You were so calm, all the way. I don't see how you did it."

I said, "I don't either, but sometimes I am like that. It wasn't that I didn't feel everything—but somehow for once I knew I must not show what I felt."

Diana said, "I know, I was ashamed of myself—but, you see, I've just come back from doing *Streetcar* and so much of the play kept coming back to me. It was all just too much."

Shortly after this she went with Tenn and Marion Vaccaro to Havana.

When she and Tenn returned to New York she was still far too thin. It was after this trip that Tenn told me, "One day at the hotel pool she swam once across and when I reached her she asked me to feel her heart. I did and it was almost unbelievable. I don't like to feel anyone's heart, even my own, and the way hers was pounding scared me nearly to death."

The columnists were having a field day after this trip. The papers had been filled with gossip items about these two, and now one reporter reached a new low, I thought, brashly crowing, "Tennessee's back and Diana's got him."

She had him, all right—but in no way anyone who was not close to this pair could have understood. She had him in the sense that he was feeling for her, as he has felt for other friends, compassion, kindness, heart-warmth, and understanding.

He was also working now on a play especially for her, having long since decided she would never be right for the heroine in *Sweet Bird of Youth*.

Diana went again to the Virgin Islands in September where she visited wealthy friends. Richard One was there, working now in a radio station, and I had a card from her which is one of the few mementos that remain. It was postmarked Charlotte Amalie. There was a picture of Trunk Bay and the beach, and the card said:

Dear Love, it is really this color. I miss you when I look at all this beauty. It should be seen with a poet. Richard and I to the beach today. Will write. Love, Diana.

She returned from the Islands looking well. Early in October, having business in her neighborhood, I stopped by to see her. Her apartment door was slightly open and when I knocked she sang out, "Come in, love."

I left my overcoat in the foyer; then, as I stepped into the living room, she danced out of the bedroom wearing nothing but a pair of boys' jockey shorts, and we both yelled as I hugged her and told her, "You wanted me to see what you looked like, all over, didn't you?"

She cried, "Yes," and ran back into the bedroom to dress.

Her nude body, unscarred from the burn, was the body of a girl, and now that she'd gained some weight she looked no more than thirty.

After a brief visit, I rose to leave, and as I pulled on the camel's-hair coat I'd left in the foyer, she helped me into it, saying as she fussed with the collar, "I never saw *this* before. You look so nice—as if you'd just come in from the country—but then, you always wear everything with an air, love."

It was all nonsense but as I kissed her good-by I thought how rare a creature she was—always, with a warm word of flattery, making a man feel as if he were a special someone.

I was often at her apartment in the late afternoons, enjoying good talk with the gay, delightful people who seemed always to be there. At these little gatherings you might find, beside Apple, the Fish, and Too, Too, such people as Rex O'Malley, Fioria, the Italian sculptress, beautiful Virginia Gilmore, and a handsome actress, Anne Francine, who was one of Diana's oldest friends.

Diana came to dinner once with Frederick and me, bringing Too, Too and Apple to meet Oleda Schrotty, an old friend of mine who was national drama director of the Girl Scouts, and afterward we all played the truth game, asking and answering intimate personal questions, some of which, in Di's case, had to do with her early life. I knew already how she'd felt about the separation of Michael Strange and John Barrymore when she was growing up, lonely and rejected, knowing that Michael preferred her half-brother, Robin Thomas, to herself, longing always to know her father.

Oleda, however, who never had read her book nor heard her speak of these things, called me next day and told me, "Gilbert, Diana is the saddest person I ever met. This girl has never had any love."

Tennessee, having retired to Key West, was absent from these autumnal gatherings, and I regretted his absence on a night when a party of us went to Jersey to see Claire Luce in *Garden District*. Diana came to dinner with a fearful migraine headache and before we left the apartment she asked me to massage her neck and back as I often did when she was enduring this special torment.

George Keathley had directed Miss Luce in *Portrait of a Madonna* and *Suddenly Last Summer*, in which this immensely gifted actress, after one week's rehearsal, was playing Mrs. Venable. The part of the madwoman in *Madonna* alone is a challenge to any actress, and Diana and I, astounded by Claire in this one-act, were further impressed when she proceeded to present old Mrs. Venable with equal authority.

I knew that Claire was as anxious as Diana was to do *Sweet Bird* on tour, even perhaps in London, so when I said, "I'd give anything if Tennessee were here to see her tonight," I was not surprised at Diana's fervently breathing, "Well, he's not, thank God."

Afterward, backstage, she embraced Claire, telling her sincerely how superb she'd been, but as we drove back to town she told me that her migraine headache was so bad that she could not join the rest of us at the little bar near Luce's place for a nightcap. She wanted *Sweet Bird*, and the mere thought of the role of Ariadne's going to another actress was not to be borne.

When Tennessee returned to town, Violla Rubber arranged to have her client read the part for him, Cheryl Crawford, and Audrey Wood. Diana was fearfully nervous the day before the audition, and, calling to tell me she had been talking to Audrey, she said, "I wonder if you see Audrey Wood as I do, Gil. On the one hand there's the cold, efficient businesswoman, but on the other there's a person of such great compassion I can hardly believe it. I told her I was so scared I didn't see how I could go through with this thing, and she said, 'Well, darling, just remember, God will be there—and I'll be there.' "

When it was over she called to tell me she'd read, lying down on the floor of the stage, for Ariadne's first-act scene in bed, and that she had been cued by the play's stage manager. She was not at all sure how she had done—but I was when Tenn told me that no one had been convinced she was right for the part. He said, "I'm writing a play for her, though, so I don't think she should be too disappointed."

The whole of this autumn was fantastically hectic. Tenn was working as usual on several projects. Each day, when I returned from Altman's, one of my would-be independent producers called to say we were on the verge of selling my screenplay, and I was also busy, evenings, editing another writer's forthcoming novel for World.

In late October I went with Frederick to the Brooklyn Academy of Music to see Bette Davis with Gary Merrill in *An Evening with Carl Sandburg*. Afterward I went back to the star's dressing room, where I found her with Guthrie McClintic, Lillian Gish, Blanche Yurka, and other visitors. When I told her who I was, she reached out both hands to me, crying, "Oh, I am so glad to see you," and asked me to wait for a moment.

The crowd quickly thinned out; she closed the dressing-room door to chat with McClintic, Miss Yurka, Miss Gish, and me, and, holding up a bottle of Scotch against the dressing shelf light, said, "Yes, there's enough. Gil, can you take a drink from a paper cup?"

I said that I could, and when her other guests refused, accepted her offered libation. We talked theater for a few minutes, and when the others had said good-by, she ran out and came back holding her husband by the hand, telling him, "Gary, this is Gilbert Maxwell who wrote *The Sleeping Trees* which I'm simply crazy about."

Her car was waiting, so we said good-by, and I promised to send a copy of the screenplay to the next town where she would be playing.

A few days later I had a letter from Charlottesville, Virginia, in which she said:

Did you send the script? Am afraid it was left at one of our million stops! We will be at the Music Hall in Cleveland, Friday, Saturday and Sunday. Am so interested to read it—my neglect in answering your letter was not lack of interest! Was so sorry I had so little time to talk to you—in Brooklyn. How nice of you to come.

The script reached her in Cleveland and Audrey shortly had a letter from her saying that she was still greatly interested in playing one of my women.

Joan Crawford had written me to say that she also, having read the script, was interested; both ladies were under the management of MCA; the producers were plugging like mad, and everyone in Tenn's and my circle was excited by the idea of these two actresses' appearing in my picture. Tenn and I talked a great deal about it; with each forward step toward the goal, Diana and Claire Luce said prayers; and the staff of Altman's silver department all became interested, too.

The Fugitive Kind, Tennessee's picture version of *Orpheus,* was to be previewed at Proctor's RKO, and on that evening he asked Diana, Cheryl Crawford, Frederick, and me to see it with him.

For some unaccountable reason which no one ever has understood, a motley array of people had assembled in the lobby after the performance, and as our party passed through, they hissed and booed. Tenn quickly called a taxi to take Diana on to the apartment of producer Sam Spiegel where there would be a second preview of *Suddenly Last Summer,* and Frederick and I walked homeward, marveling at the behavior of the hostile crowd in the theater lobby.

I had hoped that the incident would not affect Tennessee, but naturally it did, and Diana called next day to tell me that by the time they left Spiegel's place he was, indeed, in a state.

I could understand his reaction and I felt it was too bad that he'd been forced to watch both films in a single evening, but I knew my man, and I was sure that disturbed or not he was at his typewriter even as we talked, which he was.

A few days before Christmas, one of my would-be producers phoned me at Altman's to say that the money for the sale of my picture had at last been raised. The cash, in escrow, would be given to me by check when I signed the contracts, after New Year's.

I was, naturally, beside myself with joy. Everyone in Altman's silver department, as well as certain friends all over the store's fourth floor, rejoiced with me, hearing the news, and so did Tenn, Diana, and Luce, all of whom I took time out from my customers to phone.

In the days that followed Tenn sounded a brisk word of warning. He said, "Baby, don't let anything stop you from getting your hands on that check right away. I know about these things, and if there's any sort of disagreement among the people handling this thing, I assure you that money will stay in escrow."

I agreed that he could be right, but I was too elated to be seriously worried, and I looked forward to Christmas with more exhilaration than I'd felt since I was a child.

Diana asked Frederick and me for cocktails one afternoon with the Fish, and promptly told me, "I have something for you, love, which I'm going to give you this minute."

She dashed into the bedroom, emerging with a huge square box. I opened it and found, under layers of tissue paper, a crazy bottle cover of stiff brown net, topped by the long-faced, big-eyed head of a dog with floppy ears of black felt.

Everyone in the room howled, but even as she told me, "I saw it today at the Woman's Exchange and just had to have it for you," I read the little card attached to the dog's collar, feeling my throat grow taut. It said:

Dear Living Poet,

    To remind you of the hair of the dog, and me. All my love to you, dear and compassionate friend. 1960 is our year—I know it.

The few lines spoke volumes. She had often been concerned about me, as she was about any friend who sometimes drank too much, and the line about 1960 was pregnant with meaning.

The year 1959 had been hard for us both. Now, it was different, since for me there was the screenplay's sale, and for her, even if she did not get Sweet Bird, the new play Tenn was writing, with her in mind.

I turned quickly, more affected by the note than I wished anyone to guess, and told Frederick, "I brought your presents, so you might as well open them. Diana won't mind, I'm sure."

I'd given him two small things that he wanted, both expensive, and he was pleased, but even as we all sat there, filled with pre-Christmas merriment, I saw a shadow cross Diana's face, and was saddened. I knew she was hurt that I hadn't brought something for her, so I said at once, "Darling, I haven't yet bought your present, but you'll have it before Christmas Day."

She had arranged to have Tenn and me at her place the next night, and for some reason she was worried all day for fear that he wouldn't show up. She called me several times, unbelievably upset. Neither of us had been able to reach him in the afternoon at his apartment and she was sure he'd forgotten the date. I told her that she was being foolish, that he'd be calling one of us soon, but she grew more and more distraught as the hour for our meeting drew near.

He phoned me a few minutes before we were supposed to be there and said, "Gil, I guess you know we're supposed to be at The Living Actress's. I've been tied up all afternoon, so you go on and I'll follow, soon as I can shower and change."

I called Diana at once, but she only said stubbornly, "I still don't believe he'll come."

She opened the door for me, looking lovely in a new, most becoming gray dress, but I could see that she was upset, and I could not understand it. I never will, really, but I have since come to think that her agitation may have been caused by the keyed-up, over-emotional state such people as she and I, who come from divided homes, do get into at Christmas. I have mentioned this thing before, I know, but it is a phenomenon I have seen and felt many times with disturbed individuals. Christmas is for children and for people safe in the circle of a more-or-less-happy family. It is not a good time for anyone with no close ties and no protective place in the world that can truly be thought of as home.

Tenn came soon, bringing a gorgeously wrapped magnum of champagne, and I remember the startled, rueful look on his face as he stopped, set it down and said, "Oh, Lord, Diana, I brought this for you. I'd *forgotten* you don't drink.

His disconcertion was extremely funny, so we all laughed as Diana thanked him and whirled the big bottle behind the bar. It is terrible to remember, in the light of the tragic events which would follow in less than a month, the insinuations made by the newspapers about this gift, and I pause here to state, emphatically, that Tennessee Williams' champagne had nothing whatever to do with Diana's beginning to drink again through those holidays. She never opened the champagne. Still in its tissues and ribbons, this magnum ended up as a gift to her manager, under the tree in Miss Rubber's apartment.

But still and all, it was a strange evening. Tenn had brought me a gift which I sorely needed, in the form of a check for two hundred dollars. He gave it to me, and before I could half thank him, said hastily that he must make an important phone call. Diana and I went into the bedroom so that he could have some privacy—and suddenly we were both overcome. She knew how much this check meant to me, so I suppose that realization, together with other emotions, prompted her actions, for now she turned as we sat on the bed, and hugged me and cried as she wished me Merry Christmas. I asked her what she would like me to get for her, and she said she couldn't think of anything she needed, so I made up my mind, that moment, what I would do.

She had told me, "You mightn't believe it, but I've never seen the big tree in Radio City," and I now decided she *would* see it this year. I'd never been out with her and paid a check, so I'd take her for a ride down the Avenue past the tree, on to a good restaurant.

We came back into the living room and sat down to chat, but both she and Tenn seemed overwrought. When he and I'd had a few drinks, she began to talk about playing *Sweet Bird*, and I saw that he didn't know at all what to say to her.

Finally, the two of them were really at each other—Diana, on the floor by the sofa where he sat, proclaiming, "I was *made* to play this part and I'm going to have it." She shook a finger at Tenn and, quoting Adriadne Del Lago, cried, " 'When monster meets monster,' remember."

It was half in jest, all of it, but there was a desperate seriousness in her intent, and at last Tenn cried out, "All right. I've told you I don't think it's for you, but if you want it this bad I'll do all I can." He leaned forward, demanding, "Suppose you did play it in London, would you be satisfied? *Would* you?"

That rocked her. She looked at him, and shouted, *"No!"* Then she said more calmly, "No. No, I'm afraid not. It still wouldn't be enough."

It was, altogether, as I've said, a strangely hectic evening. I was feeling calm within myself, and I sat there wondering why on earth these two whom I loved so much should be tearing them-

selves apart in this way. The atmosphere gradually cleared and
they grew quieter, but I was relieved when the time came to say
good night.

Diana had been asked to spend Christmas Day with her half-
brother, Leonard Thomas, and his wife, Yvonne, but she had
decided to have their daughters over instead to see her, and after
the girls' visit she called to say she'd loved being with them.

She and I were to lunch together the next day. When I phoned,
she said that she didn't feel like going out, but I insisted she get
dressed at once, and I have always been grateful that she agreed to
this outing.

When I arrived I found her colored maid behind the bar, clean-
ing up. She asked at once, "Mr. Maxwell, can't I make you a little
old Scotch and soda?" and even as I refused, Diana said, "No,
Eva! Mr. Maxwell doesn't want a drink so early. Now, just what
are you up to, this morning?"

Eva said, "We-ll, you know, Miss Diana, you promised me fifty
dollars for Christmas. . . ."

Diana stamped her foot, crying, "Eva! Who bought shoes for
the children? Who paid for Sister's funeral?" and Eva looked
crestfallen as she went for Diana's coat.

She'd hoped, she said, for the fifty dollars because she needed it
bad. Diana shrugged into the coat, gave her a great hug and told
her, "Well, after Christmas, we'll see. I don't have fifty dollars
right now."

Out in the hall she told me, "I did buy shoes for her sister's kids
and I did pay for Sister's funeral, and it's true I won't have any
more money till my next trust-fund allotment comes after Christmas. She's just being wicked—bringing up the subject before you."

There was snow on the ground, so we took a taxi down Third
Avenue to a little French restaurant I liked, only to find it closed.
We'd let the taxi go, there was no other in sight, and I was
concerned that Diana should be out in sheer stockings and high-
heeled pumps, but she said that it didn't matter, since the streets

had been fairly cleared, and there must be some other good place in this neighborhood. We walked for several blocks on Third, then on up to Lexington, coming finally to an old bar-restaurant where she stopped and said, "Oh, yes, I remember this. I used to drink here. Let's give it a try."

The place was deserted except for us. We found a booth, and the food, when it came, was fine. Diana ate heartily of goulash, and we talked over coffee about Tennessee and ourselves.

We ended up, as we often did, reminiscing about our childhoods, and she told me several things I have not forgotten. She spoke of Michael Strange and her father, and I was amazed as she said, "You know, when I went out to Hollywood at nineteen to work in pictures, Daddy asked me, 'Trepee, why didn't you answer my letters?' and I said, 'Why, Daddy, I never had a letter from you in my life. All I ever had from you were two telegrams,' and he said, 'I wrote you, Trepee.' "

She looked at me level-eyed across the table as I said, "You don't actually mean . . ."

She nodded. "No letter of Daddy's was ever given to me."

Again, she looked me in the eye and said quietly, "When Michael was very ill in the hospital, she said to me one day, 'I was never fair to you, Diana. I always loved Robin more than I did you,' and I answered, 'Yes, Mother, you did.' I couldn't lie to her—even if she was dying."

We talked, as I've said, a long time in that restaurant, and I still remember the most important part of our conversation.

I said, "Darling, I know how low you get sometimes, but I hope you meant it when you said in your book you'd never try suicide again. You wouldn't, would you?"

She hesitated only a second before answering, "No, Gil, I wouldn't. I've thought of it, yes—but I never would, because I've already brought enough disgrace on my family. I'd never do a thing like that which would reflect, for instance, on those lovely nieces of mine I saw yesterday—and then, too, I always think 'What would Vi do without me?' She needs me, you see, as much as I need her."

After a while we took a taxi back to her place and she said, entering the living room, "I haven't opened most of my cards. Let's open 'em together, hmmn?"

There were many cards, but there was one that hurt me. It said, "Darling Diana, what would poor old Mother Moonbeam do without you?"

It was from her friend Nita Naldi, the silent-picture star, who was in financial straits.

I asked, "What does Nita mean by this?" and Diana said, "Oh, nothing. It's just that sometimes when her television set breaks down, I send the repairman to fix it."

I said nothing to that—but I was remembering Eva and the shoes for the kids, and who paid for Sister's funeral, and I wondered how much more than an occasional paid visit from the television repairman had been forthcoming for this lonely old star whom she called Mother Moonbeam.

That afternoon, I went home feeling good about my girl. She had seemed so wonderfully well, so calm and controlled, so much in possession of herself.

I suddenly remembered we hadn't seen the tree in Rockefeller Center—but there was still time for that.

On New Year's Eve, Diana called in the afternoon to say I mustn't leave the house for a while, as I'd be receiving something special from Tenn. In about half an hour a messenger came with a fifth of Scotch and a fifth of rye from the liquor store Diana usually dealt with. When I called to thank Tenn for the gift he said he hadn't sent it, and I have never known whether he had, and had forgotten it, or whether this was a generous gift of Diana's, made in his name for some highly personal reason.

I am still in the dark also, as to just what did happen in regard to me on New Year's night. Diana had said she'd like to take me to a party in the Village which Danny Blum, compiler of the well-known stage and screen photographic-history volumes, always gave for his theater friends. She said that Tenn would be joining us, and asked me not to take even one drink before midnight since she wanted me at my absolute best for the stars who'd be at Blum's. She would call me before twelve o'clock and tell me where to join Tenn and her.

Frederick, Richard Two, and I attended a party on West End Avenue where I sat waiting expectantly for Diana's call. I drank ginger ale. Ten minutes before twelve I called her at home and got no answer. At midnight, I drank a glass of champagne, and tried several more times with no success to reach someone, either at Diana's place or Tenn's.

Paul Bigelow was in town and he, Diana, and Tennessee had gone on to Blum's without me.

Next day Diana called me, contrite, making an explanation and swearing that she was not to blame for what had occurred. I spoke later to Tennessee who, extremely brusque, refused to make a definite comment. Many months afterwards, I heard an involved story from Paul about the whole situation. Diana's story and Paul's were entirely different, and since Tenn had been crossly evasive, I never knew what to believe about this peculiar instance.

I know only that when I called Tenn a few days later to ask him to my house with Diana, he said, "I'll be glad to come, Gil. Now that unfortunate New Year's Eve mess is over, maybe we can all be decent to each other again."

Diana had been keeping company for some weeks with a young actor from *Sweet Bird* named Glenn Stencel. He was constantly with her, and since I'd met him and found him a pleasant, lively sort of guy, I was happy to feel that she had someone new whom she could mother, and, at the same time, be romantically fond of. She liked cooking for Glenn, who had a true country boy's appetite, and that also seemed a good thing since she was apt to fix only a pick-up snack for herself when she ate alone.

She'd begun drinking a little through the holidays, and Tenn had told me she was rather high New Year's Eve, but I hadn't been concerned about that. Once or twice since Christmas, I'd seen her make herself a small drink and forget even to touch it as we talked together, so I was surprised, the day after New Year's Day, when she told me that Earl Wilson, at her request, had killed a story about an exchange of blows between Glenn Stencel and a singer in a club where she and Stencel were dancing. There were rumors that she as well as Stencel had been drinking, but she swore that someone had given her only a single glass of orange juice spiked with vodka, and Glenn has since told me that this was true.

I'd stayed on after Christmas at Altman's and one day Diana called the store, a thing she had never done, to ask me to come by her place for a drink at six.

When I arrived the Fish was already there, and before many minutes had passed Diana blurted out, "Well, boys, the doctor told me today that I've got a bum ticker. He also prescribed two glasses of sherry and at least one shot of bourbon daily."

The Fish and I exchanged shocked glances and both of us said that we could not understand any doctor's prescribing even a small amount of alcohol for her.

She said, shrugging, "I don't either, but it doesn't matter, because I'm not scared of the stuff. All booze tastes awful to me now—just like medicine—so I know I'll never have to be scared of it again."

One evening when we were going with Tenn to a performance of *Sweet Bird* in which Rip Torn was taking over the leading male role from Paul Newman, we dined at the Colony. I had been with her, as I've said, on recent occasions when she'd poured herself a small drink, so I was not disturbed, as was Tenn, when she casually ordered a Manhattan. I told him that I thought she was quite capable of handling a drink, but he looked troubled, and I was glad when she took one sip of the cocktail and deliberately set it aside.

Tenn likes to sit alone while watching a new performance in one of his plays, so neither of us was offended when he left us before the curtain rose.

We watched *Sweet Bird* well into the second act; then Diana began quietly to cry and I was more than willing to take her home when she asked me to. It was plain that she still could not bear the thought of not playing Ariadne on tour and that she was wretched, watching Miss Page.

Back at her house she made a highball for me and a straight drink for herself; but again she merely sipped it and set it aside, and when she asked me wistfully, "Do you think there's any danger in my taking a drink now and then? I mean, don't you think I can handle it now?" I said with conviction that I was certain she could.

We'd called Glenn Stencel and asked him to bring Tenn over with him after the show. Glenn arrived by taxi, saying that Mr. Williams had been noncommittal about coming, so I called backstage again and got Tenn on the wire. He said that he was talking to Rip Torn at the moment and that he might see us later, but I knew from the tone of his voice that he was displeased with Diana and me for having left before the play was over, so I was not surprised when he failed to arrive before I went home, around one.

Shortly after the first of the year Tennessee flew to Miami, where, with Violla Rubber acting as producer, he planned to try out *The Night of the Iguana* at the Coconut Grove Playhouse.

In the second week of January a friend called me at Altman's to tell me in excited concern that he'd heard an ugly account of Diana's being ejected the night before from the theater where *The Andersonville Trial* was playing. As soon as I reached home I called her to ask about the story.

She said, "I know you won't believe this, but it wasn't I who was noisy," and gave me the name of a girl in her party who'd caused the disturbance. Terrified that the incident would make the papers, she ended up telling me, her voice bleak with despair, "If it does, I'm completely through in the theater. You know that."

If the story appeared in any paper, I did not see it, and I felt greatly relieved that she'd somehow escaped public censure.

On the Saturday night of January 23, Diana telephoned me at home, and I had a strange feeling, from the strained sound of her voice, that all was not well. There were some friends with her, she said, naming them, and she had called just to see how I was. I asked if she'd like me to come over and she told me it wasn't really necessary, but I was not satisfied, so I asked to speak to one of the guests, a lovely blonde model named Lola, whom I liked and trusted.

I asked Lola if Diana was upset and she answered guardedly, so I said, "Tell me the truth, do you think I should come over?" and Lola said cryptically, "I don't think it would hurt, Gil," so I told her I'd be there.

The snow was deep, but I felt a compulsion, so I put on overshoes, grabbed my polo coat, and went downstairs to find a taxi.

When I entered the small apartment on 61st Street, I knew that the air was supercharged with emotion. Lola, Virginia Gilmore, and Mrs. Essee Kupcinet of Chicago were there, and Diana was in the bedroom, talking long distance to Violla Rubber in Florida.

As I remember, she had a drink on the coffee table, but she certainly was not drunk. She was restless and much too keyed-up—probably from a seconal tablet—but that was not unusual. After she had talked to Miss Rubber she became gay and high-spirited, and as she moved about the room, making drinks for all of us, she turned to point at me and cry, "Now, I know who my best friend is. He came out in all this snow and ice to be with me just because he felt I needed him."

The party was lively, and I recall with everlasting gratification one other thing that this lost girl said. She turned in the middle of the room and cried, in a voice indescribably poignant, "Oh, God, I'm so glad to have all of you here—so grateful to know at last how much I'm loved."

I have no way of surmising what had depressed her earlier, but I do know that as this night wore on she was gay, and that she felt warm and protected there with her friends around her.

On Sunday night she had another party which included Essee Kupcinet, Edward Thomajam, assistant to Elia Kazan on *Sweet Bird*, Glenn Stencel, and John Cook, an airlines pilot, a casual acquaintance of Stencel's. Mrs. Kupcinet later testified that Cook served his hostess one drink and that she took the drink from Diana's hand before leaving the apartment. At one A.M. Diana tried vainly, by telephone, to get two bottles of whisky from Gene Cavellero, Jr., one of the owners of the Colony restaurant, who refused to fill her order, telling her a sale of liquor in bottles was illegal.

Thomajam departed shortly after that and Glenn Stencel, at two A.M., went home to his West Side apartment.

At two-thirty, alone, deeply depressed, Diana called him, and Stencel later told a reporter, "She wanted me to come back to her place. I told her I had a cold and had to work Monday night. She wanted to come over to my place. I just hung up—I feel terrible about it now."

In the morning I phoned Diana from Altman's. Her voice was incredibly weak, no more than a husky whisper, so I told her, "You sound completely exhausted. Go back to sleep and I'll talk to you later."

That evening after dinner as I sat with Frederick and Richard Two, I said, "I've been worried about Diana all day. I'm going to call her."

The boys, who'd been kidding about her earlier, laughing, being somewhat facetiously critical of her as members of our circle often were of one another, said something about my being too solicitous, but I rang the apartment anyway.

A voice said, "Hello," and I said, "Diana?"

The voice said, "No, dear, this is Vi."

"Oh, Vi," I said. "I was sort of worried about Diana—is she all right?"

Vi said oddly, "No . . . it's not. I'll have to call you later, darling. I—can't talk just now."

I said, "Of course, dear," and hung up, telling the boys, "Vi sounded very formal and restrained—not like herself at all. There's something strange going on."

The phone rang almost immediately and a girl friend of mine said, low-voiced, "Gil, this is Alex Uri. Are you sitting down?"

"Why, yes," I said. "Why, Alex?"

She said, "Diana is dead, Gil. I've just heard it over the radio."

I could not speak. I do not know to this day what I finally said, if anything, before I replaced the receiver, but when I'd hung up, I sprang out of the chair screaming that my girl was dead. Frederick burst into tears as I ran about the room in a spasm of helpless, hysterical crying, and then I turned and raged at him and Richard, cursing them for having criticized her just a few moments before. I remember nothing clearly, except that I ended up yelling, "Now go get the booze, goddamn it. I want it now, *now*."

One of the guys—I don't know which—ran out, and I have no clear memory of what I did, only that I couldn't stay still, that I kept walking the room, crying, saying as people always do in the face of such a disaster, there had to be some mistake, that it couldn't be true because I'd talked to Diana, myself, just a few hours ago.

Richard made me a drink and I downed it and said, "Someone must call Tenn. He has to know."

When Richard got through to him in Key West, he gave me the receiver and I remember Tenn's saying, "Oh, God, Gil, yes. I've just heard." I don't know what either of us said after that, but I was vaguely aware as I hung up that he'd told me he'd be in New York in two days.

It was near daylight before anyone got to bed, so I did not go to Altman's. At some time in the morning, and again in the late afternoon, I went out and bought all the papers and read them, growing increasingly sick. There were hints of suicide, a statement by Mrs. Kupcinet that Diana had recently said her time was running out, descriptions of the apartment with heavy emphasis on three empty liquor bottles found behind the bar, morbid stories of a sordid past, and lies, lies, lies about all the "heavy drinking" Diana had done through the holidays.

I was grateful that I hadn't been called by the police to be interrogated, and I prayed I wouldn't be—not realizing why or how I'd been spared this ordeal. I was not called, as countless friends listed in Diana's desk phonebook were, because she had long since memorized my number, as I had hers. There was this reason—and one other for which I have always felt I must thank Vi Rubber: the police were in the apartment when I phoned on Monday evening, so she'd ended the conversation quickly, not once speaking my name.

As I sat the next evening with Frederick and Richard Two, clipping out of the papers all the cheap, melodramatic bilge, the doorbell rang.

When I had pushed the buzzer, I stepped out in the hall—and

looked down over the banister at Tennessee, running up the short
flight of stairs. It was bitter cold, yet he had flown up from Key
West wearing cotton slacks and a khaki jacket, with no overcoat
and no luggage except a small Pan-Am satchel.

He sat down to read the clippings with me and presently called
his house in Key West. He told Frank Merlo, "The papers are
saying I started Diana drinking, after a champagne binge during
Christmas." His voice was matter-of-fact as he talked to Frank and
when he laughed a little about this lie, I froze, wondering how he
could take such an ugly, unjust accusation with lightness.

It would be two years before I would learn, in talking to Audrey
Wood, that Tennessee, faced with great sorrow or some catastrophe, sometimes does laugh like that. I know now that it is the
reaction of an inordinately sensitive man who cannot—perhaps
dares not—betray what he feels.

Tenn never broke down that night, but the fact that he'd come
north in dead of winter, dressed in cotton with no outer garment
to protect him, told me more of what had been going on inside
him than I cared to think about.

He had forgotten the keys to his apartment so we called his
maid, Jean, who came down from Harlem by taxi, bringing her set.
Jean is a dear person and I was glad she was there that evening to
stay for a drink and to help us, with small talk, to refrain from
dwelling on a tragedy we all felt in such different, fearful ways.

Friday, January 29, was a clear, cold day. The solemn crowds
that surged around Campbell's East Side chapel craned curious
necks for a glimpse of celebrities or prominent socialites, and as
Frederick, Nancy Cushman, and I passed among them they gave
us a cursory glance that said plainly, "No one important."

They could not know how many small people who had come
that morning to say good-by to Diana Barrymore had seemed
vastly important to her.

As we came into the foyer I saw a girl in black, wearing a short
veil, talking tearfully to an usher. It was Alice Nunn, Diana's

actress friend who'd once been a waitress, and I touched her arm, asking, "Where are you sitting?"

She said brokenly, "Not . . . anywhere. They say they don't have a seat for me."

I took her arm and told her, "Come along. You're going to sit with us."

I was crying now myself, and I couldn't stop all through the speech by Gerold Frank, who had helped Diana write her book, or through the impressive Episcopal service which Tenn's cousin, Sidney Lanier, then the rector of St. Thomas, conducted so beautifully.

The flowers were banked high about the altar, and, in the center of one green wreath, a shiny red apple—the traditional opening-night gift which the Barrymores always sent to each other— glowed with a strange, live brightness. The apple was from Anne Francine.

The casket's blanket of two thousand violets had been sent by Tennessee, who sat directly in front of me with Violla Rubber, some members of the Oelrichs family, and Ethel Barrymore Colt.

I have since heard criticisms of Gerold Frank's speech, but it seemed to me to have both warmth and dignity, and when he finished, saying quite simply, "Good-by, my sweet, my bewildered, lost Diana," I knew that he had loved her.

At some point in the twenty-minute service a loud sobbing came from the back of the house and there was a slight commotion as someone broke an ampule under the nose of a man who had seemingly collapsed. No one knew until afterward that he was a professional mourner who made a practice of turning up at the funerals of prominent people to stage this act.

After the last prayers were said, Violla took Tenn, Frederick, and me into a private anteroom where we were introduced to some of Diana's relatives. I said to Tenn, "I'm not going to the grave-yard, are you?" and he said, "God, no. Not till they carry me there," but when we came out on the sidewalk to watch the casket being brought through a side door, Glenn Stencel caught me hard about the waist.

He said, "You have to go with me to the cemetery, Gil. You have to."

I said, "Oh, no, Glenn," but he only held me tighter, as he pulled me toward a car, insisting, "You must come with me. I can't stand it without you."

I can't recall who drove the car—some woman friend of Glenn's, I think—but I distinctly remember Lola and me, on the back seat, trying to comfort Glenn who kept on saying, "Oh, God, she called me, you know. She said, 'Glenn, please come back, I'm lonely,' and I said, 'Honey, I can't, you know that; it's three o'clock and I have to work tomorrow,' and she said, 'Then, please, let me come over there to you,' and I just hung up the receiver. I *hung up on her while she was begging me. Oh, Jesus, why did I do that?*"

At the grave I stood near Emil Sorrento, a blind man who was holding to the halter of the seeing-eye dog Diana had bought him, and almost directly beside a quiet, somber-faced woman who now and then glanced my way.

When the brief ceremony was over I turned and said to her, "I know you must be someone who was close to Diana," and she answered, "I'm Yvonne Thomas."

This was the wife of Diana's half-brother, Leonard, and something in the look on her face compelled me to tell her my name, adding, "I want you to know most of that stuff in the papers is quite untrue. She was *not* drinking heavily, and she had a good Christmas this year. I know, because Tennessee Williams and I were with her a lot of the time."

Mrs. Thomas said, "I'm glad to hear that. We wanted her to spend Christmas with us, you know, but she wouldn't. It's good to know she wasn't alone through the holidays."

Eva, the maid, came over to me and when I asked Glenn if she could drive home with us, he said of course. Essee Kupcinet walked up to me as we waited for the car, pressed her face silently against my shoulder, then turned away. She had exposed herself to unfavorable criticism among Diana's friends, in having written three tabloid articles about her ten-month friendship with Diana, and I was touched by her silent gesture.

On the way back to the city I said to the emotion-spent group in the car, "Now, all of us know Diana was a fun girl, as well as a sad person—and I feel she'd like us all to have one drink together before we separate."

Everyone agreed; and Eva said she knew of a bar in Harlem near her place, so we went there and sat about a table for half an hour, recalling certain gay, joyous times we'd had with this vivid child-woman who would never, at any time, seem actually gone to us. For though I did not know it then, I would hear more than one friend say as the months after this day merged into years, "I just keep on expecting when the phone rings, to hear that voice," or "It's not possible to feel anything except that she's away somewhere on the road, and that she'll soon be back there at her place, ready to welcome us all."

As I left the car Glenn said, "I'll be up to see you, after the show, tonight. Take care of yourself till then—and don't be alone a minute if you can help it."

There was a letter in the mailbox and I took it upstairs with me, noting there was no return address on the envelope's flap. When I sat down to read it, I found it was a letter of sympathy from an old, close Miami friend—written from an asylum where he had been recently confined. It was too much, and I reached for the phone, suddenly seized by a black, all-consuming depression that scared me. I called Tenn and told him about the letter and he said, "Oh, God, of course you couldn't take that. I'll meet you in thirty minutes at Le Bijou. We'll have lunch, baby."

I can't recall what we said as we sat wanly facing each other in that booth, but I do remember our talking quietly about The Living Actress, feeling already the grave, irrevocable weight of our loss.

Later in the afternoon Claire Luce asked me to come and be with her. We sat in the Russian Tea Room, having drinks; then Claire said, "No, you can't be by yourself. As soon as we've walked my dog, I'll go home with you."

She came and stayed until Glenn Stencel arrived at midnight. I remember little of the whole evening, or the later small hours with Glenn. I had drunk, off and on, all day, thinking I'd never really reach the blackout, mind-empty stage I was seeking, but the beer Glenn had brought was finally effective and when Frederick came home from keeping an engagement he hadn't been able to break, I was asleep—mercifully stoned, at last.

There is no saying, ever, what the death of Diana Barrymore meant to me—but I knew what it meant to Tenn when he said to me quietly and simply not long ago, "None of our lives has been the same since she left us."

On Saturday, the thirtieth of January, Sydney Fields headed his article in the *Daily Mirror*, DIANA'S BEQUESTS GIVE CLUE TO HER LONGINGS, using as his opening sentence, "The way Diana Barrymore decided to dispose of her worldly goods after death is a key to the tortured need for love she sought so desperately all her life."

Mr. Fields was right, in one way, wrong in another. She had left money to the proper friends, all right, but her desperate seeking for love from these friends and from many others had never been in vain. She had *found* love in her friends, and, thank God, she died knowing that.

What I wish Mr. Fields had pointed out is that Diana's bequests were made to people near to her who most needed financial help. They included one relative on the Oelrichs' side, two elderly actresses—Anne Andrews and Nita Naldi—and Emil Sorrento, the blind man.

It is a strange thing, I know, but I repeat that no one who loved this girl can ever forget her or even accept the fact of her physical death.

Bob Applewhite, always close to her, always a friend in need, said to me one day, "The Lord never made a warmer woman than she was," and I had hoped that Apple could help me recreate Diana in this book. He had once agreed to talk with me at length about her, but the last time I saw him in a Gramercy Park bar one summer night, he said, "I don't actually know *what* I could tell you . . ." He looked at me for a moment; then he said, "I think of her so much," and turned away.

I knew that night that Apple would be no help—that he

couldn't be, even if he tried, because now he apparently can't talk about Diana Barrymore at all.

In the winter of 1960 I wrote a sonnet for Diana, but I have never been satisfied with it. It doesn't seem good enough, so I guess I'll just keep it around until I can find the words I need to make it into something that's big and strong enough to circumscribe The Living Actress.

I've had a bad time of it, missing her these past five years, and sometimes I have even resented the existence of the few treasured, inanimate things I have that my girl gave me. It doesn't seem right somehow that a brown-net bottle cover, an autographed book, and a card from the island of St. Thomas should still exist in a world where that vibrant, vital, laughing creature no longer moves and has her being. It was a long time before I could reread the gift card that said, "1960 is our year, I know it," because I could not bear to realize that the girl who wrote that line had been buried before the first month of our year was gone, nor that she could not, somehow, have lived to appear in the play which Tennessee had been readying for her in a spirit of compassionate understanding. And of course the hardest thing of all to endure has been the question Tenn and I have often been asked, here and in Hollywood, "Why did she commit suicide?"

It is preposterous that the hints of press and radio about self-destruction should have remained in the minds of so many people, instead of the facts plainly stated to TV and in all the newspapers, which are these: the Bellevue autopsy revealed no evidence of suicide or foul play, even though both were hinted at in those sensational picture papers which a holocaust-hungry throng of readers will always plunk down their dimes for.

The truth is only that Diana, who definitely knew better, died after staying up two days and nights, on an almost continuous party. She had been warned that she was no longer in good enough health for such carousing, and she died of a heart that at last grew silent, refusing to take any more outrageous abuse.

After all the lies and salacious stories, all the tragic wailings had died down, in the winter of 1960, I kept trying to think of something I'd read somewhere that would almost, but never quite, flash into words in my head. And then one day it came to me, in fragments, from an anonymous poem I found once in an old anthology. It is an elegy for a dead girl for whom the poet beseeches his friends not to mourn too piously. Rather, he says, "Say you saw her lately, lightly kissing her last lover"—and here are his final lines, which are peculiarly fitting, I think, for The Living Actress:

> She was wild and sweet and witty—
> Let's not say dull things about her.

10

ANY NUMBER OF PEOPLE HAVE ASKED ME ABOUT THE RELATIONSHIP
of Diana and Tennessee. They were often together, and once
when the gossip columns were filled with conjectures regarding
marriage, Audrey Wood took the whole thing seriously enough to
remark to her client, "If you don't watch out, boy, I'm going to be
flower girl at your wedding."

There is no doubt Diana had convinced herself that she cherished an unending love for Tenn, but I always felt, as I have
suggested before, that she had unconsciously confused the playwright with the man in forming this dogged attachment. She had
fallen in love, long before she met Williams, with the parts of
Blanche in *Streetcar*, and Maggie Pollitt in *Cat*. She associated her
sober comeback with these roles which won her fine notices; there-

fore, being already in love with his work when she met Tenn, it was easy for her to believe she was also madly in love with the creator of these challenging female roles. In addition to this, Tennessee (as must be clear to the discerning reader by now) is a lovable man who, when he is not mentally preoccupied, often reveals great empathy for any person who is mentally or emotionally disturbed.

He said to me once, "You knew this girl better than I did, because, being always here in town, as I wasn't, you were with her much more than I." This was true, but there was another reason for my having reached with Diana an almost uncanny communication which I have never achieved with anyone else in my life: we had a bond in our mutual, concerned affection for Tennessee, and, too, because neither of us had a romantic yen for the other, that restrictive barrier was absent from our relationship. I have always felt I was spiritually in love with this girl and that she cared deeply for me. She could be a trial to people who loved her, and there were times when Violla, Tennessee, and other friends caught the full brunt of her wrath and resentful frustrations. She was never angry with me, except on the day when she was burned and hysterical, when I falsely accused her of drinking.

Often, about to say good-by to me on the phone, she'd say, on a rising note, "I love you." I'd answer, "I love you, too, Diana," and sometimes she'd tell me, in a voice that twisted my heart, "You didn't make that strong enough—say it again," and I would do so, making it triple strong. There was no solace for me in the first days that followed her death until a friend of mine who had taught her years back at the Academy of Dramatic Art called and said, "I know how you're feeling, and I have this to tell you: I knew her all her life, and, with those parents, she was doomed before she was born."

Anne Francine, on the other hand, has told me, "I knew Michael Strange, Gilbert, and I think you should know I've always felt Diana was too hard on her. It's true she kept Diana away from John Barrymore while that girl was growing up, but what would you have done under such circumstances? After all, her father was a hopeless drunk by that time."

No outsider can ever arrive at the absolute truth of any involved family tragedy, but I do think, in this case, my instructor friend was right about Diana's having been born in the orbit of a fatal star. It is terrible that this should have been true; yet I always remember that Diana, who was lonely, disturbed, scared, brave, violent, snobbish, resentful, loving, compassionate, wildly generous—being all these things—was, both in spite and because of being the daughter of a great actor and a temperamental playwright-poetess, an altogether complex creature. Tennessee and I knew her for a little more than a year before she died—and a woman must be extraordinary to leave behind her in the minds of two such hardened veterans of emotion, the conviction that neither of our lives has been the same since the bleak winter day of her passing.

In this spring of 1960 the rains of sorrow, frustration, and near disaster fell upon my house. After the Altman white sale I was out of work and out of pocket. No free-lance editing came in from a publisher; my would-be producers quarreled with their pigeon, who had the money for the screenplay's sale in escrow, and I began to see clearly that I was in the hands of a pair of big-talking, over-optimistic amateurs who would never effect a sale. I was on the phone more often with Audrey Wood than I should have been, as scheme after sales scheme cooked up by this pair, whom I'd come to think of as the Terrible Two, went glimmering, but Audrey Wood was on my side and she said to me one day, "You poor man, I wish I could get you off this hook. Maybe I can. I'll try."

Meanwhile, I went to work in a claustrophobia-begetting, tiny bookshop on the lower level of Pennsylvania station, and began to think I was indeed jinxed as a writer.

This position was at least the equivalent of Tennessee's employment in the St. Louis shoe factory, which he described as a "living death" and "a period of penal servitude," but when he asked me via long distance how I liked the job and I replied wearily that I supposed it wasn't too bad, he said, "I'm sure not. I always love to walk through that lower level of the station—it's so pretty down there."

My head whirled on that one as I hung up. Later, when Audrey and I had a session about the possibilities of getting me out to the Huntington Hartford Foundation, I repeated this remark and her eyebrows touched her hairline.

She said, "He was kidding, I hope," and I said, "No, he wasn't. He was dead serious," whereupon Audrey slowly shook her curly head and sighed.

A few days later, however, when she contacted Tenn about getting me plane fare and a little pocket money from the Organization's fund, he said that she should ask them for it, even though he had already told me, "You're going to hate that Foundation, you know."

Diana had also said, "You don't want to go out there, dear. The damn place is a nut farm." However, there were more factors than I suspected, working toward my inevitable arrival at this artist-writer's retreat—not the least being a firm-jawed determination on the part of Miss Audrey Wood.

Audrey was not only concerned about my welfare; she was damned sick of trying to cope with my screenplay and the Terrible Two who were constantly presenting us both with harebrained schemes for raising money and acquiring stars. She was handling Jack Barefield's play, *Catstick*—and, after she'd managed to get me on the plane for California, she heaved a sigh, rolled her eyes to heaven and said fervently to Jack, "Anything to get Mr. Maxwell out of town."*

This time I had to do some tall talking to the heads of the Organization, who had to decide whether or not the novel I was working on would be of sufficient worth to warrant their cutting loose with $450 to cover my plane fare and a few incidental expenses. Nevertheless, the combined efforts of Tennessee, Audrey,

---

* Audrey is always a joy. One day at an interview in the summer of 1963, I reminded her of the above remark which Barefield relayed to me. Audrey scowled, asking, "Who is Jack Barefield?" We got that straightened out and she said rather sheepishly, "I don't recall making that remark." I said, "I was hoping you could, because I think it's funny as hell and I'd like to use it in the book." Audrey said promptly, "Then go ahead, say I said it. Next question?"

and I were finally effective, and one day I found myself packing for a three-month stay in Rustic Canyon, thirty miles out from Hollywood.

For months Frederick had been laying away part of his weekly pay check toward a trip to Europe, and I shook my head sadly as he arranged for Richard Two to move in and share the apartment's expenses. I pointed out that Richard's recent exit by night via a side window from a sub-leased East Side flat should serve as sufficient warning to even the most trusting of men, but Frederick refused to believe that anyone could be truly lacking in old-fashioned principles, ethics, or basic integrity. God knows he *had* to be trusting to a marked degree since, in addition to assisting Richard in his moonlight flit, he'd been present the day before my departure when this green-eyed conniver had suggested I lend him two hundred dollars of my four-fifty grant, swearing he'd repay me out of a forthcoming income tax refund. I had merely given him a long look, telling him, "Soon, two men in white coats will come for you. Go with them. They are your friends." Frederick, however, was not as yet a burned child, so he had no protective dread of the fire.

He was to live and learn with Richard Two that he was now in the hands of one who cherished a curious conviction: namely, that in the harsh winter, the autumn-hoarded earnings of a friendly, diligent bee should be shared with a profligate grasshopper who'd fiddled the past summer through.

I loathe flying and I am not ashamed to say the ominous silence of the jet to California seemed to me a positive portent of doom. Worn out from the recent frightening days, and heartsick still about Diana, I looked, I'm sure, not only apprehensive but rather like my own granddad on this flight. The stewardess sat on the arm of my chair and gave me a lot of defensive statistics about the accident odds of air travel being practically nonexistent in comparison to the holocausts of the rails and highways, but I was buying little of what she had to sell, so she tried a new tack, asking politely about my destination.

When she learned where I was headed, and that I wrote books, she glanced at the screenplay beside me and asked, "Oh, do you write for pictures, too?" I made a mental note that writing for pictures was one thing, *selling* to pictures another, as I murmured modestly, "Yes, but I'm still green at the game. This is really my first screenplay—but I'm pretty hopeful about it, since Bette Davis and Joan Crawford seem anxious to make the picture together."

The stewardess said then, as everyone always did upon hearing this news, "Oh, wouldn't it be fabulous to see those two in the same film," and added, "By the way, Hal Wallis and Lizabeth Scott are flying with us today."

I leaped with joy, told her that I knew these two, and asked if I could go up to first class and see them. She said in effect that unfortunately us tourist white trash weren't allowed up front with the quality, but that she'd be glad to deliver a note. I scrawled something and she returned to tell me Miss Scott would be back in a few minutes.

When Lizabeth appeared, she greeted me warmly, but remarked, her voice trailing ruefully off as she glanced at my face, "You're looking—er—quite well."

I restrained myself from telling her that I knew how bad I looked, and asked about Mr. Wallis.

She said he'd be back as soon as he'd had a short nap. We talked of our Florida yacht cruise with Tennessee; I told her that he and Audrey were sending me to the Foundation, and we spoke of Diana. Then Liz asked, "Are you scared of flying, Gil?"

I said, "I'm terrified, as I guess you can see."

Liz said, "Well, I'm not any more, but I still catch myself praying when I get on a plane, and thinking about what a bad girl I've been—the time I've wasted, all the big things I've wanted to do in pictures—and how I've never even got started."

She stayed with me for nearly an hour, then went up to first class again, so that Hal could come and sit with me.

Wallis came back and chatted, saying that he was sorry he hadn't been able to see his way clear to buying the rights to my novel. I said, "I've got a screenplay I've made from it right here, and those two fabulous gals still want to play it," so he said, "Then send it to my studio, addressed to me personally."

By the time he'd left me, my spirits had risen and I even finally got up nerve enough to look out the window at the marvelous Rockies as we zoomed over them.

At the Foundation, as Tennessee and Diana had predicted, I failed, for reasons I need not go into here, to be either inspired or contented. I worked hard every day for six weeks on my novel, then, in the second week of April, said farewell to Rustic Canyon and drove into Hollywood to stay with my old friend Bill Hughes, in his New England style residence set incongruously in another canyon called Laurel. There I continued to write in the sun-flooded patio of Hughes' peaceful house, watched television in the quiet evenings, or ran about a bit with my host and his friends; but I was always nostalgic for New York, and more than once, after a couple of drinks, I could be heard wailing, "What in God's name am I doing here, when New York's just five hours away by jet?"

Bill, who was also sick of the Coast, was getting ready for a trip to Europe, so we planned to fly East together. I had, in fact, already made plane reservations when I received a surprise phone call from Tenn in Manhattan.

He said that since he'd be out in two days with his mother, Dakin, and Dakin's wife, he'd like me to stay on for a few days. I agreed to do so, and he said he'd call me when he arrived at the Beverly Hills Hotel.

He rang us on his first evening in town, and Hughes and I drove down to see him just after dinner. He seemed preoccupied, withdrawn, and more than a little weary.

I lunched with him alone next day and he explained that he was in Hollywood to discuss a business deal he wasn't quite sure about. He'd planned to take Miss Edwina to Europe, but had asked her, instead, to join him for a California vacation. She'd be arriving with Dakin and Joyce next day and he would like me to join his party for a visit to the Twentieth Century Fox studios.

We spent the afternoon swimming and chatting with a young

man who was writing the screenplay of Summer and Smoke, and when, at one point, I said something that tickled T.W. enormously, he told the screenwriter, "Sometimes I think Gil's the last man I've got left on this earth to really laugh with."

At noon next day, he introduced me to a photographer and a young actor who would accompany us to the Fox lot, and we all gathered at the elevator to await his family's descent. The car reached the ground floor and Miss Edwina, stepping out first, gave me her tiny hand, crying, "Oh, my, here's my partner." I shook her hand; then, when I'd greeted Dakin and Joyce, she said to me gently, "Gilbert, it was terrible about Diana. I know how you must feel."

I said, "It hasn't been the same world to me since she left, Miss Edwina," and she nodded, answering, "No, nor to me either. I loved every minute of the week she spent with me last year in St. Louis."

I gave Miss Edwina my arm and we all walked out to the car.

As we sat at lunch in the Fox commissary, I spied a blonde head at a table across from us in the annex and felt my heart jump.

Joyce Williams asked, "Gil, is there anyone famous here today?"

I said, "Yes, I think so," and asked, as the waitress came up, "Who's that blonde over there, dear?"

The waitress said, "It's Marilyn Monroe," and Tenn, overhearing, cried, "What? You mean Marilyn's here?" He got up at once, went over to her table, and came back with her to ours.

She was wearing a big white mohair sweater with slacks and when she paused under the ugly fluorescent ceiling lights I stood up with the other men in our party, amazed by her beauty. As I looked full into that fabulous face she gazed level-eyed into mine; Tenn introduced me, and when we shook hands she gave me a grip as strong as a man's. What's more, it is God's blessed truth that while she stood there talking to all of us, her eyes never left mine, and I've wondered why, ever since. I have always felt, with humility, that maybe she sensed the empathy I felt for her the instant my fingers touched hers—and, actually, this doesn't seem to me too far-fetched a conjecture, since we know now that in the last years of her life she was a lonely, pathetically seeking, truly sad human being. Anyway, regardless of the reason her blue eyes held to my own, I can state simply that mine stayed riveted to hers because I was transfixed by this unique creature whose appeal was legendary.

Miss Edwina said, "Marilyn, you're just as pretty as you were when I saw you at Tom's party in New York, five years ago," and Marilyn sighed, small-voiced, "Well, I'm kind of tired right now. I've been dancin' all mornin' and I can't dance."

She turned then to Tenn and said, "My set's supposed to be closed, but would you all like to come over and watch us a while?"

All of us cried yes in chorus, and she said, "Then I'll tell the guard you're coming, but I have to run now 'cause I'm almost late."

She left us, waving good-by, and I let out a long sighing breath, saying to Joyce, "Lord, she really is beautiful. She *has* to be, to look like that under *these* lights," and Joyce fervently agreed.

We drove across the Fox lot past the ghostly store and saloon fronts of a Western town, to the building where *Let's Make Love* was in progress.

The guard at the door let us through the barnlike place to a theater-in-the-round set, and we all took regular theater seats facing a center platform. Tenn introduced us to George Cukor, who explained that the picture's plot revolved around the doings of an off-Broadway group, and Cukor in turn introduced us all to his assistant, a good-looking young woman whose soft, deep-voiced drawl compelled me to ask, "Where are you from down home?" She answered, "Macon, Georgia," and in the next two minutes we became practically kissing kin, having found out that both of us had been friends of Margaret Mitchell's.

Edwina was chatting gaily with Mr. Cukor and I was gabbing with Miss Macon and Tenn, when a door across the set suddenly opened and Marilyn slipped through, wearing long gloves and a diaphanous evening gown cut to the base of her spine. I gasped and whispered, "Good Lord, Tenn, I can see her *skin* through that dress."

Tenn said, "Sure, that's what it was made for," and the two of us watched, fascinated, as Marilyn, holding her long skirt off the floor, crossed the platform and came toward us, for all the world like a little girl dressed up, imitating a movie star.

I said, "That sure is one hell of a dress, Miss Monroe," and she said eagerly, "Do you like it? The designer made it—right on me."

She flashed us a smile and went to the platform to begin work with her dancing instructor, Jack Cole. Her voice came sweetly over the loudspeaker, crooning, "You have to specialize," and we watched as, following Jack Cole, she faithfully mimicked his movements. Perhaps she was not a dancer, but she was certainly a graceful girl and certainly I have never seen such incredible peach-glow skin as was hers.

She did the same few steps over and over with Cole, docile, smiling, seemingly tireless, and I wondered if all the stories I'd heard about her being difficult and temperamental hadn't been rather exaggerated.

Presently the lady from Macon leaned over to Tenn and me and said, "You all come with me a minute. I have something to show you." As we walked off the set, I said, "Miss Monroe seems to be a very sweet person," and our guide said simply, "Yes, she definitely is."

She took us around back of the set and showed us a round, linen-covered table in the center of which stood a white cake ornamented with two tiny figures of a man and woman. There were paper napkins and paper cups beside the cake and Miss Macon told us, "It's Marilyn's birthday, and we're giving her a little surprise. We're having champagne, so I do hope you'll stay for the party."

Tenn and I said that we'd love it. Yves Montand suddenly appeared, twinkling-eyed, urbanely smiling, and Miss Macon introduced us; then Dakin came and said to Tennessee that Miss Edwina seemed to be getting awfully tired, so he thought we'd better be going.

I said that Miss Edwina seemed to me to be having the time of her life, but Dakin insisted I didn't know her as he did, so there was nothing for it but that we must all take our leave.

I hated like hell to go without having a chance to talk further with Marilyn and Mr. Montand—but this was Tenn's party, so naturally I had to leave when he did.

When we reached the Beverly Hills Hotel the photographer, who'd offered to drive me into Hollywood, remarked as we walked down the hotel's curving drive, "Well, Gil, Mama's a real darling, isn't she?"

I said, "You bet she is, and I love her. I didn't want to leave out there, but Dakin was adamant about Miss Edwina's being dangerously overtired."

"Oh, really?" the photographer said. "I didn't get that impression at all—as far as I'm concerned, she was the life of the party all day long."

I made a mental note to relay this compliment to Miss Edwina as soon as I could, and regaled my newfound friend with anecdotes about her all the way into town.

Next day Tenn and I did some browsing in a bookstore on Hollywood Boulevard, then sauntered down to a quiet bar where we could talk in a leisurely way about all that had been happening to us since we'd last been together, in March.

He told me that he was more than a little concerned about the problem of accepting or rejecting a package deal for two pictures and when he told me the price he'd been offered, I whistled, adding, "That sure ain't hay, T.W."

"No," he said, "but have you any *idea* how much has to come out of that before I can touch one cent?"

I said that I hadn't, and as he reeled off all the different ways, including an 87 per cent federal income tax, in which the full sum would be divided, I said, "Looks to me as though there's not going to be much left for you."

"Exactly," Tenn said, "but I'm such a lousy mathematician I can't figure out just what I *will* be getting."

I said, "I'm no Einstein, either, but we'll try to do something, anyway." I asked the bartender for pencil and paper and set down all the pay-out fees as Tenn enumerated them, then deducted the sum from the proposed amount—and we both stared, aghast, at the figures.

"There, you see," Tenn said. "There's really not going to be much left for me, and the hell of it is I might've gone ahead with the deal, if we hadn't done this little job of arithmetic."

He went on to say that the newspaper reports of his yearly income and lifetime earnings are always exaggerated and that no one would believe how little he had left each year, after the government, MCA, and his lawyers had been paid. He told me in detail about his personal living expenses, and by the time he'd finished I was really amazed. Although he'd obviously never be without an adequate income from his many plays and pictures, it was also plain that he was not a tremendously wealthy man. He had earned a great deal of money since 1945, and when he told me what he was worth on paper, I said, "Well, that's damned little to've ended up with after writing every day for thirty years—especially since fifteen of those years were unrewarding, money-wise."

When we left the bar he insisted on taking me home in a taxi to Laurel Canyon. He got out for a minute to take a peek at Bill's house perched high above its sloping terraces, then said good-by, reminding me that I'd be joining him and his family for cocktails at the Beverly Hills on the morrow.

Next day Hal Wallis entertained him and his mother on the lot, and when they returned to find me waiting in the lobby, Miss Edwina cried out, blue eyes all aglow, "Oh, Gilbert, what a lovely day this was. I've just had my picture made with Elvis Presley."

The photographer friend came later to make more pictures of the whole Williams family, and after that Tenn walked with me through the shop-lined basement of the hotel to the front, to say good-by. He seemed unusually tired and harassed, but he said things would be better the next day, when he and Miss Edwina would be going down for a stay in La Jolla.

During my last few days in Hollywood, there was a positive flurry of letters and wires from the Terrible Two and their lawyer, in New York. I was on the phone talking to a famous director who'd read the script and was interested; the Two had teamed up with Carmel Myers and her husband, who were well-known producers; everyone was sure that we were now about to hit pay dirt, and my immediate presence in New York was absolutely imperative.

I told myself not to believe one bloody thing I was hearing, and got on the plane, burdened with my usual fearful apprehensions of death and destruction.

Back in New York, with one hundred bucks to my name, I took a tiny room on 18th Street and went furiously to work on my novel. I met Carmel Myers and liked her. There seemed no doubt that she was honest and businesslike. She had just lunched with Joan Crawford, who still was enthusiastic about making the film with Bette Davis, and I finally had to admit that the future did look rosy.

When Tenn came back to town, Carmel had him and me over for a drink on the terrace of her midtown penthouse and afterward he told me, "Well, I must say you seem now to be in much better hands than I'd dared to hope for, baby—so maybe this really is going to be it at last."

He said he'd take the screenplay and read it all through, which he did, making many marginal notes and suggestions. Then he sat down and talked to me in detail about some changes that he felt had to be made, and I made them promptly. Carmel took me to see Danny Mann, who said he loved the script, and that it didn't read in any way like any man's first screenplay. He also said that if he weren't tied up for three pictures in the next year, he'd be glad to direct mine, and Carmel and I rode home, hopeful.

When Tenn heard what Mann had said, he nodded and told me, "He's right. Your script is better than ninety per cent of the screenplays I've read in the past few years."

Bill Hughes returned in June, and he and I took a suite at the Irving Hotel in Gramercy Park. I was lucky enough to get a few good free-lance editorial assignments, and Carmel soon nosed out the Terrible Two by insisting that MCA and I give her an exclusive three months' option on *Summer's Day*.

Throughout this summer and fall Tennessee was working toward the production of his comedy, *Period of Adjustment*. Kazan, who'd been set for the play, had been called to Hollywood because of a prior commitment to direct a film, so Tenn had selected as his replacement George Leroy Hill, a young man who'd recently done a fine job on the musical *Greenwillow*.

T.W. gave a great party at Nicholson's Café honoring the casts of *Period*, *A Taste of Honey*, and Brendan Behan's *The Hostage*, to which I went with Bill Hughes. Frank Merlo acted as co-host with Tenn who seemed merry as a grig all evening, and his hospitable gaiety spilled over on everyone present. I sat at a table with Maureen Stapleton, Barbara Baxley, and Carson McCullers' sister, Rita Smith, of the editorial staff of *Mademoiselle*, watching the later celebs arrive.

Tallulah breezed in, embraced Tenn and told him, "You can't fool me, Tennessee, this whole thing's deductible," then took her place at a table where she was at once surrounded by six young actors and writers, including the novelist-playwright James Herlihy.

Frank Merlo, who'd introduced Herlihy to *Go Looking*, brought him over to me and I felt momentarily like The Living Poet again as this talented young man told me graciously what he thought of my work. He and Frank suggested that I hop over to see Tallulah and I said that I would as soon as her circle thinned out.

Geraldine Page was seated on a banquette near the front door and I glanced at her now and then, thinking of Margrit Wyler on a certain day about six months after *Sweet Bird*'s opening when she'd called me, in evident distress.

Whenever I'd been with her of late she hadn't seemed too discontented serving as a stand-by for Miss Page, but on this day she said, "My darling, I have to leave the show. The money is all right, but I simply cannot sit there any longer, doing nothing, watching another actress play the part I had hoped would give me my big chance in New York. I like and admire Miss Page—it has nothing to do with that. It is only that I cannot go on with this torment."

I'd remonstrated with her but she was adamant. She was also close to tears as we said good-by.

I'd hardly hung up the phone when it rang again. This time it was Tenn, hoarse-voiced, saying without preamble, "Gil, if you have any influence over Margrit, for God's sake beg her not to leave me. I've given her my word I'll see that she plays this part."

I told him I'd call Margrit, and he said, "Please do, baby. I'm almost knocked out with bronchitis, and I just can't stand the thought of Wyler's leaving."

He sounded greatly troubled, so I rang up Margrit at once and repeated what he'd told me.

I said, "Sweetie, Tenn has made you a serious promise, and he's never made one to me that he didn't keep. I think you ought to stay," but it did no good. Margrit broke down as she told me, "I just cannot, Geelbert. I cannot depend upon promises. I must go back to Germany where I am a known and respected actress."

She said good-by in a choked voice, and I dreaded having to call Tenn again. He was more than ever dispirited, but he said only, "I know how she feels. I can't blame her. . . ."

Margrit Wyler was in Germany now. I missed her sorely—and here I was, looking with a kind of resentment I couldn't help at Geraldine Page. I got up on a sudden impulse and went over to her. I told her my name and said, "Miss Page, I was one of your first-night audience who stood up and cheered you in *Sweet Bird*, and believe me this is an accolade, because *I* saw Margrit Wyler as Ariadne."

I don't know what I'd expected Miss Page to reply to this, but I was charmed with her when she squeezed my hand and told me, "Oh, I know. You can't imagine how I felt, knowing that great actress was out there, standing by for me. One day we met in the corridor backstage and when I stretched out both my hands to her and tried to say something, I started to cry. She cried then, too, and neither of us could say much of anything, but somehow I knew she understood all that I was feeling and couldn't say."

It was a simple, sincere speech and I had a swift insight into Geraldine Page, whose fame had steadily increased since her fine portrayal of Alma Winemiller in *Summer and Smoke* Off Broadway. It takes more than talent and temperament to make a star, and to me an utter absence of bitchery is not the least of true stellar qualities.

I left Gerry Page, moving on to Miss Bankhead's table where Tenn suddenly rose and cried, "Oh, Gil, yes, sit down. Tallulah, dear, here's . . ."

"I know, Tennessee."

Tallulah's small hand came out to mine as she told him, "It's my perennial poet. Sit down by me, Gil, darling."

Having appeared in James Herlihy's play *Crazy October* she asked at once if I'd read his book *All Fall Down*, and, when I said no, demanded, "What do you mean, you haven't read it?"

I said that I'd read parts of it, standing on one leg in the Columbia University bookstore where I was presently employed, and that I meant to read it all as soon as I'd tossed off a rewrite job on a movie star's autobiography which I was doing for a publisher.

Miss B. nodded quickly and went on to ask me how I was really making out, staving off the wolf on my doormat.

She seemed quite composed and I'd seldom seen her in better spirits. In Key West, Jim Herlihy'd had her up early of late, skin diving, eating Southern breakfasts of bacon and eggs flanked by hominy grits, and she looked extremely healthy.

As the various groups milled around, Elia Kazan arrived and Tenn, leading me up to him, said, "Gadge, you remember Gil Maxwell."

To our joint surprise Kazan said blandly, "No, I don't."

Tenn and I chorused, "But you must—from Miami and *Sweet Bird*," but Mr. K. said again, "No, I don't remember anybody. As a matter of fact, tonight I can't even remember my own name."

He passed on, leaving Tenn and me aghast. Kazan is a man who simply doesn't drink; therefore, neither of us, to this day, has been able to make head or tail of this incident.

Bill Hughes was timid about meeting Miss Bankhead, so I grabbed him by the hand, yanked him into the back room of the café where she was now holding forth with Brendan Behan and cried, "Tallulah, say hello to Bill Hughes." She sang out, deep-voiced, "Hello, Bill Hughes," and shook his hand.

A few minutes later I heard Bill calling from the other side of a group of people, "Gilbert, for heaven's sake, Miss Bankhead's trying to get your attention"—and as I swerved, there she was, on tiptoe, peeping over some tall person's shoulder, waving and calling, "Good night, Gilbert darling, good night."

As I have remarked before, though I can't lay claim to being a particular friend of Tallulah's, I've found that whenever we meet after a lengthy absence, she is always the same. She thinks of me as a poet, and consequently treats me with a kind of fond regard which I find most agreeable.

Bill and I said a grateful good-by to Tenn at the close of his party and set off for home glowing with that special aura of enchantment which never fails to suffuse such stage-struck blokes as we, after an evening spent with the ultra-sophisticated, curiously childlike people of the theater.

Period of Adjustment opened in November with Barbara Baxley, Robert Webber, James Daly, and Rosemary Murphy as the two young married couples desperately trying to adjust to the storms and rigors of a first matrimonial winter.

I escorted Jo Healey on opening night and the two of us were charmed from the moment the curtain rose on Mielziner's interior-exterior set of a living room gay with Christmas decorations, just back of a ramp where snow was falling fast.

On a Williams opening night, you will find him at intermission having a drink in the near-by bar with old friends to whom his house seats have gone, and on this night Jo and I sat with him, Frank Krause, and a couple of other people who'd known him donkey's years. Mr. and Mrs. Brendan Behan were also with us and I remember Brendan's repeating my name over and over, musing, "What a fine name that is."

Tenn and I exchanged winks, guessing that B.B. had never heard the fine name before; then, as we rose from the table, I looked at T.W. and made the familiar radio-and-TV O with my thumb and forefinger, which told him just how I felt about *Period*.

Some very rich young man whose name I never knew gave a lavish after-theater party that night at the Plaza, and Jo and I sat at Miss Edwina's table.

When Tenn came in, I rose and rushed toward him. He looked unreservedly happy, and as I approached he stretched his arms out wide on either side to give me a mammoth hug. There seemed no doubt that his play was a joyous hit, and the air of the Plaza's banquet room was one of general rejoicing.

Next morning I skidded into Altman's silver department after two hours' sleep, still giddy and phosphorescent from the fabulous night before. Everyone asked, "How was it?" and I told them, "An absolute delight. A sort of surprise Christmas gift from Tennessee to a troubled world."

The newspaper critics were unanimous in praise of this offering and the majority expressed astonishment at its "romantic, human, touching" qualities.

Apparently not one of them had expected Williams to come up with anything like this.

A re-examination of *You Touched Me* or *Tattoo* might have been revealing to all of them, since in both these vehicles, Tenn had already established himself as an able creator of romantic, human, touching comedy.

11

All through the summer and fall of 1960 Carmel Myers had worked with the heads of various major picture studios, with Joan Crawford, and through her MCA agent, with Bette Davis. Time and again the whole setup looked good; time and again something happened to monkey-wrench a carefully worked-out package project.

In January, I wrote to Tenn in Key West that I was eating snow ice cream right off my hotel window sill and that I now had a hankering for Florida. He and I had already discussed the possibility of my returning to Miami to set up some private classes; now he called me long distance to say that he would personally be delighted if I'd come down since we could again be together in a relatively peaceful, relaxed atmosphere. He sent me railroad fare,

301

and, shortly after my arrival in Miami, again dug into his own pocket to make me a little more comfortable while I was getting the classes started.

I found a small apartment in the same house on Fifth Avenue where I'd been when he'd first visited me in 1950, and began to teach creative writing to a small, fluctuating group—first in a friend's downtown office, later at my own small place.

My weekly income from these activities was minor and unpredictable, but the cost of living in Miami is less than half of what it is in New York, so I continued to get by, writing steadily on my third novel when I was not teaching or ghosting some manuscript.

Tennessee was in town a great deal, working constantly on *Iguana* and other things after a recent bout with pneumonia.

I went down one day to the Towers Hotel just after he'd finished his morning stint and found him in a room littered with papers and manuscripts, half-empty coffee cups and highball glasses, in a state of near collapse. He fell heavily back on one of the studio beds and groaned, "Oh, baby, I just can't *tell* you how I feel this morning. You just can't imagine."

I said that I thought I could, and suggested we go right down to the poolside.

He sat with me in the restaurant patio, his tired eyes hidden by dark glasses, and stared out at the Miami River, making dull small talk, but I sensed that he was unbearably depressed, and I could only guess at a few of the reasons. He had been very ill; he was having some family trouble, and he was working unusually hard, but I guessed that this was not all, and sure enough, he soon came out with a sordid story.

A reckless friend of his, in trouble with the police in a midwestern town, had called asking for help the night before. I knew that this man had been involved in a similar mess before, so I said flatly, "Well, I know I've no right to judge, but since this character seems to be just damn stupid about his life, I honestly don't see why you feel you have to do anything."

Tenn said, "You don't understand. Last night he told me on the phone, every friend he had out there has deserted him—and unless somebody helps him, he'll not only lose his job, but will go to jail.

The poor guy was crying so hard he could hardly talk, so I told him to go on to bed and stop worrying. I *had* to, Gil. I just can't stand by and see a man's whole life ruined."

I said, "No, I guess you can't." And then I added, depressed: "God knows life's no picnic for anybody. I keep writing and rewriting this novel, seeing the end but never reaching it, and worse, seeing quite plainly nothing's really going to happen after all this heartache, even with the goddamned screenplay. I'm a jinxed failure as a writer—just as I've been telling you for years."

Tenn said, "No, you're not. After all, there's still your poetry."

I said, "I haven't so much as sent out a poem to a magazine since I don't know when. I just write poems and put 'em away in a drawer. I haven't felt like a poet for years. And anyhow, as you said once, 'Poetry is something you do when you're young.'"

"Nevertheless," Tenn said, "I hope you won't start feeling a lot of self-pity. . . ."

I cut him off. "I don't. What I feel is a profound frustration, and worse, a kind of constant, inner rage at circumstances of all kinds—at publishers, editors, and Hollywood producers—at the callous indifference manifested on every side toward a man who was a successful published writer when he was twenty-three years old. That's what I feel and I know it's justifiable. If I were a lazy man, it would be different. I'm not, and never have been."

"No, you're not," Tenn said. "You've worked all your life, just as I have." He looked out at the pool from behind his protective glasses and went on sadly, "I still don't think you should feel too bad, though. Think about me—up there in that hotel room, *killing* myself, and for what? *Just to stay where I am.*"

It was a gloomy lunch hour and I was glad when it ended.

I was with him later in the hotel suite when he called Audrey Wood in New York about the friend who was in trouble and told her quietly, "I think you'd better make it a thousand. And get the money off right away, won't you, dear?"

I was deeply moved by this action on Tenn's part, not only because it was indeed true that he was the last resort in the case of this obsessed, unhappy man, but because I knew of additional S.O.S. signals he had personally answered in the past few months.

There was a friend who'd been forced to go to a mental institution, and I'd been in his New York apartment on the night he'd assured her on the phone that she would be taken care of. He had just come forward once more to give me a leg up, and I guessed that there'd been others whose urgent needs he had answered.

Later, Audrey Wood was to tell me, "No, it's not just one or two people, by any means. It's a whole group he's helping, and it goes on all the time."

Yes, Williams was being his own truly generous self during this period, but he was having more than one kind of personal trouble, and soon I was to be the unwitting target of his turbulent inner griefs and suspicions.

One evening when he'd been asked to dinner at my place, he walked into the room, said howdy to a man he'd never met before, fell back on my bed and asked, "Why do you hate me?"

I was busy at the stove, and I almost dropped the hot dish in my hand. I banged it down on the sink shelf, clenched my jaw while I counted slowly to five, and then I said, "Nobody on earth hates you. Certainly I don't, and you ought to be ashamed to lie there and ask me such a venomous question. There's not a damned thing wrong with you right now except that somebody you're fond of's been making you feel inferior, and filling your head with lies. I've watched you for days, running yourself down around here—and now you've reached rock bottom where you're hating yourself so much you're taking it out on me."

He tried to break in, but I'd have none of it. I said, "All your life you've believed yourself unattractive, that nobody loves you for yourself, that everyone's really against you—and these are all nothing but figments of a monstrous imagination. Not only are you the Tennessee Williams, an attractive man, with a warm, even a scintillating personality when you're in good enough shape inside to reveal it—you are always a lot more amusing, attractive, and lovable than someone you care about whom I suspect you of comparing yourself to at this moment. Now, top that if you can."

He said slowly, "None of that's true, and you know it."

"It is all true," I said firmly, "and I'm not going to let you go on feeling so inferior and self-hateful inside that you can turn on me

with false accusations of hatred. Get up off that couch, pour yourself a drink, and *forget* it."

He did have the drink and he did forget it, I think, for a long
time. But the same accusations would be made more than once in
the future—and each time I had to find a new way of defending
myself against a supposed sin of which I am, as far as he is concerned, completely incapable.

Altogether, this Miami experience was disappointing to me
because of a number of things. I could never find any of my old
buddies who used to brighten my evenings; the classes were always
uncertain, due to the irregular hours my students worked at their
various jobs; Carmel Myers was finally forced to give up the ghost
on her last valiant try with the screenplay at Columbia Pictures,
and I came back to New York, on a federal income-tax refund
check, still burdened with an unfinished novel.

Tennessee was out of the country all through the hot months,
still at work on *The Night of the Iguana*, which was done in mid-
summer at Spoleto.

I worked a few weeks, helping with the inventory at the
Columbia University bookstore, and after that there was nothing.
Summer is no season in which to expect free-lance editorial work
from publishers, and this summer was especially barren. Richard
One was back in town, having his own troubles too, so when
things got tough for the two of us we went out to stay in the
apartment of an elderly Southern lady I'd known for some years,
whom I shall call Miss Effie, while she was on a visit to Alabama.

All of which leads me to a major disaster in my life, of which I
shall speak in sparing terms, mainly because I cannot bear either to
remember it or to recount it in lengthy detail.

Miss Effie returned from the South, and Dick and I stayed on
with her for a fortnight.

I managed at last to pick up a few paltry writing jobs; I was
interviewed in late August for a job with a literary employment
agency, then, on August 31, just after dark, crossing the street

toward Effie's place in Brooklyn, I was struck down by a speeding motorist and whisked off, maimed, in an ambulance.

Because Miss Effie has heart trouble, not one of the neighbors in her apartment house would tell her that I had been seriously hurt, so it was past midnight before I could get word to her from the Long Island College Hospital in Brooklyn Heights, where, in the emergency ward, I'd been X-rayed and slapped into a tubular leg cast.

Not a soul I knew was in town over this Labor Day weekend, so I spent the first four days in the hospital ward minus a comb and a toothbrush.

After a consultation of five doctors, including a famous bone specialist, on the second morning I was rushed into the operating room where a young surgeon after three and a half hours managed to put my shattered right knee back together.

As soon as my friends got back to New York, they came out in pairs and groups. Seeing me surrounded by books, lamps, dressing and writing tables, Effie remarked that she'd never before known anyone to set up housekeeping in a hospital; and it was true that I'd been receiving unusual attentions from the doctors and nurses who were interested in what I was up to on the typewriter. They'd never had a writer around before and some members of the staff were fascinated by the knowledge that a novel was being created, right under their eyes, in a corner of the central ward.

One night I was eased into a chair and wheeled to a booth phone down the hall to answer a call from T.W. He seemed in a jovial mood and told me at once, guffawing, "I was talking to Bill Liebling, today. He says we'll have to get you a wig and a wheel chair and send you out on the road to play Mrs. Venable in *Suddenly Last Summer.*"

For the second time in my life I was speechless in the face of an unbelievable attitude. I had not merely broken my knee in three places; I had just undergone an extremely serious operation after being told that if a second set of X rays hadn't revealed more damage than had been recorded on the first set, there'd have been no operation—in which case I'd have had a locked knee for life.

On the first morning when my private physician had asked me how I felt, I'd answered with desolate honesty, "I want to die."

Now, here I was, listening to flippant badinage from by best friend about a whole series of situations which could only add up to tragedy. I made what conversation I could, hung up, and rolled myself back toward the ward more hurt and bewildered by Tennessee than I'd ever been in my life.

When he and Jo Healey called me jointly the next night, he said that he'd be out one day soon to see me. He asked me what I needed, and I said, "Well, you might bring me some typewriter paper, so's I can get on with this novel."

He came one afternoon, wearing his dark glasses, with a twenty-five-cent typewriter tablet he'd picked up at the hospital stationery stand, and a dog-eared paperback copy of a biography of Marie Antoinette.

As he strolled into the ward, finding my lawyer, two doctors, and a couple of nurses with me, he said brightly, "Surrounded as usual, I see."

We talked casually, but he never took off his dark glasses. After a while, he got up, wandered to the windows of the ward and looked out, saying wearily, "Well, the hot weather's about done, I think."

When he said that he must leave, I asked him to stay about five minutes more until they got me and my cast into bed. He did so, and then told me good-by, saying as he departed, "Haven't seen you looking so young and well in five years, Gil."

I lay for a long time after he'd gone, trying not to think about this visit. If he had been moved, I had been unable to detect any evidence of concern in his face about my plight, which was serious in more ways than one—but then, of course, his eyes had been hidden behind the dark glasses.

It may be (as Paul Bigelow and Richard Two contend) that Tennessee, unable to bear the sight of illness and suffering, must always make light of it. He *is* inclined to joke about his own serious ills, and when he does I seem to sense, back of the bravado, a kind of ironic, wry acceptance, as who should say, "Well, it's no more than I expected of life," so this may indeed be his attitude, as well, toward the disasters of others. However, these are no more than conjectures. There are whole areas of Tenn's inner consciousness to which I have never had access.

Everything was being done for me in the hospital, but I'd had little cash in my jeans when I was struck down, and I was beginning to wonder how I should manage when I was released from the ward. Effie had said that I was to come to her, but I knew that her own funds were limited and that I must find some way of paying for my board and keep. And so, once again, I turned to Audrey Wood.

I wrote her on September 16, telling her what I was up against and asking if she could think of any way of getting me a weekly stipend. I said that since Tenn had come to my rescue so many times in the past, I'd prefer that she shouldn't approach him, and thanked her in advance for anything she might be able to do.

On September 18, one day after two friends had moved me by taxi out to Miss Effie's, I received this from Audrey:

Dear Gil:

I am so sorry to hear about your accident. I can't tell you how sorry I was to hear this distressing news.

I have one or two ideas about securing funds for you, which I will get on at once. I know how anxious you are to receive word from me, so I will do my best to get back to you quickly.

I had been injured on August 31, yet Audrey apparently had known nothing about my accident until she received my letter.

Some ex-students of mine in Miami, hearing my bad news, began to send me small checks tucked into letters of sympathy. Audrey phoned to say I'd be hearing soon from the lady who headed the Organization, and sure enough, I did. She told me that money was tight at the Organization's headquarters, and asked, since I was at Miss Effie's, if I could manage on $25 a week which she thought the board might grant me for a twelve-week period. I said that I could and would be most grateful.

The answer to all this was simple: Audrey had phoned Tennessee in Key West, and he'd said, "Ask them for five hundred dollars for Gil."

So, once again, via Audrey, Tenn had come through for me. Once again, out of all the friends I had—and there were some who were by no means unaffluent—none but Tennessee Williams had been there for me when cash was a primary necessity.

When he came back to town for *Night of the Iguana* rehearsals I heard from him rarely. Throughout the last half of September and through October my visitors were Bill Hughes (who once brought with him a droll new lady friend named Rita Livingston), Richard One, and Frederick, who had recently returned from Europe. Alex Uri (the girl who called to tell me of Diana's death) phoned me faithfully every day, and on a few occasions, Jack Barefield and another friend, Gerald Peters, came mercifully to take me for long drives in their cars.

I'd never learned how to manipulate stairs with my crutches, so I invariably bumped myself down on my derrière, an object of round-eyed interest to a half-dozen kids and their parents who lived in the old house, but I was never disturbed by their gawking. For me anything was better than being cooped up in Miss Effie's small apartment where I lay in a tiny back room beneath a plaster-flaking ceiling, or in the living room, striving to retain my sanity while my hostess, a marathon monologuist, talked to me about her family or goaded me, with gleeful intent, into violent arguments on subjects about which we held opposite views.

Miss Effie is in her eighties, clear of mind, stout of spirit and body, fundamentally kind. She is also (as I was to learn, lying helpless) possessed of the extraordinary notion prevalent among Southern ladies, that all men are children, to be dominated, shouted down, controlled with a whip hand by their womenfolk. When I complained of being thus used, she countered with the old, cunning trump card, "You're just like a member of my family, and family members have a right to say anything they please to each other."

It was of no use whatever for me to reply that this was precisely the attitude in my own family which had driven me far from home

at the age of twenty-one, and I dreaded the day when our relationship should become unbearable.

In the last days of October, several things happened that were
to affect my future in devious ways. One night as I sat with Effie,
Richard One, and Bill Hughes, Tenn called to ask me how he
could reach Frederick. He was lonely, he said, and badly in need of
some company. I said that since Frederick was in process of
moving, I didn't yet have his new phone number. Then, as the
group in the room chorused, "Why doesn't Tenn come on out
here?" I relayed this suggestion. He said that he was too tired to
make it, but that he'd come soon and we'd go to the St. George
Hotel for dinner. He went on to tell me about the rehearsals of
Iguana, which were beginning to be more than lively, and hung
up, again devoutly promising to come to see me ere long.

I was not to see him again until Christmas week, when he came
back to New York after the tryout road tour of *Iguana*. The gang
tried several times before he left town to get him out to Effie's,
but he was always too beat from his bouts with rehearsals to
manage a trip to Brooklyn. I could scarcely believe that he'd leave
town without coming out at least once to see me. He did,
though—and the mystery of his absence was cleared up for me in
part when Jack Barefield, in Birmingham, Alabama, tried to reach
me one night by long distance. He called Tenn to ask for my
phone number, and according to him, Tenn said, "Jack, baby, I
can't help you. Gil's staying with some old lady way out in Brooklyn, and I don't *have* his number. I just can't see Gilbert these
days—he depresses me too much."

T.W. has since sworn to me that this is all untrue, but I think
his memory is faulty. I am quite sure he made these remarks to
Jack, and that he was too depressed by my plight, plus the *Iguana*
rehearsals, to bear the thought of me and my broken leg—in
Brooklyn.

One Sunday, when I opened the *Times* and found a front-page
book section review of two critical, semibiographical books on
Williams, I felt my heart sink. In Miami the past winter when
someone had said that I should be doing a biographical book on

him, Williams' eyes had gone steel blue as he stated, "Well, he's not going to, I can tell you."

Now, on the sofa at Effie's, I laid the *Times* book section across my plaster cast, asking myself, "Maxwell, are you man or mouse?" Here were two published books on this man, written by people who never had known him—and here was I, with all sorts of sugarplum stories dancing about in my head. Rage and frustration boiled within me as I pulled myself up from the sofa, reached for my crutch and stumped out to my dreary bedroom to pick up from the table the few rough pages of the novel I'd written the day before.

I was the forgotten man and the forgotten author, all right, but I swore I'd somehow change these conditions, once I'd got my leg back.

A few nights after this, Frederick, out with Richard One and Bill Hughes, said that he'd been at a small gathering the previous Sunday which Herbert Machiz had given in honor of Miss Bette Davis, one of the stars of *Iguana*.

My name had come up, and Miss Davis had said, "I think Mr. Maxwell's screenplay is one of the most brilliant scripts I've ever read. I'd still give a lot to play one of his leads, with Joan Crawford."

"Oh?" said I. "And what did Tennessee say to this?"

"I don't recall his words exactly," said Freddie, "but I *think* he said, 'I'm worried about what's ever going to happen to Gil, but I don't know just what I can do,' and then he added, 'I guess his work will be appreciated, after he's dead.' "

Everyone in the room burst out laughing, including me. I, alone, however, knew how much it cost me to laugh at this ghoulish anecdote. It was as if at the Machiz gathering, I'd already been relegated to a Chinese house of the dead—and suddenly as the group around me went on talking, I grew morosely silent.

I know now that on this evening I made up my unconscious mind that somehow, leg or no leg, come poverty, hell, or high water, I'd be a published writer again. Something of mine again would appear between covers, to be read, discussed, and criticized, at least by the few thousand people to whom, as a poet and novelist, my name had once been familiar. All that I had now for comfort was the dubious knowledge that my four published volumes of verse, all out of print, were collectors' items—and that was truly cold comfort. I squirmed on the sofa and told myself, "The hell with what's going to happen after I'm dead; I want the flowers now, while I can smell 'em, and I'll even take a few weeds with 'em, if that's how it has to be."

For me the acclaim of posterity has always held slight appeal. I was down, this fall, but not out—and the Good Lord being my helper, I'd be some sort of Living Writer again before I reached that last bed where I'd be laid to die.

12

IN EARLY NOVEMBER, WHILE TENN WAS OUT ON THE ROAD WITH *Iguana*, I learned that there were one or two friends in New York whom I could no longer reach by phone. Miss Audrey Wood was by no means one of these.

By November 15, Miss Effie and I had reached a point of mutual intolerance which required a drastic move on my part. An elderly lady, worn out from waiting on me, she had come to the end of her tether and was now using all the verbal weapons at her command to remove me from her premises. One morning she dealt a last blow, ending a tirade, "And what's more, Mr. Maxwell, I don't think you were ever much of a writer, or you'd never be where you are now."

I said, "This does it. If you don't move out of this room on the

313

double, my girl, I'll let you have it, smack on the head with my crutch. In fact, I think I just will, anyway."

I reached for the crutch—and Miss Effie vamoosed at a speed which would have done credit to an ingenue, much less a character-dowager past eighty.

That afternoon Jerry Peters moved me to a small room in a hotel in Brooklyn Heights, where for the next few weeks I would live a rugged but peaceful life. My gang shopped for me at a near-by Bohack's, and I cooked, for myself and sometimes for them, three meals a day on an electric two-burner.

An appeal to Audrey, relayed by her to Tenn, out in Detroit with *Iguana*, brought me additional funds from the Organization.

The snow piled up, but this did not deter Bill Hughes, Frederick, Rita Livingston, George Hodge, and another old, dear friend of mine named Babs Beatty, from coming to take me to the hospital by taxi, first for the removal of my cast, later for therapy treatments. Jerry, Frederick, Bill, Babs, and Rita got me into New York for weekends at their several apartments. Richard One came to see me, and so did Richard Two, down from northern New Hampshire where he was now residing, and I was with a crowd on Thanksgiving.

When Tenn returned in Christmas week, I talked to him from the apartment of a friend who'd loaned me the place while he was away with his family.

The stories Tenn told me of his troubles with *Iguana* on the road were fantastic. He said he'd try to make one of the parties I was being hauled around to through the holidays, but I had a feeling he'd never get to the West Side where these festivals were to be held. I was sure that last-minute rehearsals of the play before its opening would have him hogtied, and I was right. He called finally to ask if I'd like seats for opening night, and I said that of course I'd be grateful and glad to come.

Bill Hughes and I went together. I was on a cane now, and wildly happy to be off crutches.

The play, with Margaret Leighton, Bette Davis, and Patrick O'Neil, was lovely and sad, and I was moved by Alan Webb in the

role of Nonno, "the world's oldest practicing poet," since h
portrayal was almost a prototype of Grandfather Dakin.

Bill and I were in the mezzanine, so by the time we'd made our
slow way downstairs, most of the crowd had thinned out. Tennessee, in full dress, was standing alone by the soft drink stand in the
lobby, and I could see, among the people coming up the center
aisle, Dakin, Mrs. Williams, Jo Healy, and Carson McCullers;
then, as we approached Tenn I came face to face with Audrey. She
looked at me, smiled, and said softly, extending her hand, "Well,
well, well, look at this, will you. How wonderful, my love."

Bill and I talked with her for a moment before we moved up to
Tenn. He shook hands with us both, acknowledged our congratulations, and turned to Carson, asking her if she'd like to come to
his place for a glass of champagne.

I had stepped back with Bill—and now as we said a rather
timorous good night, Tenn said, "Good night, Gil. I'm not having
a party—just going straight home, you know."

I had never before felt so intimidated or so depressed in his
presence.

I said to Bill, "Come on, let's get out of here"—unable even to
wait and greet Miss Edwina.

I was sure that Tenn's absent-faced look of unsmiling preoccupation as he slouched there by the soft-drink stand had nothing to
do with me. His mind was on *Iguana*, and he was by no means
happy, I guessed, with this play.

Still, this was like no opening night of Williams' that I'd ever
attended, and I said to Bill, "I don't understand all this, but I
think it calls for a drink, so let's go and find one."

Tennessee left town at once for a desperately needed respite in
Key West. Audrey had made a third and last request through him
from the Organization for a little more money, which would hold
me until March 1, when I hoped to be self-supporting. The board,
however, was slow in making up its mind about this request—so I
was forced to move from the Brooklyn Heights hotel, one week
when the rent came due, to a large apartment owned by two guys

in uptown Manhattan. There, it seemed, I would finally succumb to being a full-time burden on my valiant, small group of good friends—but again, the unexpected happened.

One day, by phone, I received an assignment to do a rewrite job on a book manuscript, and fifteen minutes later the Organization heads called to say I could have a little more loot.

Tennessee was in town for the weekend, so I phoned in the evening to tell him the news, and he said that he was pleased to hear it. This was late February, and I hadn't seen him since Christmas, so I delayed taking the old bit in the teeth. Lying awake that night I thought things over, and next morning, called him.

I asked flatly, "Tennessee, are you angry with me?"

He said, as though greatly surprised, "Why, Gil, of course not. Why?"

I said, "Well, since I haven't seen you in two months, I assumed something had to be wrong. . . ."

"Oh, no," he said. "Look, why don't you take a taxi down to the King of the Sea? We'll have a nice, long lunch."

I met him and we did not talk about the silent months before and after the holidays.

Instead, I told him, "I've been thinking ever since last winter, of that time in Miami when you bounced into my place and demanded, 'Why do you hate me?' I handled you wrong that evening. I should have walked to a chair, sat down and said, very slowly, 'We-ll, now, let me see.' "

Tenn guffawed, but his eyes were warily watchful as I continued, "I should then have gone on to say, 'I hate you, my friend, for having made my life glamorous since 1950, with marvelous, famous people, first nights at your plays, meals in superb restaurants, fun evenings in night clubs—and, most of all, for never having failed to come through for me financially when nobody else I knew did. These are the reasons,' I should have said, 'why I hate you, friend Williams.' "

I looked up and saw he was still silently watchful.

I said then, "I know there's a school of thought that contends one man may hate another for being generous to him—especially, money-wise—but I've never understood this reasoning. I am a man who has never been anything but grateful for any friend's acts of kindness, great or small. If you don't know this by now, you ought to."

Tennessee nodded, still silent, still looking me in the eye—and now I asked, straight out, "Who tells you I hate you, Tenn?"

He answered slowly—giving me the two names I'd expected to hear, of two people as close to him as I'd once felt myself to be.

I said, "But you see, since these people have always been jealous of this old friendship between you and me, I naturally never see them. Therefore, how could they possibly know how I feel about you? I should think it would be more fair to ask the people who are constantly with me—the people who *have* been, all through this wretched, confining illness. I'm convinced you'd come closer to getting an honest answer from them."

I said it all out, there at the King of the Sea, and was glad, the moment the last words left my lips. I'd had it with Tennessee and this strange attitude of indifference, anger, resentment, whatever the hell it had been since my accident, and now I was almost past caring how he took the real truth from me.

Fifteen minutes later we were walking merrily up Third Avenue in the sunshine, and for the nonce, all was once more as it should be, with Yours Truly and friend T.W.

Later, as we sat in a bar, we got to talking with a couple of people near us. The conversation turned to man's inevitable inhumanity to man, and I said, "I don't agree with all that. I've just been through an experience with a serious illness, in which everyone I'm fond of was unbelievably kind to me."

Tennessee said promptly, "Ah, but you have a genius for that."

Two drinks later, a guy on my left complained of the difficulty of making a living, and, at the same time, doing one's real, creative work in a quality sort of way.

Williams flung an arm about my shoulder, leaned toward the guy and asked, "Why don't you be like my boy here? He's a poet and he never works—except at *his real work.*"

I stiffened under that arm's weight and turned very slowly.

I said, "T.W., you could have lived a long time without saying that," and the look on his face, as I eyed him, seemed to me enigmatic.

For weeks now, still on a cane, I'd been traveling by taxi through falling snow, over streets sheathed with ice, from West 91st to the Columbia University Library and the downtown libraries doing a research job for World. What I'd been doing was essential to my existence—and as far as I could see it had little to do with poetry.

The warmth I'd felt between my friend and me, as we'd left the King of the Sea, had vanished as we sat through twilight in that East River bar.

In March the free-lance editorial work gave out, along with the Organization's stipend. I moved from uptown to a room in a Broadway hotel in the sixties—and now, devastation and despair set in with a vengeance. There was no work and I couldn't seem to finish the novel, so I was living on small sums borrowed from this or that faithful friend. I'd sworn, with my leg in a cast, that if I was ever mobile again, I'd never be sunk so deep in despair as to think of death in terms of release.

I had almost reached that point, however, when Tenn, returned from a trip to New Orleans, called me up and asked me out for an evening. We went to a penthouse party and while we were there, Don Windham rang up for Tenn.

Tenn put me on for a moment while I congratulated Don on his recently published book of short stories; then he grabbed the phone again and told Windham, "I wish you could see this character. He's *had* a broken leg, but he hasn't got one anymore—and right now, sitting here on this sofa beside me, he looks about nineteen."

I was feeling at least sixty but I decided that Williams—for once—should not know how I felt.

A few days after this I reached an absolute nadir. Then, all in one day, I called an editor and told him exactly how things were going with me.

He said, "I'd no idea anyone alive could feel as low as I do today, and I also had no idea you were desperate. I have work for you—so come to see me, tomorrow. I'll get you going on two projects that will pull you out of that hole."

Within a month I was able to give a party at Barefield's for all the old friends in town who'd loaned me small sums, slipping into the hands of each a small envelope containing some greenbacks.

And a few days after that, I sat down to begin these memoirs.

When Tennessee returned from Europe in the fall of 1962, my half-finished manuscript was with a publisher. He and I spent a rousing, rambunctious evening in Chinatown in which he gave me at least twelve reasons why the book should not be written, repeating over and over, "For God's sake, with all those articles, two books last year, and now, Mother's book coming out, don't you see this isn't the *time*, Gil? Why, the public must be just fed right up to *here*, with old T.W."

I said, "The public hasn't met the old T.W. I know, but they're certainly going to, and you may as well give me your blessing, or I shall proceed without it."

The evening was one that should be allowed to fade, unmourned, into limbo. Words were exchanged 'twixt Williams and me which blued the air of the restaurant, the taxi uptown, and, later, the telephone wires as we spoke together that night.

In the morning I phoned and held the receiver away from my ear while T.W., uninterrupted, accused me of all sorts of evil intentions. I then spoke my piece and said quietly, "For the first time in years I've got money to take you to lunch. Will you have it on me, today?"

The voice on the wire crescendoed, "Who cares who pays for the lunch? I'll tell you this, though—no matter who pays, it'll be one hell of a meal if it's anything like last night."

I said, "There's no need for that, if you'll just let me bring you the manuscript."

Silence. Then T.W. said quietly, "All right. I'll see you at one o'clock at the Isle of Capri."

As I entered the restaurant he rose from the table, arms outstretched, face wreathed in smiles, crying, "Baby! Come on, have a drink, and let's look at this thing."

I sat, slowly sipping a martini while he read the first few pages of a rough draft. He gurgled and chuckled a little, made some penciled notes, then laid the manuscript down and told me, "This book's going to be simply delightful. All I ask is, you'll let me see it all before it goes to press, and that you won't put back anything after I've cut it out."

We finished lunch and walked slowly down Third Avenue, window shopping, reminiscing about old times.

Since then we have talked a great deal about all that I have set down here—and most of the time, he has seemed to be pleased. To date, there have been only six explosions. Now we are near the end, and I trust there will be no more.

13

I HAD SCARCELY FINISHED DRAFTING THE CLOSING SEQUENCE OF THIS
book when a long-expected but nonetheless shattering event came
to pass: Frank Merlo died, with merciful suddenness, before the
pain of lung cancer became too great for him to bear, or for
Tennessee to watch, in a Manhattan hospital.

Tenn had been constantly at the hospital, and on the day of
Frank's going he'd stayed, as usual, through the afternoon visiting
hours. He and I had planned to meet for dinner at Cavanagh's
restaurant where he would read the closing pages of the manuscript, and when I called to verify the appointment, he said in
reply to my query about Frank, "I'll tell you now, and we won't
talk about it any more when we meet. He couldn't stay still today.
He was jumping every ten seconds from the bed to a chair, and

back again—plainly breathing with difficulty. He said to me, 'My heart's going, now, I think. . . .' It was terrible to watch him. I'm so afraid of what he may have to suffer, even in spite of the drugs."

After dinner Tenn came home with me to my hotel, where we were joined by Frederick and the two Richards. We all sat around for a while and then went out to a boring night club where we were when Frank Merlo, sitting up to take his medication at 11:30 P.M., fell back lifeless against his pillow.

I had told Tennessee that I'd be available at any hour if he should need me, and on the next morning, when I picked up a message asking me to call his Butterfield number, I knew in reason, even before I rang up, that Frank had gone.

In the months that have elapsed since Frank's passing, Tennessee has said those things that anyone says who somehow happened not to be there when a loved one drew a final breath. He has felt that he *should* have been there, despite the doctor's having assured him, "Even if you'd been in the corridor, Mr. Williams, you couldn't have reached the bedside in time."

In saying farewell to Frank Merlo, Tenn was relinquishing the affectionate presence of a man who had been, as I have said elsewhere, his secretary, his traveling companion, his utterly loyal friend since 1940. However, since this unusual man was not a part of that particular small group of Tennessee's friends of which I am a member, I did not know him well and for this reason I here reproduce the following eulogy, read at Campbell's as a part of the service for Frank Merlo, by the Reverend Sidney Lanier of St. Clement's Church, as "a recollection written by someone who knew and loved him. . . ."

He was a man of honor.

He had a clearly defined code of behavior which nothing in life or death could make him alter. His character was as strongly and distinctively cut as the Sicilian features of his face. A friend of Frank Merlo's would have to learn his nature as one learns certain inalterable, empirical truths such as "I have to turn this way and then that way and then back this way again to get home from such and such a locality." The way would not change. It could not be changed. And when you had learned it, you knew that it was right.

In some persons such an inalterable character might be irritating. In the case of Frank it was, on the contrary, a source of unfailing reassurance as a beacon light in a harbor.

He had no onstage part in the theater: he didn't act for it or write for it. But for more than fifteen years he was a vital part of it. He loved people in the theater and he knew their names, first and last names, and a star meant no more to him than a player who had just a walk-on. He knew the first and last names of the men on the light board, the stage manager, the propmen, the stage doorman.

He had a unique capacity for knowing and liking people, and all he demanded of them for his understanding and liking was a decent honesty in them, and he had a unique gift for drawing out of them the best that they had to give.

Being above all honest, he had a phenomenal instinct for that quality in others. And he had a personal warmth and sweetness that could evoke those sometimes timid qualities in all whom he knew and accepted.

There was something about Frank Merlo that would not accept the untrue, that immediately and instinctively rejected whatever was contrary to his practically infallible sense of the truth in people. He was a man to whom you would go for the interpretation of whatever was obscure to you in the quality of anyone you knew, because he knew them better than you did.

He was a giving person, always giving of himself and whatever he owned. The generosity of his heart, and its gift for understanding, made him superior to us in a way he probably never knew.

He had the kind of pride which is nobility and it was never broken once by the illness that has ended his living, visible presence. Those of us who knew him during his nine months' approach to life's end all wonder how it was possible for any man living, who lived and understood living as amazingly well as Frank did, to retain, as he went to his death, such a never-breaking vitality.

The afternoon of the day when he died, visitors to his hospital room found him sitting up in a chair. He would return to his bed for a few moments, and then go back to the chair, but he said nothing of pain or fear, he only said, "I feel restless."

One time on a two-motor plane flying over high mountains, one of the plane's engines suddenly failed. His companion, as the plane lost altitude steadily over the mountain range on its way back to its point of departure, found it necessary to wash down two pills with the contents of a pocket flask of whiskey in order to endure the apparently imminent prospect of crashing in flame. But Frank sat quietly reading his book, after saying casually, "Oh, I've flown back over the South Pacific, after a bombing mission, on a four-motor bomber with only one or two motors working a lot of times, and made it home safe. Drink? No, I don't want a drink. There's nothing to worry about."

And it was the proudly unafraid face of his companion that kept Frank's friend from giving in to his panic, not the medications and the liquor, but that seemingly casual reassurance and that seemingly calm concentration on the book that he held before his beautifully, strongly cut face.

As an epigraph to the poem of Frank's life and death, his plane companion, over mountains and oceans, can think of none more suitable than Stephen Spender's line: "I think continually of those who were truly great."

14

Now (AS I HAVE SAID BEFORE), THOUGH IT HAS NOT BEEN MY
intention to criticize or discuss the work of Tennessee Williams in
these memoirs, I feel impelled to state his message as it has come
across, personally, to me.

In his plays and stories he has repeatedly used as a theme the
unjust cruelty of man toward his fellows because he has been
haunted, first, by nightmarish fears that his sister may have been
subjected to harsh and terrible treatment in sanitoriums, and
secondly because, obsessed with a fearful revulsion at the thought
of deliberate cruelty (Blanche du Bois speaks of it as "the one
unforgivable thing"), he has been impelled to face it unflinching
as he has grown older, and consequently to cry out in the loud
voice of a possessed reformer against it. In portraying scenes of

abominable, outrageous beastliness, he has been fighting fire with fire; and surely with such a motive, he has been justified in shocking the prudish, the hypocritical, the stubbornly blind or misunderstanding members of his audiences—at least for a space of three hours—out of their habitual apathy, their acceptance of intolerable things as they are in the world today. It will probably be true, of course, that the majority to whom he cries out will be disturbed for no more than a matter of hours, but there is also, always, the hope that some few may have heard and heeded what he has had to say. He has tried to drive home his basic message, as in *Orpheus Descending*, by such devices as posses of bigoted men mobbing an innocent victim with blowtorches and blood hounds, and with gossiping, ignorant women destroying a man or a woman's character; with a wretched neurotic (Blanche du Bois) paying all her life for having, with one awful accusation, driven her young husband to suicide; with the police in *Camino Real* attacking homosexuals and the street cleaners trundling them out in ash cans; with self-righteous, corrupt, powerful, small-town citizens castrating a simple, mixed-up boy in *Sweet Bird of Youth*; with the naked, starving children devouring the corrupt poet Sebastian, in *Suddenly Last Summer*.

He has done all this—and more—and he has never done it to be sensational, to shock the good citizen or, through flamboyance, to become notorious, famous, or rich. He has done it because he was impelled to shout (and let the damned chips fall where they may) to a selfish, self-centered, materialistic audience of millions everywhere, "This is your world, and here is what happens within it each hour that you live, going deaf, dumb, and blind about your personal affairs, self-imprisoned in your own thick skins. This is your world, which you made, so now, if not for the sake of that kind, omniscient God you no longer believe in, at least for your own sake, *try to do something about it.*"

15

The time has now come for me to give, as objectively as I can, an evaluation of my friend, Tennessee, and of our long, roller-coaster relationship.

It is my belief that having reached this concluding chapter, the reader must be aware by now that Tennessee Williams is a man with fewer major faults than many less interesting people. For this reason, I shall not hesitate to deal with his shortcomings, as well as with my own, in a forthright manner.

In his *Post* articles Robert Rice made the statement which follows here, and I have chosen to use it as a sort of faulty springboard from which to take my plunge into a possibly perceptive analysis.

He is undoubtedly one of the most trusting, suspicious, generous, egocentric, helpless, self-reliant, fearful, courageous, absent-
minded, observant, modest, vain, withdrawn, gregarious, puritanical, Bohemian, angry, mild, unsure, self-confident men in the
U.S.

Now, first of all, he is inclined by nature to be *trusting* of the
essentially good self within those he loves; however, the word
suspicious when applied to T.W. is a tame, inadequate adjective,
as anyone who knows him will testify. Every friend and business
associate of Williams has at times been suspected of such motives
as envy, jealousy, and deliberate desire to wound. In a single year I
have seen him three times leave a gathering outraged by a remark
or action of some person present. In two cases, he truly misjudged,
misread, or misheard the accused, and was unjustified in departing
without giving the poor devil a chance to defend himself. In the
other instance, he was partially right about an insult, since the
person involved was a resentful stranger, who (as sometimes
happens) found himself intimidated by Williams, the playwright.
The worst of it is that Tenn, convinced that he has been inten-
tionally hurt, insulted, or even subtly speared, remains indignant
for days. When a man attempts an explanation, he is not allowed
to make it before he has been subjected to a blast of recrimina-
tions. And if the accused is innocent, he is naturally outraged in
turn, not only by being misjudged, but by the injustice of being
forced into a defensive position about something he did not deliberately do. He rages inside all through the tirade against him
and comes up aghast as T.W. finishes piously, "Now, I never hold
malice, I really don't; you know that."
Well, this situation for the accused is well-nigh intolerable, or
would be, if the following comical aspects of the real truth were
not evident: when Tenn says he never holds malice he is kidding
himself, because, though he may finally say (once you have been
sufficiently apologetic or fiercely indignant to convince him of your
innocence) that he is willing to forgive and forget, he is going to
do no such things. Forgive, he may, but you can lay your last buck
on it that some day, somewhere, when you least expect it, you will

hear again about the terrible thing you did to him in your cups last Christmas, or on St. Walpurgis night.

What the whole situation amounts to is this: Williams neither forgives nor forgets. It is simply that in the man there is a natural friendliness, a kind of compassion, which overshadows and transcends the unforgotten, the unforgiven word or action.

With me it is not so. I, too, flinch at times when my friends (including Tenn) come up with something that I'm convinced amounts to a veiled insult, a deliberately cruel remark, a slyly subtle jibe, but I do not, as a rule, storm out of a room enraged. I treasure these matters, and on some clear summer evening when all seems serene I down the third highball and let go with a blast that rocks the rafters, pouring forth upon friend or acquaintance a conglomerate tirade compounded of many injustices, secretly hoarded and brooded upon for months or even years. For this reason, Tenn and other friends have been heard to groan, "If you were a bastard all the time, it wouldn't be so awful when you cut loose loaded. It's because nobody's sweeter than you are sober that all this vitriol comes as such a blood-chilling surprise."

All of which simply adds up to one conclusion. As I have remarked earlier in these pages, it seems extremely doubtful that any unforgotten remark or action has been forgiven. Therefore, if forgiving means also forgetting, neither T.W. nor I ever will be forgivers.

So much for *suspicion*. As to the word *generous*, I can hardly do better than to quote my stenographer. I asked, "How does my friend emerge to you thus far in this book?" and he answered, "Well, first of all, it's apparent that *generosity* is this man's middle name."

As I have mentioned earlier, Tenn is financially generous with a bevy of people. He is generous with both his time and his talents, in regard to less fortunate writers; he is extremely careful about the sensitive feelings of some poor, scribbling devil whose work has come to nothing—and always he is the champion, in any area of human endeavor, of the misfit, abused, downtrodden underdog.

He is selfish, too, but only because of a fanatical preoccupation with the all-self-absorbing process of creation. If he becomes seemingly callous or indifferent toward his family or his friends when he is deep in a play or on the road with a new production, it is only because, as he says, "At these times, I just don't think about *anything* except the play." In all fairness, therefore, I suppose he cannot be blamed for such an attitude, since indeed, if it were not for this absolute absorption in his work, he would never have reached a degree of success where he could afford to be so lavishly generous, financially.

The accusation of *egocentricity* is one which always bores me. Certainly Williams is egocentric, and so is the latest Miss Subways, genus Brooklyn, who has nothing about which to be egocentric except a pair of oversized boobs and the puss of a bisque baby doll. Why shouldn't this man be egocentric? If he weren't he would not be a creative artist.

Helpless, no. This boy has never been helpless since the days when the father of whom he was mortally frightened installed him in a St. Louis shoe factory—and the reader may recall that he even managed by means of a psychosomatic heart seizure to effect a permanent escape from that dismal trap. Once when I asked him, "Do you suppose you could live without money now?" he thought a moment and answered, "No-o, I don't think so." I am inclined to believe he was wrong about this. I am, in fact, convinced that if he went bankrupt tomorrow, Tennessee would pitch right in and make himself a new fortune. I also think that if he should suddenly go out of fashion—as certain playwrights have done—he would discover a new way of writing and astonish his public with a kind of play no one had dreamed he could write. No, he is not helpless. True, there was a time when he allowed Paul and me to lead him around (apparently in a state of vague preoccupation) by a literal or figurative hand, but this was because he was smart enough to accept our duped ministrations while wandering free in the wild, sweet country of his absorbing fancies.

Self-reliant he definitely is, except at those times after the day's work is done, when the grayness of boredom or loneliness settles about him in the disquieting dusk. It is then that he reaches for the phone to call any warm, sympathetic friend who may be around; and *fearful* he is of course—of disease, of death, of faithlessness or betrayal in those he loves, of violence, which he loathes, and of the future, which ever must be, to him as to every man, a chartless realm.

Courageous he is, as he had to be, faced for years with a constant struggle for existence, with serious illnesses that might have been fatal, with certain hopeless conditions of life that he could not change. But then again—though courage is admirable, I am constrained to remember that this personality asset is as necessary to any human being's survival as the shell is to the tortoise. He must grow courage who would remain alive, and so courage does not seem to me much more than a defensive requirement in each of us who lies down at night unsure of waking, or waking, faces a fathomless day in which death, disease, or emotional disaster may be lying in wait.

Absent-minded, says Robert Rice. Well, yes and no. When Williams appears absent-minded, it's usually because he's forgotten the group and wandered off to pick his metaphorical daisies, but since his mind is *presently* fixed on a scene in a play, it can't actually be said to be absent at all. It's simply that he is present in the flesh at the cocktail or dinner party, absent from there in mind, present in mind elsewhere. Absent of mind: what after all does it mean except that one is not present of mind where one is sitting or reclining? And often of course one might as well be mentally absent from the banal, repetitive group in which one's mind is likely to find itself.

Observant, yes. Williams is observant as the writer always is —evaluating, summing up the friend, the acquaintance, the family member, in terms of a character who may be used partially in a composite portrait. Most writers are guilty of this sort of observation which is sometimes so evident as to make the victim squirm, and sometimes so inaccurate (especially if the writer is creating a specific character) as to cause unjust evaluations and miserable misunderstandings. But then, good writers are like this, and though the clinical act of using one's friends and dear ones in this way is deplorable, the writer must be forgiven, because the end in art so often does justify the nefarious means.

Modest, again both yes and no. Tennessee is extremely modest about his person, his looks, his personality; and there are times when he speaks deprecatingly about his work, but I think that he would have to be something of a fool (which he isn't) to be modest about the best of his plays, in view of the accolades that have been heaped upon them and himself. Of vanity, I would say that he has little. He has no personal vanity, and he has always worked too hard on his plays to feel anything so shallow in regard to them. He feels a pride in the best of them and a deeply regretful affection toward the less critically favored ones upon which he labored as hard and long as those which were most successful. No, he is not a vain man.

Withdrawn and gregarious. Yes, both. When he is withdrawn in company he is either brooding regretfully over the irrevocable past, or plotting the impenetrable future wherein always there appears through the darkness the star of hope.

Gregarious he frequently is—but only in the presence of old, affectionate friends. This is a facet of the man which few people are privileged to know, but I am here to say that those who have not seen him leap from a shower clad in a bath towel, as Madame Sarah Bernhardt, cupping her ear for her cue; or as Amanda, rushing in on Laura and the gentleman caller with her pitcher of lemonade; or, when he sports a beard, charging into his New York living room in a terrycloth robe, like a prophet of old, bawling, "Repent, ye whores of Babylon," have not known the true old T.W.

He might well have been a fine actor, if he had not been a poet-playwright.

Puritanical, Mr. Rice? Well, no-o-o. Not anymore. He may have been until he left St. Louis at the age of twenty-six, but after that, he went to New Orleans. You do not remain, in the French Quarter, to any degree puritanical. That is to say, if you are puritanical you do not remain in the French Quarter more than a couple of hours.

Bohemian he may be, but not nearly so much so as people have been led to believe. Many of us think of ourselves as Bohemian who are fundamentally quite something else. Williams, like me, is at heart a conventional man. There is a difference between being puritanical and being conventional. Although one might be both puritanical and Bohemian, I am inclined to doubt it. To be at once Bohemian and conventional is almost to be expected. Williams and I, like a vast majority of more freakish beatniks who consider themselves real far out, were raised in the shadow of the church with the fear of God, a knowledge of the seven deadly sins, and an ingrained awareness of certain ironclad virtues and values. These include personal cleanliness, a love of good food, comfortable lodgings, and nostalgia for what it used to be like down home when the world was young. No, I do not think Tennessee is a true Bohemian.

Angry, mild— angry, good God A'mighty, yes. And when there's a tantrum I prefer to be elsewhere—if possible in the next county. Sometimes, as I've pointed out, the anger is justified, and sometimes not. As for mildness, yes, on many occasions when affection surrounds him and everyone present is being sweetness and light; but since I am ever aware of the volcano beneath the surface, I keep myself alerted—expecially when I am out with this boy at any place where even one other person is present. When we are alone there is mildness and peace, of a sort, for then I am less likely to be suspect. It is only when an extra ingredient is added that one need fear the atomic holocaust.

Unsure, of course. There is no man alive who is not.

And now that we've come to the end of Mr. Rice's necklace of adjectives, what is there to be said? Only this—that no truly creative man has less than six separate selves within him; but what is truly important is the self that emerges most often. In Tennessee Williams' case, it is the good, generous, compassionate, kindly self that is most often in residence, and because of this I feel that most of us who love him should be forever grateful.

To quote James Branch Cabell, "If you have been yourself you cannot reasonably be punished." And Tennessee has never been anything but himself, no matter what self was foremost, all his life.